Towards 2000

TOWARDS 2000

World Business Leaders Speak Out on the Future of Free Enterprise

Compiled, Edited with an
Introduction by Ruth Karen

Hutchinson
London Melbourne Auckland Johannesburg

Published in Great Britain in 1986 by Century Hutchinson & Co Ltd
Brookmount House, 62–65 Chandos Place, London WC2N 4NW

Century Hutchinson Group (Australia) Pty Ltd
16–22 Church Street, Hawthorn, Melbourne, Victoria 3122

Century Hutchinson Group (NZ) Ltd
PO Box 40-086, 32–34 View Road, Glenfield, Auckland 10

Century Hutchinson Group (SA) Pty Ltd
PO Box 337, Bergvlei, 2010, South Africa

Printed in Great Britain by
Redwood Burn Ltd Trowbridge Wiltshire
and bound by WBC Bookbinders Maesteg Mid Glamorgan

ISBN 0 09 165500 5

Contents

Introduction

At Business International, we have been monitoring global interdependence, particularly the role of multinational corporations in creating and sustaining that interdependence, for thirty years. As the international debate sharpened on where this global interdependence was taking mankind—and where it should be taking mankind—it occurred to us that one important perspective was missing from the dialogue: the perspective of those who are arguably the main actors in this arena, that is, the business and banking leaders around the world whose ideas and activities transcend national boundaries every day. It was important, we felt, to contribute to the debate the insight and practical knowledge of these men.

This, we decided, could not be done by forming a consensus. Nor could it be done by eliciting views through questionnaires. A meaningful contribution could best be made by identifying some of the most innovative minds in the private sector around the world and engaging these minds in a one-on-one dialogue.

With the help of a committed and creative Advisory Board, representing a range of countries, industrial sectors and, most important, viewpoints,* we set out major issues that business leaders could address with expertise and credibility, and identified the people who could address them. Elliott Haynes and I then conducted individual conversations with these men and

*The Advisory Board consisted of the following members: Umberto Agnelli, Vice Chairman, Fiat; Warren Batts, President, Dart & Kraft; Atherton Bean, Chairman, International Multifoods; Antoine Bekaert, Chairman, N. V. Bekaert; Romuald Burkard, Chairman, SIKA; Dorman Commons, President, Natomas Company; Edwin Dodd, Chairman, Owens-Illinois; Arthur Fürer, Chairman, Nestlé; Robert Galvin, Chairman, Motorola; A. H. Heineken, Chairman, Heineken; John James, Chairman, Dresser Industries; Samuel Johnson, Chairman, S. C. Johnson & Son; Duane Kullberg, Chairman, Arthur Andersen & Company; Ivan Lansberg Henriquez, Chairman, The Lansberg Group; Gregorio Lopez Bravo, Chairman, SNIACE; Jose Mindlin, Chairman, Metal Leve; Juan Miro, Managing Director, Union Explosivos Rio Tinto; Hans Rausing, Chairman, Tetra Pak Group; Antoin Riboud, Directeur Général, BSN Gervais Danone; H. Smith Richardson, Chairman, Richardson-Vicks; John Roberts, Chairman, American International Group; Peter Wallenberg, Industrial Adviser, Skandinaviska Enskilda Banken; Robert Wilder, Chairman, National Forge Company; and François Zannotti, Directeur Général, SCOA.

women in their homes, clubs and offices around the world. The list of interviewees is on pages 18 through 22.

We called this enterprise the International Business Initiative. In 1983, we issued a report, entitled *Toward an Unlimited Future,* which summarized the major thrust of the conversations and led to the formulation of A Call to Action. The Call appears on pages 23 through 31.

Also in 1983, the Advisory Board of the International Business Initiative recommended that the enterprise become an ongoing effort. To carry on this effort, it was decided to form The Global One Hundred, a group of business and banking leaders around the world who would, in their individual capacities as concerned citizens, address global problems and offer solutions in areas where they have standing. The mission and mandate of The Global One Hundred is described in detail on pages 33 through 49.

The Global One Hundred issued its first statement, on the debt problem of the developing world and the deficit dilemma of the industrialized nations, in December, 1984. The statement, a distillation of two original research studies, and the signatories to it, appear on pages 47 through 53. The Global One Hundred roster is still in formation. The Advisory Board engaged in constructing the roster is listed on pages 45 and 46.

This book offers the complete text of thirty-three conversations conducted between June, 1982, and December, 1984. These conversations were chosen for their original ideas and particular perspective. None has ever before appeared in print.

Industrial Statesmen from Five Continents

Lazlo Akar, Director General, Ministry of Finance (Hungary)

Dr. Ernesto Amtmann Obregon, President, Laboratorios Sanfer (Mexico)

Dr. Amadeo Ancarani Restelli, Chairman, Regina (Italy)

Dr. Hannes Androsch, Chairman, Creditanstalt-Bankverein (Austria)

Bernard Asher, General Manager, The Hongkong & Shanghai Banking Corporation (Hong Kong)

Thomas Bata, Chairman, Bata International (Canada)

R. von Bennigsen-Foerder, Chairman, VEBA (Germany)

G. P. Birla, Managing Director, Birla Brothers Pvt. Ltd. (India)

Naftali Blumental, Chairman, Koor Industries Ltd. (Israel)

Dr. Josef Bognar, President, Institute of World Economics, Hungarian Academy of Sciences (Hungary)

Dr. Lewis M. Branscomb, Chief Scientist, IBM Corporation; Chairman of the Board, National Science Foundation (USA)

Willard C. Butcher, Chairman and Chief Executive Officer, Chase Manhattan Bank (USA)

A. W. Clausen, President, International Bank for Reconstruction and Development (The World Bank)

Neville Cooper, Director, Standard Telephones and Cable PLC (U.K.)

Rodolfo M. Cuenca, President, Construction and Development Corporation of the Philippines (Philippines)

David M. Culver, President and Chief Executive Officer, Alcan Aluminum Ltd. (Canada)

Dr. E. E. David, Jr., President, Exxon Research and Engineering Company (USA)

Denis Defforrey, Chairman, Carrefour (France)

Sir Alistair Down, Chairman, Burmah Oil (U.K.)

John Elliott, Chairman, Elders, IXL (Australia)

Sir Alastair Frame, Chairman, Rio Tinto Zinc Corporation (U.K.)

Maurice Raymond Greenberg, President and Chief Executive Officer, American International Group (USA)

Akira Harada, Executive Vice President, Matsushita Electric Industrial Company Ltd. (Japan)

John Henry Harvey-Jones, Chairman, ICI (U.K.)

Yamani Hassan, Chairman, Unilever (Indonesia)

Dr. A. M. Hegazy, Chairman, Association of Commerical Professions; Chairman, Bank of Commerce and Development; Chairman, Chloride Egypt; Chairman, Islamic Council for Trade (Egypt)

Robert Ingersoll, Former Chairman, Borg-Warner; former U.S. Ambassador to Japan and U.S. Assistant Secretary of State (USA)

Ahmed Joda, Chairman, SCOA (Nigeria)

Sir Trevor Holdsworth, Chairman, Guest, Keen and Nettlefolds (U.K.)

Reginald H. Jones, Former Chairman and Chief Executive Officer, General Electric Company (USA)

Dr. Mostafa Khalil, Chairman, Arab International Bank (Egypt)

S. L. Kirloskar, Chairman, The Kirloskar Group of Companies (India)

Cha Kyung Koo, Chairman, The Lucky-Goldstar Group (Republic of Korea)

Dr. Stefan Koren, President, Austrian National Bank (Austria)

Dragutin Kosovac, President, Energoinvest (Yugoslavia)

Dr. John R. Lademann, Executive Vice President, Bank Leu Ltd. (Switzerland)

Celso Laffer, Political Scientist and Director, Metal Leve (Brazil)

John A. Landesberger, Managing Director U.S. Rubber Uniroyal Holdings; Vice President and Manager, Uniroyal International (USA)

Ivan Lansberg Henriquez, Chairman, Lansberg Group (Venezuela)

Gerard Lefort, Former President, Directeur Général, SCOA (France)

Dr. Fritz Leutweiler, President, Swiss National Bank; Chairman and President, Bank for International Settlements (Switzerland)

Dr. T. S. Lin, Chairman, Tatung Group (Republic of China)

Keshub Mahindra, Chairman, Mahindra and Mahindra (India)

Manuel Marquez Balin, Chairman and Managing Director, Standard Electrica (Spain)

Mashhour A. Mashhour, Chairman, Suez Canal Authority (Egypt)

Dr. Ettore Massacesi, Chairman, Alfa-Romeo Auto (Italy)

Konosuke Matsushita, Chairman, Matsushita Electric Industrial Company (Japan)

Dr. Helmut Maucher, General Manager, Nestlé (Switzerland)

Shane T. A. McNeice, Chief Manager, Corporate Finance, Australian Resources Development Bank Ltd. (Australia)

Dr. Manfred Meier-Preschany, Member of the Supervisory Board, Dresdner Bank (Germany)

José Mindlin, Chairman, Metal Leve (Brazil)

Dr. Juan Miro, Managing Director, Union Explosives Rio Tinto (Spain)

Mario Monti, Economic Adviser, Banca Comerciale Italiane (Italy)

Shuzo Muramoto, Adviser and Former President, Dai Ichi Kangyo Bank (Japan)

Shigeo Nagano, Director and Honorary Chairman, Nippon Steel Corporation; President, Tokyo Chamber of Commerce and Industry (Japan)

Sir David Nicolson, MEP, Chairman, Rothmans International (U.K.)

Jaime V. Ongpin, President, Benguet Corporation (Philippines)

Osman Ahmed Osman, Chairman, The Arab Contractors; Chairman, Osman Ahmed Osman and Company; Chairman, Syndicate of Egyptian Engineers; Chairman, Popular Development Committee of National Democratic Party (Egypt)

Michael Wong Pakshong, Managing Director, Straits Trading Company (Singapore)

J. Palmstierna, Managing Director, Skandinaviska Enskilda Banken (Sweden)

Sir Alastair Pilkington, Director, Pilkington Brothers (U.K.)

Dr. Louis von Planta, President, Ciba-Geigy (Switzerland)

Dr. Bharat Ram, Chairman, Delhi Cloth and General Mills Co. Ltd. (India)

Charles W. Robinson, Chairman, Energy Transition Corporation (USA)

Jose Maria Ruis Mateos, Chairman, RUMASA (Spain)

Dr. Mohammad Sadli, Secretary General, Indonesian Chamber of Commerce and Industry (Indonesia)

Dr. Rolf Sammet, Chairman, A. G. Hoechst (Germany)

Juan Sanchez Navarro, Chairman, Cerveceria de Mexico (Mexico)

Enrique Sanchez S., President, Sanchez & Compania (Venezuela)

Herta Lande Seidman, Managing Director, International Trade Services, Phibro-Salomon, Inc., former Deputy Secretary of Commerce (USA)

Mario Henrique Simonsen, Banker-Economist, former Minister of Finance (Brazil)

Sir Leslie Smith, Chairman, BOC International (U.K.)

Soedarpo Sastrosatomo, President Director, NVPD Soedarpo Corp (Indonesia)

Dr. Joseph Staribacher, Minister of Foreign Trade (Austria)

Fuat Sureh, Chairman, Transtürk Holding (Turkey)

Washington Sycip, President, S.G.V. and Company (Philippines)

Dr. Ivan Szasz, Director General, Ministry of Foreign Trade (Hungary)

Rafael Termes Carrero, President, Spanish Association of Private Banks (Spain)

W. Paul Tippett, Jr., Chairman and Chief Executive Officer, American Motors Corporation (USA)

Dan Tolkowsky, Vice Chairman and Managing Director, Discount Investment Corporation, Ltd. (Israel)

Peter I. Walters, Chairman, The British Petroleum Company, Ltd. (U.K.)

Y. C. Wang, Chairman, Formosa Plastics Group (Republic of China)

Ralph Ward-Ambler, Managing Director, McPherson's Ltd. (Australia)

Hans Werthen, Chairman, Electrolux, Sweden; President, Swedish Federation of Industry (Sweden)

R. Bruce Williamson, Treasurer, Australian Resources Development Bank Ltd. (Australia)

Tanku Dato Ahmad Yahaya, Group Chief Executive, Sime Darby Berhad (Malaysia)

A Call to Action

The business leaders interviewed share a profound conviction that, despite the problems and challenges confronting the human race, the global society can cure its ills and create a sound and equitable life for all mankind. In their view, there is no limit to the good our future can bring us, if we approach it wisely.

At the same time, they believe that certain attitudes and conditions must prevail if free enterprise is to continue to be successful. In assessing their suggestions about needed modifications of policy and behavior, the reader should bear in mind several things.

First, while there was a remarkable degree of unanimity concerning these suggested changes, they do not represent a consensus: They are a compilation of ideas put forward individually by one or more of the interviewees.

Second, many of these suggestions concern needed improvement in the attitudes and behavior of their own business colleagues.

Third, as realists, these leaders recognize that the changes they propose cannot be accomplished quickly, or in their entirety. Elected officials, for example, cannot be expected always to take the long view; modification in attitudes and behavior by individuals in all sectors of society is a slow and often painful process. Hence the compilation below should be viewed as a roadmap pointing to goals, the achievement of which will require extensive research and debate. We anticipate modification and compromise rather than exact replication of the suggestions offered here.

SUGGESTIONS FOR MODIFICATION OF POLICY AND BEHAVIOR BY THE PUBLIC AND PRIVATE SECTORS

I. Enhance Competition

Competition—the struggle for corporate survival and growth—is what makes the private sector an unparalleled force for the development and creation of social products. Competition is the lifeblood of the system. It needs to be strengthened on an international basis in ways that recognize and foster global interdependence. Specific recommendations:

A. Internationalize the rules governing corporations with respect to:

1. Environmental law;
2. All forms of government subsidy;
3. Other laws, incentives and regulations that materially affect competitiveness.

Competition is damaged when companies do not all play by the same rules, and do not all suffer or gain from the same government-created costs and benefits, within whatever marketing area is theirs—including, for international business, the international marketplace. While some poorer nations may be unable as yet to impose the costly burdens of environmental protection on their corporations that the richer nations can afford, internationalization of environmental protection laws should at least be effected within the Organization for Economic Cooperation and Development (OECD) countries now.

B. Eliminate barriers to the free international flow of goods and services and to the means of their production. This calls for the following actions:

1. Reverse the present tide of trade protectionism;
2. Upgrade the General Agreement on Tariffs and Trade (GATT) to the status of a full-fledged international organization with greater sanction powers;
3. Create a global organization for foreign investment, or expand GATT's functions into this area.

True freedom of movement for goods, services and the resources for their production would have an electrifying effect in improving standards of living everywhere in the world. It would speed the demise of unprofitable "sunset" industries in the rich countries; open the door for the competitive exports of developing countries; permit multinational corporations to assist developing countries in exploring, exploiting and exporting their raw materials as well as products fabricated from them; and generally bring about a more efficient and equitable allocation of production resources on a global scale. The structural adaptation to economic reality which eliminating protectionism entails would inevitably cause disruptions in production and employment; but these could be eased by government and private industry programs, the cost of which would be offset by the overall benefits derived by rich and poor countries alike.

C. Educate the private sector itself to the need for, and benefits of, an open, competitive world economy.

Too often, corporations will praise competition in general but claim that their company or industry is the exception that proves the rule. Responsible business leadership must measure up to this challenge and take the initiative in educating all businessmen about the benefits to society as a whole, as well as to corporate growth and profits, of an open world economy.

II. Strengthen the Private Sector: Government Action

As the proven instrument for wealth and job creation, private corporations and their management function most efficiently and effectively when given maximum freedom to respond to the forces of the marketplace. Therefore:

A. Taxation of corporations should be minimized or eliminated. Companies create wealth, they do not consume it. In addition, corporate taxes represent double, and in some cases triple, taxation. If, in the absence of corporate taxes, companies chose to pay sharply increased wages, salaries or dividends, the individuals involved would automatically pay higher taxes. If companies chose instead to lower prices to consumers and reinvest their untaxed earnings in research and development, modernization of plant and equipment, and new plant and job creation—which they undoubtedly would do in a competitive environment—employment, living standards and thus government tax revenues would be likely to show a substantial increase. An econometric model exploring this subject is needed.

B. Anti-monopoly laws should be strengthened.

1. Legislation regarding monopolies and cartels which leaves them alone so long as they "act in the public interest" should be scrapped and replaced by laws enforcing competition. Whether or not a company is offering the best possible price, quality and service—i.e., acting in the public interest—can only be determined by the litmus test of competition. And lacking the whiplash of competition, monopolies and cartels almost invariably place unwarranted cost and other burdens on their customers.
2. Laws against labor monopolies should be strengthened. In some countries, labor has acquired monopoly powers which, like business monopolies, must be thwarted. As part of this effort, sanctions should be instituted when warranted for breach of contract.

C. Government deficit spending should be eliminated. Perhaps the greatest deterrent to the private sector in spurring economic development is massive and continued deficit spending by national governments, which results in inflation, high interest rates and a stultifying tax burden. Welfare statism (which, with defense spending, is responsible for these deficits in most countries) cannot and should not be abolished, but it has clearly gotten out of hand. Specifically:

1. A cap should be put on new or expanding welfare programs;
2. Efficiencies should be effected in existing programs, such as contracting their execution, where feasible, to the private sector;
3. Except for the poorest segment of society, recipients of transfer payments should be taxed on these receipts;
4. The reward system for providers of social services should be changed to encourage cost effectiveness. For example, doctors should be rewarded for preventive medical practices;
5. Most importantly, constitutional (or equivalent) limitations should be adopted by nations on annual increases in total government spending.

D. State-operated enterprises should be required to compete—or be scrapped.

Because they are mostly monopolies burdened with governments demands regarding employment, pricing and other sociopolitical objectives, state-owned enterprises (SOEs) generally provide poor, high-cost goods and services, and their losses, offset by government subsidies, place a high burden on taxpayers. The private sector suffers both directly from the inefficient and costly provision of goods and services, and indirectly from the distorting competition that government subsidies enable SOEs to offer. SOEs should be forced to compete with private enterprise on an equitable basis, including annual reports of their operations.

III. Strengthen the Private Sector: Business Action

A. Companies must strengthen their ability and willingness to forecast market trends and plan long term. This is necessary to cope effectively with change, thus assuring profitability and avoiding the need to dismiss workers for economic reasons.

B. Companies must persuade stock market and security analysts to measure their worth not on the basis of quarterly earnings but on the basis of the energy and resources they devote to long-term growth and profitability.

C. Companies must carefully balance their dividend policies to attract investors on the one hand and provide for sufficient reinvestment on the other to meet technological and market changes. Ultimately such a policy provides the greatest benefit and constitutes the greatest attraction for investors.

D. Companies must strive to find a way to internationalize their stock ownership (this may also require changes in governmental regulations). Eliminating conflicts of interest among shareholders of numerous subsidiaries of a single international corporation would go a long way toward making companies even more efficient allocators of resources on a global scale and forcing them to respond in a practical way to the fact of growing international interdependence.

E. Companies must devote more resources to coping with such social needs as economic enrichment of the poor and environmental protection. Though government will always be needed to rescue the truly disadvantaged and to lay down ground rules for corporate behavior in the public interest, the private sector could obviate much legislation by taking the initiative in meeting those needs which it could meet more efficiently than government could. It would of course have to add the cost of doing so to the price of its products.

F. Families who own or control corporations—representing more than 90 percent of the private sector worldwide—should determine in a systematic way what they want their company to achieve as a social organism; what the role of professional management in it should be; what their relationship with that management should be; how to cope with the question of succession; and they should carefully work out policies that will make the company a responsible member of society.

IV. Curtail Armament Expenditures

The private sector has a profound responsibility to advance peaceful accommodation among nations and to reduce the threat of nuclear annihilation. International corporations, in particular, must do more to make clear their dependence on a peaceful, integrated global society, and utilize their knowledge and experience in dealing with peoples and governments in the North, South, East and West to help bring about such a society. In doing so, companies should stress the enormous stimulus to human well-being that would result from diverting current armament expenditures to peaceful pursuits.

V. Strengthen the International Financial and Monetary System

The near-chaotic state of exchange rates today and the possible bankruptcy of a number of countries is one of the greatest deterrents to stable economic development. Business leaders share a responsibility to push for improvements in the system, among them:

A. Strengthen the International Monetary Fund in terms of both its financial resources and its sanction powers;

B. Create a mechanism that will ensure that the total foreign indebtedness of nations is clearly visible;

C. Create a system which, to the maximum possible extent, permits exchange rates to be determined by the normal forces of supply and demand;

D. Introduce mechanisms that will require greater discipline by national fiscal and monetary authorities in terms of adherence to sound economic policies. This includes politically independent central banks.

VI. Upgrade and Expand Education

The private sector has a vital stake in stimulating and/or directly providing more and better education in at least four important areas:

A. Training for the new technological age.
Business should step up the training and retraining of its own workers in conjunction with its expansion into new products and technological innovations. It should also spur improvements in technical and scientific training at all levels of education.

B. Correcting, at the grade school and secondary school levels, the serious failure to provide adequate basic skills training in reading, writing and mathematics.

C. Education in economics.
An understanding of basic economic reality is sadly lacking throughout society worldwide. What is needed is a value framework for the economy, a modern economic philosophy, which in turn may require the emergence of a new economic genius to articulate it. Lacking this, business should encourage the teaching, with the best tools available, of economics at all levels of education, and should expand its own efforts to instill an understanding of economic reality—including the role and meaning of profit—in college faculties, international forums, the media and other segments of society, as well as in the public at large.

D. Management education.
Perhaps the greatest single deterrent to development of the poor countries is their lack of entrepreneurs with management skills who can mobilize the human and material resources these countries possess. Hence business in the industrial countries must help to develop new and expanded programs of management training in the less developed countries (LDCs). At home, they should question the increasing tendency of business school to turn out "paper entrepreneurs" more adept at putting together finan-

cial deals and mergers than creating new facilities, products and services.

VII. Speed Economic Development in the Poorer Nations

The private sector, and particularly international corporations, have a responsibility to seek profitable ways to put their skills and other resources to work in helping developing countries attain genuine self-development. Two approaches would seem especially crucial in this respect:

A. A push for equitable investment conditions in the developing countries that would include minimizing or eliminating equity-ownership limitations; providing guarantees against expropriation; easing limits on profit remittances; and in general creating a legal and regulatory system that gives fair and equal treatment to indigenous and foreign investors alike. One way to achieve this would be to make creation of such an investment climate a condition of World Bank, IMF and other governmental assistance. Another would be formulation of an international code of behavior regarding foreign investment, which laid down rules of conduct for both investors and governments.

B. An imaginative search for new forms of cooperation among corporations, governments, international agencies and other groups, which would stimulate private investment, domestic and foreign, by helping to overcome such obstacles in the host country as weak market demand and lack of human and material infrastructure. The goal would be to supplement or gradually replace massive government-to-government aid programs, which have generally proven ineffective in stimulating development, with smaller, market-oriented investments, managed by the private sector and brought to fruition by profit inducements rather than by regimentation or compulsion.

The Global One Hundred: Its Purpose

During the last several decades it has become increasingly clear that mankind is losing its power to manage events and assure its well-being and perhaps even its survival. Seemingly insoluble deprivation, poverty and starvation grip more than two-thirds of the earth's population. A major contributing factor—exponential population growth—continues almost unabated. To meet even the minimal needs of the existing world population we are depleting nonreplenishable raw materials and energy sources and are destroying renewable resources such as farmlands, rain forests and fisheries. Global pollution infests the air we breathe and the water we drink. The threat of nuclear annihilation hangs ominously above us. Radical technological advances raise the prospect of profound change and disruption in our employment, lifestyles and sociopolitical systems. More immediately, unemployment, underemployment, inflation and economic stagnation are rife. International indebtedness and national deficit spending threaten to plunge the world into economic chaos.

It is little wonder, therefore, that the perception has been growing that events and developments of unprecedented severity are outpacing mankind's ability to deal with them. Part of that perception involves the notion that our economic, social and political systems have not kept pace with technological developments; the resulting problems and challenges transcend national boundaries and are clearly not susceptible to solution on a nation-by-nation basis. Inevitably, a growing international dialogue has arisen as to how these challenges can be met. Over the past few years, dozens of studies have been published and debated throughout the world by such groups and organizations as the Brandt Commission, the Club of Rome, the OECD, the United Nations and others. Careful analysis reveals that most of them share two fundamental conclusions. The first is that overcoming the magnitude of these global problems will require major alterations in the way in which mankind manages its affairs. The second conclusion is that the private sector will play an ever-diminishing role in the emerging new systems. To one degree or another, these studies suggest that profit is an inadequate motivator and regulator in today's world; that competition is harmful and must be replaced by cooperation; and that government planning and control must supersede the market system as an allocator of resources and rewards.

The cumulative thrust is illustrated by three examples. Summing up what is happening, a 1981 United Kingdom report entitled *Global Strategy for Growth,* headed by Lord McFadzean of Kelvinside, has this to say about the Brandt Commission's study:

> There is a belief that the existing international economic order operates in a way that frustrates and impedes the process of development in poor countries. There is a persistent, if implicit, belief in the efficiency and benevolence of governmental central planning and direction as the engine for economic progress and development. There is a pervasive mistrust about the working of the market and an assumption that it will, almost automatically, produce "wrong" results. This seems, in turn, to rest on an assumption that competition is in itself harmful and should be replaced, wherever possible, by regulation. Indeed, there is an implicit distaste for, and distrust of, the structures and processes of private enterprise.

The second illustration emerged at a 1982 meeting of the Club of Rome in Washington, D.C., where Dennis and Donna Meadows, the econometricians who wrote *Limits of Growth,* asserted that the period since that study's publication had done nothing to undermine its validity. They proceeded to note that MIT Professor Jay Forrester's global econometric model, which served as the basis of their work, was the first ever to be produced. Ten years later, over thirty such models had been created—in Eastern and Western Europe, Asia and Latin America, as well as in North America. A meeting attended by the Meadows, along with twenty-two of these model-builders, resulted in unanimous agreement on thirteen propositions, including the proposition that any hope of solving the world's economic problems would require competition to be replaced by cooperation. This conclusion was reached despite the radically different political, economic and social systems and values from which these econometric models originated.

The third example of the direction in which world opinion is moving is an article published in *The New York Times Magazine* in August, 1982, by the influential economist Robert L. Heilbroner, entitled "Does Capitalism Have a Future?" After suggesting that capitalists have survived over history only by eliminating or suppressing competition; after calling for price, wage and dividend controls; and after insisting that it is time "to haul down the flag of free trade," Professor Heilbroner had this to say: "To put it boldly, just as the strategic vehicle of accumulation in Adam Smith's day was the pin factory, in Henry Ford's time the national corporation, and in our own day the multinational enterprise, I think tomorrow's vehicle will be the state corporation."

It is entirely possible that the widespread and growing dissemination of ideas such as these, if not forcefully countered, will lead to an increasingly collectivist society and diminishing managerial authority and freedom. The process by which this could happen was aptly described by Alfred North Whitehead in writing of the abolition of slavery. That major sociopolitical change did not occur overnight. Rather, what Whitehead called an "invisible climate of opinion" developed over the years concerning the evil and self-defeating nature of slavery, and the quiet, almost unnoticeable spread of this opinion created a climate in which slavery simply could not survive. As the ideas cited above gain wider recognition and acceptance, a similar fate could await the private sector, or at least the private sector as we know it today.

On examination, it becomes clear that the groups advancing these ideas are composed overwhelmingly of bureaucrats, politicians, academicians and intellectuals. Missing from this international dialogue has been one vital voice, the voice of the business community, particularly the international business community. Its absence has not only given free rein to the proponents of collectivism but, equally important, has deprived those genuinely concerned about global threats to human well-being of the practical experience of leaders of the private sector, whose knowledge can make a creative contribution to the quest for a better, safer and more equitable world society.

In recognition of this, a group of prestigious and innovative businessmen in Europe, North and South America and Asia have come together under the name of "The Global One Hundred"* to ensure that leaders in government, labor, academia and other groups benefit from the experience of the private sector in the search for solutions to world problems. The group's intent is to tap the best thinking of business statesmen throughout the world and inject it into the international dialogue through publications, seminars, round-table discussions and speeches and, in the process, subject it to critical appraisal and analysis by these other segments of society.

The first endeavor of The Global One Hundred was to collect the thoughts of business statesmen throughout the world concerning solutions to the threats to human well-being and survival. More than eighty top executives were interviewed on five continents and the results published in a document entitled *Toward an Unlimited Future: Mankind Can Manage.* The overriding conviction of these executives is that competitive, profit-motivated companies operating under the market system constitute the most dynamic engine of development. They expressed a passionate belief in the inherent capacity of the private sector to create wealth and distribute it equitably; to find solutions to the shortage of energy and other natural resources; to create and sustain employment; to combat pollution; and to move the international economy forward in stable,

*The list of Advisory Board members is given on pp. 45–46.

sustained growth. Corresponding to this powerful affirmation of the market system was the equally strong conviction that government central planning, control and operation of economic enterprises paralyzes progress and the effort to improve the human condition. Although these leaders have no doubt that business, working for profit, can create an unlimited future for mankind, they are equally insistent that its success in doing so is seriously threatened by negative attitudes and behavior both within and outside the private sector.

While they are convinced that the lifeblood of the future is competition, they also believe that the struggle for corporate survival demands sensitivity and rapid response to market needs and demands, efficient allocation of human and material resources, and legitimacy in the eyes of all the constituencies the corporation serves. All too often, while giving lip service to the principle of competition, companies abandon it by seeking government subsidies in one form or another, especially by demanding protection against imports. "Free trade is fine—but my company is an exception," goes the refrain. In the view of the business statesmen interviewed, however, true freedom of movement of goods, services and the resources for their production would have an electrifying effect in improving standards of living everywhere in the world. It would bring about a more efficient and equitable allocation of production resources on a global scale, thus speeding the demise of unprofitable and wasteful "sunset" industries in the rich countries, opening the door for competitive exports of developing countries, and permitting multinational corporations to assist developing countries to explore, exploit and export their raw materials and, more important still, products fabricated from these raw materials.

Two corporate leaders in England made the point succinctly. One said: "Think what would happen if the United Kingdom unilaterally declared total free trade tomorrow. Both management and labor would be put on their mettle and forced to face economic reality. The pound would drop precipitously, boosting exports and slowing imports. Among others, the British steel industry would vanish, freeing precious resources for more productive use and saving British taxpayers hundreds of millions of pounds sterling now used to subsidize that albatross around their necks." His view was echoed by another U.K.

business leader: "The steel and aluminum industries have little validity in Europe, the United States and Japan, and will essentially vanish from those places as a matter of course. Why not now? With truly free trade, we would quickly help Central Africans and others who possess the requisite and cheaper energy sources, to become major exporters, and galvanize their economies."

These and other business leaders agree that elimination of protectionism would entail major structural adaptations in industry, and inevitably cause disruptions in production and employment. But they believe the resulting hardship could be eased by private and government programs, the cost of which pales in comparison to the overall benefits that would be derived by rich and poor countries alike. For example, the increased ability to import which developing countries would enjoy would significantly help the developed countries to switch to "sunrise" industrial production. For all these reasons, the interviewees, together or separately, called for the following actions (summarized below) to enhance competition:*

- First, spur education of the private sector itself to the need for, and benefits of, an open, competitive world economy;
- Second, reverse the present tide of trade protectionism;
- Third, upgrade the GATT to the status of a full-fledged international organization with greater sanction powers;
- Fourth, create a global organization for foreign investment to ensure the unrestricted international flow of the resources of production—or expand GATT's functions into this area;
- Fifth, since competition is threatened or becomes impossible unless all companies play by the same rules and suffer or gain from the same government-created costs and benefits, they urged internationalization of the rules governing corporations in respect to environmental protection regulations and all other laws, incentives and requirements that materially affect competitiveness.

Another threat to the private sector arising from within it, in the view of many interviewees, is the failure of too many

*The full text of the Call is given on pp. 23–31.

companies to follow good management practices. The private sector, they insist, must eschew the pursuit of short-term gains at the expense of future growth and profitability. It must strengthen its ability and willingness to forecast market trends and engage in long-term planning, thus enabling it to shift to profitable endeavors and never, in the words of one interviewee, "have to fire an employee for economic reasons." It must persuade stock markets and security analysts to measure corporate worth not on the basis of quarterly earnings but in terms of the energy and resources devoted to market position and earnings five and ten years hence. It must balance dividend policies to attract investors, on the one hand, with the need for sufficient reinvestment of earnings to meet technological and market changes on the other. It must strive to find ways to internationalize parent company stock ownership, since eliminating conflicts of interest among shareholders of numerous subsidiaries would spur more efficient allocation of resources on a global scale and, in the process, enable corporations to respond in a practical way to the fact of growing global interdependence. Finally, the private sector must devote more resources to cope with social needs such as environmental protection and unemployment, adding the cost of doing so, of course, to the price of its products. In the view of many of these business statesmen, while governments will always be needed to rescue the truly disadvantaged and to lay down the ground rules for corporate behavior in the public interest, the private sector could obviate much social and environmental legislation if it took the initiative in meeting society's needs, which it could do far more efficiently and inexpensively than government.

The business leaders interviewed by The Global One Hundred expressed the view that, in addition to the spur of competition, the inherent strength of the private sector lies in the self-perception of its managers, or at least its better managers. These managers see their companies as social organisms and themselves as stewards, with profound responsibility for the production of a social product and for equitable treatment and service to customers, employees, shareholders, the communities in which they work and the public at large—worldwide. It is this that gives the private sector its legitimacy. While these business statesmen insist that corporate profit is the sine qua non of their contributions to society—and hence their first responsibility as managers—they insist with equal fervor that profit is not an end in itself but a means. Typically, a leading Venezuelan, founder and owner of his family business, conducted a two-year program of study and discussion within the family to clarify how it viewed the company and its role in society, what family members expected from the company in the way of prestige, money, and so on; and how they viewed the question of professional management and its relation to the family: the question of succession. He hopes by his example to lead others to do the same, since more than 90 percent of the private sector worldwide is family-owned or controlled—including a good portion of the Fortune 500 companies in the United States. As a person who has a profound belief in the value of the art and science of management, this same leader has persuaded several hundred Venezuelan companies to earmark a percentage of their earnings each year for a fund called "Dividends for Society," the principal purpose of which is to upgrade the management skills of various organizations outside the private sector such as hospitals, schools, and eleemosynary institutions.

Another perspective is provided by the chairman of a large, publicly held Swiss chemical company which has ordered its subsidiaries worldwide to follow the same expensive practices as the parent in areas such as worker safety, employee benefits and environmental protection, even when the competition does not burden itself with such costs. Market position and profits are maintained by the subsidiaries through better product design, quality and service. When the chairman took office, he told his managers that it was their duty never to have to fire a worker because of bad planning. The prescription: good market research, long-range planning, and flexibility in creating new products to replace dying ones. His injunction has been met.

A Taiwanese business leader, whose company's name is a Confucian phrase meaning "Help others as you help yourself and the world will be like a family," illustrates the fact that a business statesman is a Renaissance man whose sense of responsibility is global. He quoted Thomas Carlyle to the effect that business is a sacred profession because businessmen replaced priests as society's leaders after the industrial revolution. Managers, he said, have a religious duty to help the LDCs. Through perseverance and imagination, his own company has found a variety of ways to earn a profit while helping numerous countries in Africa, Latin America and elsewhere to move toward self-sustaining growth.

In the view of The Global One Hundred interviewees, the largest external threat in the long term to the private sector and its ability to serve the public interest is the growing climate of opinion concerning the shortcomings or evils of the profit motive, competition and the market system. These business statesmen are not afflicted by self-doubt. They do not cringe at the word "profit" or attempt to find euphemisms for it. They are proud of the market system and the entrepreneurial vigor it permits and inspires, and they believe the system is fundamental to individual liberty and human freedom. At the same time, they are realists. As hard-nosed, successful businessmen, they recognize that the realization of their ideas for a better world will be a long time in coming—if it ever arrives. For example, they know that it is impossible for every country in the world today to adopt the same environmental protection laws, given the costs involved, and hence would urge as a start that at least the OECD countries adopt uniform legislation in this area. With regard to corporate tax reduction, let alone elimination, they know that elected officials—like the rest of us—cannot always be expected to make rational decisions and take the long view, and that any action in this sphere will be gradual at best. Most important, with respect to their suggested improvements in laws and regulations, they are aware that modification in attitude and behavior by individuals in all segments of society is a slow and painful process.

In getting the message of the private sector across to governments, labor, academia and the public at large, however, they are finding that economic reality is becoming a powerful ally. In China and at least some of the countries of Eastern Europe, there is a rapidly growing recognition of the imperative of the market system to stimulate individual effort, spark development and encourage productivity. In Hungary, for example, ranking government officials insist that the "second economy," as they refer to it—that is, the private sector—is essential to the country, is being rapidly legitimized, and must become much larger than it is today.

Nor is the private sector without a growing number of allies in academia. In 1982, the Nobel Prize was given to George

J. Stigler, an economist at the University of Chicago, who validated Adam Smith's claim that an invisible force operates in the market system to balance supply, demand, prices and wages. In this context, the former chairman of General Electric in the United States reminded The Global One Hundred that, in addition to *The Wealth of Nations,* Smith wrote a book about "countervailing forces" in the marketplace—referring to competition—to support his belief in economic freedom.

Recognition is growing that these fundamentals operate in the developing nations as well as in the industrialized countries. Professor Hans Thorelli, a pioneer in international business education and a Fellow of the Academy of International Business, after conducting a two-year study entitled *Consumer Emancipation and Economic Development: The Case of Thailand,* concluded that traditional, massive government-to-government aid programs, while occasionally needed for dams, roads and other major infrastructures, do not truly stimulate economic development. He argues that small, market-oriented investment projects by the private sector—local and foreign—are the only true path to growth and prosperity. In the final chapter, "A Policy Program for the Mixed Economy," he makes a number of important observations:

> Whatever the relative shares of the managed part and the open-market part of the economy in a given country, when doubt exists as to whether a given activity should be managed or open the rule should be that those wishing to extend the managed sector assume the burden of reasonable proof that this is preferable to open-market operation of the activity. This principle is vital for several reasons. Open markets can represent a potent force in development, but only as long as the open sector is larger than some minimum threshold in size relative to the managed. Another is the related belief that *in general* an industry or trade will grow faster if the role of the government is to provide the general rules of the game and serve as its umpire rather than continuously to regulate the play and the players or, indeed, get into the act itself. Further, many observers have noted that the bureaucracy in the LDCs [less developed countries], while invariably large, would typi-

cally not deserve high marks for efficiency. It is also a commonplace observation in MDCs [middle developing countries] as well as LDCs that governmentally operated economic ventures tend to have somewhat obscure performance criteria and be removed from detailed public scrutiny as well as the fresh winds of competition. Finally, and this is an important practical matter, the more detailed the governmental regulations the greater are the opportunities for corruption.

Indeed, when a decision has been made in favor of extending government regulation or operation in a given case, ideally some kind of a "sunset" provision should be attached ensuring that the decision will be *automatically* reconsidered at suitably frequent intervals.

While he recognizes—and indeed identifies—the shortcomings of multinational corporations, he is profoundly convinced of their value and utility:

What, then, may be the contribution rendered by the MNC [multinational corporation] at its best? As in the general development orthodoxy of the past, people have been thinking almost exclusively in physical or near-physical terms: the transfer of goods and engineering technology to the LDCs, the orderly development of their natural resources, the building of differential advantage for the LDCs in international markets by the establishment of export industries, and so forth.

No one can deny that such contributions are important. But potentially even more significant is *the transfer of values conducive to development.* The absolute key role that may be played by the MNC as a change agent is in the building of an open-market system. The MNC can serve as a catalyst in the transformation from crypto-capitalism to open-market capitalism in the private sector. These firms have not just provided incentive goods. They have provided job opportunities in an atmosphere relating reward to effort and results and rendering fatalism obsolete. They have demonstrated the importance of quality, delivery, service, and, not least, maintenance. They have fostered independent domestic suppliers and helped educate local retailers, stimulating entrepreneurship and a spirit of progress in their wake.

These and similar supporters of the market system notwithstanding, the need for business to put its own house in order, and to educate society's leaders and the general public to the contributions and requirements of the private sector, is clear and urgent. This is why The Global One Hundred got together to ensure that leaders in government, labor, academia and other groups benefit from the experience of the private sector in the search for solutions to world problems. They hope and expect that this continuous effort will lead to a better understanding of the nature and value of the competitive market system, and so bring about improvements in attitudes, laws and regulations enabling business to make greater contributions to employment, living standards and the quality of life in all countries of the globe.

At the same time, they are convinced that this will only be achieved if peoples everywhere are persuaded that their destinies are inextricably linked; that self-serving national interests are self-defeating; and that an agenda for the world must be created to identify the common interests of all mankind. This is the challenge The Global One Hundred have accepted.

Elliott Haynes
Executive Director
The Global One Hundred

THE GLOBAL ONE HUNDRED ADVISORY BOARD

Dr. Umberto Agnelli, Vice Chairman, Fiat SPA (Italy)

Giovanni Auletta Armenise, Chairman, Banca Nazionale dell' Agricoltura (Italy)

Warren L. Batts, President, Dart & Kraft Inc. (USA)

Atherton Bean, Chairman, International Multifoods Corporation (USA)

Antoine Baron Bekaert, Chairman, N. V. Bekaert (Belgium)

G. P. Birla, Chairman, Birla Brothers Pvt. Ltd. (India)

Romuald Burkard, Chairman, SIKA AG (Switzerland)

Dorman L. Commons, Managing Director, A. G. Becker Paribas Inc. (USA)

Neville Cooper, Director, Standard Telephones & Cables PLC (U.K.)

John B. Curcio, President, Mack Trucks, Inc. (USA)

Sanjay Dalmia, Chairman and Director, Golden Tobacco Company Ltd. (India)

Carlò De Benedetti, President, Olivetti SPC (Italy)

N. M. Desai, Chairman, Larsen & Toubro Ltd. (India)

Edwin Dodd, Chairman Emeritus, Owens-Illinois (USA)

Yuksel Erimtan, Chairman, Gama Imalat AS (Turkey)

Arthur Fürer, Chairman of the Board, Bank Leu (Switzerland)

Alexander F. Giacco, Chairman and President, Hercules Incorporated (USA)

A. H. Heineken, Chairman, Heineken NV (The Netherlands)

Samuel C. Johnson, Chairman, S. C. Johnson & Son (USA)

Dr. Neel Kalyani, Chairman, Bharat Forge Company (India)

Duane R. Kullberg, Managing Partner & Chief Executive Officer, Arthur Andersen & Company (USA)

Ivan Lansberg Henriquez, Chairman, The Lansberg Group (Venezuela)

Barry MacTaggart, President, Pfizer International Inc. (USA)

Keshub Mahindra, Chairman, Mahindra & Mahindra (India)

William Miller, Executive Vice President, Bristol-Myers Company (USA)

Nerio Nesi, President, Banca Nazionale del Lavora (Italy)

Hugh Parker, Chairman and Chief Executive Officer, Business International Corporation (USA)

Sir Alastair Pilkington, Chairman Emeritus, Pilkington Brothers Ltd. (U.K.)

Edward B. Pollak, Chairman, International Group, Olin Corporation (USA)

Antoin Riboud, President, Directeur Général, BSN Gervais Danone (France)

John J. Roberts, Chairman, American International Group (USA)

M. E. Viora, President, Societa Reale Mutua di Assicurazioni (Italy)

C. R. Ward-Ambler, Managing Director, McPherson's Ltd. (Australia)

Robert O. Wilder, Chairman, National Forge Company (USA)

Professor Gianni Zandano, President, Istituto Bancario San Paolo di Torino (Italy)

François Zannotti, President, SCOA (France)

A STATEMENT OF THE GLOBAL ONE HUNDRED

We, the undersigned international businessmen, believe that the world is drifting toward financial chaos and an economic collapse more serious than the Great Depression of the 1930s. Mounting international indebtedness, already estimated at $810 billion, holds out the threat of a chain of defaults, resulting in global economic anarchy. Deficit spending by nations throughout the world continues on a vast scale, pushing interest rates up, absorbing financial resources needed by enterprises to create more wealth, and threatening renewed inflation and deeper unemployment.

To date, stop-gap, short-term palliatives have been directed at these profound threats to human well-being; root causes have been ignored. Equally serious is the growing tendency of nations to seek solutions which they deem to be in their own self-interest, disregarding the fact that in an interdependent world such behavior is ultimately self-defeating.

Fundamental change and improvement in policy is urgently needed in four areas:

> First, industrial nations must reverse the downward trend of their economic and technical assistance to poverty-stricken countries; only with such help will they reach the point of self-development and begin meeting their debt obligations.
>
> Second, less-developed countries must accept the fact that such concessionary aid is only a preliminary to the true engine of development—market-oriented investment by the private sector—and that they must create a climate favorable to such development.
>
> Third, the present trend toward protectionism must be reversed; expanded international trade and investment is the best, if not the only, hope of resolving the debt problem and ensuring the health and vigor of the entire world economy.
>
> Fourth, national budgetary processes must be subjected to new forms of discipline—particularly in the

developed countries—if continual and growing over-spending is not to result in economic catastrophe.

We believe it is imperative that these fundamental changes take place. What is missing is the will, characterized by realism and courage, to put them into effect. Therefore we call on the leadership of the principal industrial and developing nations to join forces in drafting and implementing an international agenda for human betterment. Specifically, we urge that this agenda include the following:

First, a multilateral Marshall Plan of concessionary aid to less-developed countries, with responsibility for creating and implementing national programs—as in the case of the first Plan—placed squarely on the shoulders of the recipients themselves;

Second, modernization of the International Monetary Fund (IMF) in terms of its authority and sanction powers, and further substantial increases in its lending resources;

Third, resumption of progress toward free trade, particularly in respect of elimination of non-tariff barriers and of the requirement of so-called "voluntary" export restraints; such a program should give priority to upgrading the General Agreement on Tariffs and Trade (GATT) into a full-fledged, powerful agency along the lines of the IMF;

Fourth, creation of an international organization to create and enforce rules for foreign investment, as GATT does for world trade, with powers to protect the rights and security of investors and of host countries;

Fifth, meaningful discussion between the NATO and Comecon powers to halt, and then reverse, the weapons race, whose economic cost is damaging their standards of living and sapping their ability to raise—in their own self-interest—the living standard of the developing world, and which could lead to nuclear annihilation of the entire world;

Sixth, agreement to move in concert toward sound fiscal and monetary policies through reduced government expenditures and, if absolutely necessary, increased consumption taxes; importantly, such agreement should include a commitment by larger nations to impose constitutional or other effective strictures on their budgetary processes—given the seeming inability of politicians in the western democracies to curb spending, this is an idea whose time has come.

Such a program may sound visionary. It is anything but. The realities of the current situation dictate immediate and incisive action if we are to halt the present drift toward calamity, and harness the creative energies of people everywhere in building a safe and prosperous world.

SIGNATORIES TO THE STATEMENT

Dr. Umberto Agnelli, Vice Chairman, Fiat (Italy)

J. E. Andriessen, Chairman, Royal Packaging Industries (The Netherlands)

Carlos Auto de Andrade, President, Vale do Rio Doce (Brazil)

Percy Barnevik, President, ASEA (Sweden)

Warren L. Batts, President, Dart & Kraft (USA)

Francesco Bignardi, Director General, Banca Nazionale del Lavoro (Italy)

C. K. Birla, Senior Executive, Birla Brothers Pvt. (India)

J. T. Black, Chairman, Molson Companies (Canada)

Jean Boucau, Directeur Général, Schlumberger (France)

A. L. Burridge, President, Sterling Asia—Pacific (Philippines)

Patrick P. Byrne, Vice President, Ford Espana (Spain)

Dr. Donal S. A. Carroll, Chairman, Carroll Industries (Ireland)

Dorman L. Commons, Former Chairman, Natomas Co. (USA)

J. E. Cunningham, Chairman, McDermott International (USA)

John B. Curcio, President, Mack Trucks Inc. (USA)

Sanjay Dalmia, Chairman, Golden Tobacco Company (India)

John F. Daly, Chairman, Hoover Universal (USA)

Carlo De Benedetti, President, Olivetti (Italy)

W. Dekker, President, Phillips' Gloeilampenfabrieken (The Netherlands)

N. M. Desai, Chairman, Larsen & Toubro (India)

Carlos E. Dietl, President, Pasa Petroquimica (Argentina)

Adan Elizonda, Executive Director, Cydsa (Mexico)

Yuksel Erimtan, Chairman, Gama Imalat (Turkey)

L. G. Estenfelder, President, Gates International (USA)

B. Fenwick-Smith, Director of Finance, Thyssen-Bornemisza (Monaco)

J. M. Fleming, Chairman, Vauxhall Motors (U.K.)

Dr. Reinhart Freudenberg, Director, Freudenberg & Co. (Germany)

Daniel Goeudevert, Chairman, Ford-Werke (Germany)

Brenton S. Halsey, Chairman, James River Corporation (USA)

Robert A. Hanson, Chairman, Deere & Company (USA)

W. R. Harris, Senior Vice President International, PPG Industries (USA)

Sir Anthony Hayward, Chief Executive Officer, Private Investment Corporation for Asia (Singapore)

Thomas A. Holmes, Chairman, Ingersoll Rand (USA)

M. G. Hulme, Jr., President, Mine Safety Appliances (USA)

Ambassador Robert Ingersoll, Former Chairman, Borg-Warner (USA)

H. W. Jarvis, President, Sybron Corporation (USA)

Vicente R. Jayme, President, Private Development Corporation of the Philippines

Samuel C. Johnson, Chairman, S. C. Johnson & Son (USA)

Dr. Neel Kalyani, Chairman, Bharat Forge (India)

Shigekuni Kawamura, President, Dainippon Ink & Chemical (Japan)

Dr. Mostafa Khalil, Chairman, Arab International Bank (Egypt)

C. C. Knudsen, Vice Chairman, MacMillan Bloedel (Canada)

Koji Kobayashi, Chairman, NEC Corporation (Japan)

Yotaro Kobayashi, President, Fuji-Xerox (Japan)

Philip Kramer, President, Amerada Hess Corporation (USA)

Robert Krikorian, Chairman, Rexnord (USA)

Duane R. Kullberg, Managing Partner, Arthur Andersen & Co. (USA)

Norbert von Kunitzki, Member of the Board of Management, ARBED (Luxemborg)

.P.A. Linck, Director, Dutch Baby Milk Industries (Malaysia)

Barry MacTaggart, Chairman and President, Pfizer International (USA)

Keshub Mahindra, Chairman, Mahindra & Mahindra (India)

Frederick J. Mancheski, Chairman, Echlin (USA)

William May, Former Chairman, American Can Co., Former Dean, New York University Graduate School of Business (USA)

Donald R. Melville, President, Norton Company (USA)

George P. Mitchell, Chairman and President, Mitchell Energy & Development (USA)

Robert K. Mueller, Chairman, Arthur D. Little (USA)

Lee Myung-Bak, President, Hyundai Group (South Korea)

Sir David Nicolson, Chairman, Rothmans International (U.K.)

Jaime Ongpin, President, Benguet Corporation (Philippines)

Hugh Parker, Chairman and Chief Executive Officer, Business International Corporation (USA)

Sir Alastair Pilkington, Former Chairman, Pilkington Brothers and British Chloride (U.K.)

Dr. Louis von Planta, President, CIBA-GEIGY (Switzerland)

Edward B. Pollak, Chairman, International Group, Olin Corporation (USA)

Bharat Ram, Chairman, DCM (India)

José Miguel de la Rica, President, Petronor (Spain)

John J. Roberts, Chairman, American International Group (USA)

Lorenzo Rossi di Montelera, Director, Martini & Rossi (Italy)

Ing. Andres Marcel Sada, President, Cydsa (Mexico)

Herta Lande Seidman, Manager, International Trade, Phibro-Salomon Brothers (USA)

Sir Leslie Smith, Chairman, BOC (U.K.)

Jacques Solvay, President, Solvay (Belgium)

S. J. van Eijkelenburg, President, Netherlands Federation of Christian Employers

Washington Sycip, Chairman, SGV Group (Philippines)

Dr. Susumu Takamiya, International Academy of Management (Japan)

Dan Tolkowsky, Managing Director, Discount Investment Corp. (Israel)

S. Viswanathan, Managing Director, Seshasayee Paper and Boards (India)

Hans Werthen, Chairman, Electrolux Sweden (Sweden)

S. C. Whitbread, Chairman, Whitbread & Co. (U.K.)

J. A. Winfield, Chairman, Brockway (USA)

Gianni Zandano, President, Istituto Bancario San Paolo di Torino (Italy)

TOWARD AN UNLIMITED FUTURE

I. THE NEW REALITY: NO EASY CHOICES

Industrial statesmen in both the developed and the developing countries concur: The era of easy choices is over.

A representative assessment comes from the industrial world, in North America:

> I believe 1981 was a watershed year in the economies of the industrialized countries. From the early 1950s to the early 1980s, we had a world that could afford, and did indeed take, soft options whenever it came to a fork in the road. I think we are now entering a period where we will once again choose and address the hard options rather than the soft ones. I find this encouraging, because history seems to show that societies that take the soft options for any length of time eventually are overrun by societies that live by the hard options.

And from the developing world:

> It is true that in the past few decades we have all been too easy in choosing the soft options. We gave in to demands without insisting on responsibilities. I refer specifically to the responsibilities of productivity. This was true both domestically and internationally. It is not possible anymore.

Free enterprise had a significant role in creating soft options and now has a major responsibility to lead the way on the path of hard choices.

From a Third World industrialist:

> The dream/myth of the free enterprise system is that it leads to an instant affluent society for all. The myth leaves out the effort it takes and the long, hard slog that is necessary to get the performance that makes possible the results of the dream.
>
> As the dream is propagated now, it leads to expectations, particularly in the Third World, that really cannot be fulfilled. Free enterprise needs to be presented for what it is, and is not. It is *not* like giving candy to children. It is hard work to create wealth, but it is the best path to wealth. What free enterprise offers is the prospect of a better society, but it requires a work ethic to create that society. In the Third World we must create a concept of the work ethic, a desire for achievement, and the idea that there is reward in labor per se.

In illustration of what has gone wrong, three observations from industrialists in Europe—East and West.

First, a Yugoslav executive, looking at oil-rich Norway:

> The richer these [oil-rich] countries get, the more they spend and the deeper they get lost in a morass of debt. Take Norway. Norway's windfall of oil income was supposed to eliminate its balance-of-payments problems as well as its national budgetary problems. It did neither. Instead, Norway today is suffering from one of the biggest balance-of-payments and budgetary

> problems in Europe. This is because they cut taxes, raised welfare payments and wildly overspent.
>
> The reality is that it is impossible to re-create the growth rates of the 1950s and 1960s. We are going to have to live with less growth. The problem is that no country—and particularly no democratic country—seems to be willing to accept this fact of life and tell its citizens that they will have to cut their living standards.

Second, a U.K. business leader, in the oil industry:

> In the past thirty years democracy in the West has deteriorated into social demagoguery. It has used resources that simply aren't there, building up welfare states without creating the productive base and the wealth to sustain these states.
>
> The welfare state, and the rhetoric that prompts it, has become a theology. This theology has put a crushing burden on the private sector and has severely limited its capacity to respond to the social needs that do indeed exist and that depend on the private sector for a productive and lasting solution.

And finally a Swiss banker:

> Youth today, at least in Europe, has been so brainwashed and pampered by the incredible advances in wealth of the last thirty years that young men and women simply do not recognize the need to work and to take responsibility. The young are intent on settling down comfortably under the security blanket provided by the state. Today, the educated young of Europe believe that their personal comfort and security must be provided by the government. They are not educated to believe that they themselves are responsible for the future—their own or that of society.

In sum, industrial leaders in North America, Europe and—significantly—the developing countries agree that while the revolution of expectations, which has brought unprecedented achievements for unprecedented numbers, must continue to be nurtured and nourished, a new balance must be found. That balance must match rights with responsibilities, dreams and desires with effort and accomplishment.

1. ILLUSIONS

In facing the new reality, illusions must be recognized for what they are. For example:

It is an illusion that countries do not go broke.

They do. And when they do, their bankruptcy must be addressed in much the same way that the bankruptcy of a company is addressed. Sovereignty is not a shield against economic reality.

It is an illusion that rhetoric will bridge the North–South gap.

However impassioned and inspired, the rhetoric that demands a new allocation or reallocation of resources is basically destructive for all. As a German industrialist notes:

> A redistribution of the world's riches won't make the poor rich. It just means that, deprived of incentives, the producers will no longer produce. There will be mammoth waste. And the poor will remain as poor as ever.
>
> What we in the North need to do is to try to teach the South how to produce and to make the people of the South understand that there is no future—for them or us—in policies that proceed on the assumption that others sow, and I reap.
>
> In the final analysis, redistribution as preached in the rhetoric of the South is a form of charity, and charity is not a way of life that anyone enjoys. More important, it is not a solution to an economic problem.

It is an illusion that profit is unnecessary and undesirable.

From an industrialist in the public sector in Italy:

> Our industrial relations with the trade unions have created a situation where the trade unions declare emphatically that they do not want to contribute to the company's profit. In fact, we are losing money, for which the taxpayer picks up the tab. Profit, after all, is the last item on the balance sheet, after labor, raw materials and the cost of money.

What we in the public sector must try to make people understand—our employees, our customers, indeed our political bosses—is that profit is a reward for effort and a yardstick for competence. Most important, it is needed for reinvestment in the continuing health of the company. Without profit, there are no jobs; there is no new technology; there is, in fact, nothing. The problem is that people think of profit simply as a reward, and very often an unearned, disproportionate and unwarranted reward. This is an illusion that badly needs correction.

The fact is that companies create a social product in every sense of that word: not only in the wealth they create for their countries and the goods and services they produce for their societies, but also in the concrete allocation of their resources. In the industrial countries today, in most industrial sectors and in all service industries, the largest portion of corporate resources goes to employees; the larger part of what remains goes to government in the form of taxes; a smaller amount goes to shareholders for the use of their money; and the smallest amount, unfortunately and dangerously for the health of the world economy, goes into reinvestment.

Another fact—and companies throughout the world know this—is that profit is a minimum requirement, not an optimum goal.

The goal is growth: growth of the enterprise; growth of the people in the enterprise; growth in the community in which the enterprise is located; and growth of the society that the enterprise serves.

A Canadian industrialist offers a personal definition: "The real objective of an enterprise is to use the minimum requirement of profit for sustained job creation, for sustained creation of challenges, and, above all, for the sustained creation of opportunities for people to grow."

2. PROBLEMS

While illusions must be discarded, problems must be faced. Some examples are:

Global interdependence is real and increasing.

It would be best served with a free global economy. Maximum movement toward a free economy is therefore desirable. But a totally free global economy would have to include the free movement not only of capital, goods and services, but also the free movement of labor. On a world scale, this does not seem to be a practical possibility for the foreseeable future. Therefore, we will probably have to accept as well some constraints on other aspects of a free economy.

Protectionism.

Developing countries do have to protect infant industries and, perhaps even more vitally, nascent agriculture. Developed countries, as they restructure their industries and economies, do have to strike a socially acceptable balance between protecting the old and encouraging the new.

In this process, private enterprise has a special obligation. It must be consistent. It cannot, on the one hand, argue generically against protectionism and, at the same time, demand protection for its own specific industry or company.

Planning.

Developed countries are probably served best when planning is least, although some developed countries have operated effectively with indicative planning suited to their cultural givens.

In this area, developing countries may have different needs. An industrialist in Africa suggests:

> In North America and Europe, I don't think you need periodic development planning. Industry functions and development occurs without government interference. In the developing countries, however, there is need for central planning, guidance, the allocation of resources to priority sectors. These aids, or crutches if you like, are necessary until a country reaches a certain level from which the private sector can operate on its own.

The mismatching of savings and investment on a global scale.

At present, too many savings are diverted, not into real capital formation but into meeting current deficits. This in turn has produced an excess of consumption over production worldwide.

The problem of inadequate capital accumulation leads, in the first instance, to financial crisis; and, in the second, to an even deeper structural dilemma, that is, the inadequacy of productive capital.

The mismatching of problems and the time element with which they are addressed.

An industrialist in Asia notes:

> The time frame that is needed to address some of the major problems that face mankind is longer than the time frame that is available to most political and governmental systems. Governments deal in medium-term solutions. Most of the world's fundamental problems require long-term solutions. It is the difference between these time frames that creates most of the discontinuity in addressing global problems.

Education.

Often, and in many places, education is designed to frustrate and negate individual aspiration and accomplishment instead of enabling individuals to create and contribute.

In the developed world, education has focused excessively on macroissues that individuals can do nothing about, instead of microissues that would enable individuals to act. Psychologically, it has encouraged community fragmentation and splinter group concerns, rather than creative commitment and social cohesion.

In the developing world, education is too often abstract rather than job-related, and knowledge is imparted by rote rather than through exercises in problem-solving.

In both worlds, freedom and individuality are concepts that are frequently either distorted or obfuscated in the educational process.

As an industrial statesman in Europe puts it:

> Education has to teach that freedom is an individual concept. It has personal, political, social and economic ingredients that are interdependent. Human beings are individuals. They need individual challenges that span all these ingredients. Only freedom provides these kinds of individual challenges.

3. SOLUTIONS

While industrial statesmen everywhere concur that the era of easy choices is over, they concur as well that devising solutions is not beyond the wit of man. To do this, they hold, requires the recognition of three facets of reality:

First, the solutions to global problems cannot be tackled nationally or through ad-hocery.

> We have the competence. What we need is the will.

Second, knowledge does not diminish through dissemination.

> If there is anything in the world that does not reduce its stock through distribution, it is knowledge.

Third, there are no limits to growth.

> Natural resources are a matter of technology and price. Technology reduces the price.
>
> The human mind is a resource that, for practical purposes, is infinite. We have barely begun to tap it.

II. STRUCTURING THE WORLD ECONOMY

1. AN ECONOMIC ORDER THAT WORKS FOR ALL

Four ingredients characterize economic order, everywhere and at all times: agriculture, industry, services and leisure. In devising an international economic order, the question is how are these ingredients structured and what relative role are they assigned, both within the developed and developing countries and between them?

And, how can the developed and developing countries be integrated, effectively and expeditiously, into a world economy that works for all?

World Bank President A. W. Clausen suggests three principles for a sound and sustainable international economic order at this point in human history:

> First, if our goal is sustainable development, our perspective must be global;
>
> Second, human development must allow for continued economic growth, especially in the Third World, if it is to be sustainable;
>
> Third, sustainable development requires vigorous attention to resource management and the environment.

In substantiation of the last point, Mr. Clausen makes a vital observation that is frequently disregarded by activists and advocates in the developed countries who claim to speak for the welfare of mankind:

> Third World leaders are absolutely right to point out that poverty is the very worst pollution that faces us on earth today. Only about a quarter of the people who live in developing countries, for example, have access to clean water.
>
> In the Third World, disease typically takes up a tenth of a person's potentially productive time. Disease causes suffering, dampens initiative, disrupts education, and stunts physical and mental development.
>
> Poverty also puts severe—and often irreversible—strains on the natural environment. At survival levels, people are sometimes compelled to exploit their environment too intensively. Poverty has often resulted in long years of mismanagement of natural resources, evidencing itself in overgrazing, erosion, denuded forests and surface water pollution.
>
> Our experience at The World Bank seems to indicate that it is much easier to deal with the negative environmental effects of development than with the negative environmental effects of pervasive and persistent poverty.

Industrial statesmen in the developing countries approach the issue from the vantage point of production and demand.

On production, a Brazilian industrialist argues:

> An important tool to integrate developing countries into the world economy is joint ventures by industrial country companies with developing country companies. This includes, although it is not limited to, joint ventures in which local entrepreneurs have majority equity. In this kind of arrangement, money becomes not an end in itself but a tool for development.
>
> Right now we are in the situation, not only here in Brazil but worldwide, where the financial sector attracts resources that should be going into productive use. At the extreme end, we then get wealthy countries accumulating additional wealth, while there are others that have nothing to eat or to wear. It is the classic, deadening touch of Midas.
>
> What is needed for economic growth is a different fiscal treatment of financial investment and productive investment in order to attract resources into productive investment. At present, it works the other way round.

On the demand side, an Indian industrialist notes that for a large array of goods, demand in the developed world is largely saturated, while demand in the developing countries is both enormous and voracious. The problem that needs to be addressed, therefore, is how the demand that undeniably exists in the developing countries can be turned into purchasing power.

Undoubtedly this calls for a measure of restructuring in the world economy that makes sense for all. It means, *inter alia,* that production processes that have high energy requirements should be located where cheap energy is available. For instance, in addition to the obvious example of a petrochemical industry based in Saudi Arabia, there is Zaire, with cheap hydroelectric power potential that could be used to produce aluminum. The European industrialist who cited these examples adds that "These changes must come, painful as they may be to the North." And a Swiss industrialist, concurring, notes:

> The real problem with protectionism is that it does not protect. It is a dangerous misnomer for a Band-Aid that covers a scratch but does not heal the wound. Protectionism does not cure unemployment; it causes it. The strength of the private sector lies in its constant change and adaptation to new circumstances, and protectionism cripples that ability. What happens when governments try to conserve existing industries through protectionism is that no new industries emerge.
>
> Take the example of my own country, Switzerland. In the late 1930s, Switzerland was a country of textiles and watches. During the depression of the 1930s, the Swiss government decided to protect the watch industry but not the textile industry. As a result, textiles all but disappeared, except for a few specialty items. Also as a result, the watch industry failed to adapt and is now in deep structural difficulty. Protected, it did not keep pace with change.
>
> At the other end of the spectrum, my city, Basel, did keep pace with change and is today a world center of pharmaceutical and chemical industries.

Developing countries must make their own contribution to this process of restructuring so that it can work for all. A Mexican industrialist points out:

> The current Mexican crisis is due in part to the overprotection of Mexican industry. We must learn to increase productivity and improve quality so we can become competitive in the international market. Protectionism prevents, or at least discourages us from doing this.
>
> Developing countries must become more aware of the need to restructure their economies to enhance their comparative advantage so that they can participate as full and equal partners in the international market. As the saying goes: We must learn to get our own act together.

Adding another facet to a parallel viewpoint, a Venezuelan industrialist observes:

> The main problem in many developing countries, and emphatically here in Venezuela, is the transfer of activity from the private to the public sector. As a result, salaries and wages go up, while productivity does not. Being thus made noncompetitive, protectionism becomes mandatory, at least from a political point of view. This protectionism then produces an artificial industrial structure, which is costly in the short run and untenable in the long run.

Both the Mexican and the Venezuelan industrialist agree that developing countries that want to "get their act together" in order to compete in the world market must also address the problem of pervasive corruption, which can make its own corrosive contribution to hampering productivity and distorting economic reality.

Since multinational corporations are at present the most important and effective problem-solving instrument on both the production and the demand side of the equation, the logical follow-up question becomes: How can their effectiveness be enlarged and enhanced? An Australian industrialist offers a novel suggestion:

> Multinational corporations should be given the maximum opportunity to function, the greatest freedom to compete, and perhaps in return be levied with a supertax that could be put into a capital fund designed for investment in developing countries.
>
> The problem with harnessing such a capital base is that it is, in itself, not enough. You also have to get people to use it competently and productively. Multinational corporations are clearly best equipped to do that. So perhaps the capital in this fund should be put at the disposal of companies to make possible investments in developing countries where the risks would otherwise be too great.

A Swiss industrialist, whose company has extensive operations in the rural areas of dozens of developing countries, agrees that it would be helpful to put together what he describes as "a bouquet of incentives." This would consist of the World Bank and other international financial institutions providing funds for such large-scale physical infrastructure as roads and dams; specialized international agencies helping with such human infrastructure projects as education and training in job-related skills; and host governments offering incentives in the tax area. If such a "bouquet" were put together—in joint consultation, including multinational companies, to make certain that the package devised would be pragmatic and realistic—then, he asserts boldly: "There is no country in the world that does not offer an investment opportunity of some kind."

From a French industrialist comes another idea:

> We can use the tax system of the industrialized countries to help the developing nations concretely, productively. . . .
>
> What happens now is that governments transfer taxpayers' money in government-to-government aid, and nothing changes. Take the most extreme example: government aid for disaster relief in Africa. Disaster is temporarily, and not very effectively, alleviated; but the basic problems remain and it is only a question of time before disaster strikes again.
>
> If a government used only part of the money allocated to, say, hunger relief in Africa, to allow a large tax deduction to a food company going into the disaster-ridden country to attack the problem at the fundamental level, i.e., local food production, it would be much better for everyone. Unlike government, that company's aim is to do the job well permanently. That is where its success lies—as well as that of the country in which it contributes to the solution of a basic problem.
>
> A less drastic but equally relevant case: Say a company invests in Brazil. It is a huge market, but it is not yet easy to get started there and it is difficult to get money back for some time. So an investment in Brazil shows up in the balance sheet as a loss for many years. If the tax system allowed the investment to be depreciated, if it became tax-deductible, a lot more investment would go into these countries where it is needed, with everyone benefiting.

> Really large investments, and especially large-scale investment by many companies, would also reduce political risk. Right now, for example, companies in France, especially medium-sized companies, might invest in Latin America if they saw a payout in a five- to ten-year period. They won't invest in a project that stretches over fifty years. But if there were more investment in Latin America, particularly by big companies, smaller and medium-sized firms would consider their own investments to be safer. This investment depreciation schedule I have in mind should be tied to the political risk the country represents for an investor.

Given the vital role of multinational companies in the integration of developing countries into the world economy, many industrialists both North and South believe that a global code governing the behavior of international companies *and* the countries in which they operate is probably desirable. Corporate behavior in consonance with such a code can be enforced by law, both national and international. But how can the countries' behavior be enforced? An industrialist in Switzerland proposes that enforcement be structured along the lines of conditionality now applied by the IMF. If a country breaks the global code, all loans to that government, by international institutions and by commercial banks, are halted until conformity to the code is reestablished.

In principle, the United Nations and its agencies are the ideal and proper institutions to promote the effective integration of the world economy and to police the behavior of the participants in the integration process. The problem is that the UN, as it is currently constituted and, more important, as it functions at this stage, is long on irrationality and rhetoric and short on soundness and effective action. The inevitable result, in the words of the Brazilian banker who is a former Minister of Finance, is that "We have a situation in which the UN is important when the problem is unimportant, but . . . is marginal, at best, when the problem is important."

In that context, a Canadian industrialist offers a ray of hope:

> In some functional areas, sovereignty is being surrendered to achieve reasonable objectives. I think of such

> areas as aviation, conservation, anti-pollution measures, weather observation. It seems that nations can work together where there are realistic objectives and where what needs to be done does not touch political pride and ambition. This proves that the possibility exists of increasing recognition of the need for cooperation for purposes that are clearly beneficial for all.

And from a senior corporate scientist in the United States, this suggestion:

> One way of going about addressing this problem would be the creation, and above all empowering, of more decentralized international organizations with a focus other than that of safeguarding sovereignty or bolstering national pride and ambition. Multinational corporations, with their focus on productive enterprise, are of course a classic case in point. But there is a whole range of nongovernmental institutions that exist and even play a role in the United Nations system. The tragedy is that the role played by these nongovernmental organizations at the UN is peripheral. In fact it is modest to a point of being meaningless in the current UN approach to the world.
>
> If these nongovernmental organizations, with concerns and objectives in many areas that really cut across national borders and the limitation of sovereignty, were allowed to play a more vital role at the UN, their constructive contribution to the integration of the world economy would be substantial.

In both the developed and the developing countries, industrial statesmen point out that if the money and resources the world spends on armaments could be funneled into productive purposes, much—probably all—of mankind's present peaceful needs could be met.

The comment is usually limited to the military expenditures of the superpowers. The distressing reality is that many developing countries spend an even larger part of their GNP on armaments. (Two examples: Chad, with a per capita income of $140 a year, currently allocates half of its budget to military expenditure. India, having recently drawn on the IMF for $6 billion, immediately spent the lion's share of the money on a fleet of military aircraft.)

From a Japanese industrialist, an observation that reaches beyond the waste inherent in preparing for war and deals with the profound challenges of peace: "True peace is not a state of non-war. Peace is a state in which people understand each other, help each other, and share wisdom and power with each other."

An economic order that works for all would constitute a major component of such a true peace.

2. FIXING THE FINANCIAL SYSTEM

Necessity has prompted both action and thought to deal with the needs of, and dangers to, the international financial system. Essentially, these revolve around close to $600 billion of debt with which an array of countries cannot cope under present conditions. While the best way to meet the current emergency is debatable, the need for lasting solutions is evident.

The first of these is a better way to keep track of the full extent of a country's exposure, to include short-term, medium-term, and long-term indebtedness of both the public and the private sectors. What the world must have in order to prevent present and future calamity or chaos, industrial statesmen agree, is a comprehensive and dependable early warning system that provides knowledge—the same knowledge—to both borrowers and lenders.

One practical proposal comes from a banker in Spain:

> The main problem of the international financial system is a matter of information. Take Mexico, for example, and its problems. We all thought that Mexico was a better risk than Brazil. It had oil. It had a sound political system. But we had no information about its debt structure, particularly its short-term debt structure. By we, in this case, I mean the lenders, all the lenders.
>
> As the international financial system operates today, the only organization that has this kind of information, or at least an important part of it, is the IMF.

> For political reasons, under current rules, the IMF cannot make this information available to others, including commercial banks who make loans to these countries. Obviously, the IMF and the World Bank cannot make this kind of information available publicly. It has to be handled with great sensitivity. But I believe it would be a good idea if the IMF set up a kind of warning system that would alert concerned parties. In Spain, we have in the central bank a Risk Information Center that knows what the credit exposure is of all companies in Spain, private or public. That Center cannot publish its information. But if someone in the banking system with a legitimate interest asks, the central bank does give out the requested information. I would like to see a comparable system, on a global basis, established by the IMF.

A top-level financial executive of the public sector in Singapore analyzes how such an early warning system could be implemented and policed:

> The current institutional structure of the international financial system is adequate to solving most problems, but it lacks leadership and commitment.
>
> The main problem lies in borrowers, especially countries, being unwilling to reveal their full debt to international institutions or commercial banks. Without this information, it is impossible to make sound lending decisions. Banks have played their own deleterious role by being too meek to demand such information as a condition for lending. Thus, the world needs to clarify the rules for international lending. Unless the world has a clear picture of exposure from a borrower, that borrower, that country, should not get money from international institutions.
>
> And unless a bank is willing to share its information on a borrower, it should be penalized by international and national authorities.
>
> All of this would be fairly easy to organize, if a person or group had the moral clout and intestinal fortitude to put such a system together. Such leadership probably has to come from the World Bank or the IMF.

In addition to cooperation on an early warning system, a closer connection between international financial institutions, such as the IMF, the World Bank, the IFC, the regional development banks and commercial banks, seems indicated in other areas.

One banker who is a former Minister of Finance and an adviser to the IMF proposes that "There should be much closer cooperation between the IMF and the commercial banking system worldwide. Specifically, this can be accomplished by the commercial banks buying IMF long-term bonds." Suggesting a different form of synergy, a German banker suggests that commercial banks should continue to make, and expand, their loans to developing countries, but have these loans guaranteed by the World Bank or the IMF. And a number of industrialists, in both borrowing and lending nations, recommend more joint loans by the World Bank and commercial banks, and the introduction into regional development banks of their own version of the IFC.

The most complete consensus emerges—again, both from borrowers and lenders—on the subject of conditionality, that is, the disciplines imposed by lenders on borrowers, whether in the public or the private sector.

From an industrialist in the Philippines:

> What seems to be the most fundamental flaw in the international financial system, particularly as we have lived with it in the past couple of years, is that with interest rates as high as they were, it was difficult to justify productive investment. And without investment there is no development, and no growth.
>
> What is vital now is that we devise a financial structure that is designed to help productive growth, not hinder it.
>
> One way of doing this is to arrange for patterns of co-financing by commercial banks and the World Bank and its regional affiliates, where joint conditions are devised that reflect both sound commercial practice and sound development policies. And that these conditions be firmly policed for all loans, but especially for loans made to developing countries.
>
> It is quite clear here in the Philippines, for exam-

> ple, that commercial lending in the past did not have the required disciplines, with the result that a great deal of money was wasted. I am convinced that unless international lenders, especially commercial banks, clamp down on country lending with sound rules of conditionality and impose stricter discipline, that problem will not be solved.
>
> It is important for the borrowers as well as for the lenders to have sound disciplines imposed on them. As we in the developing countries tally up the debts that we accumulated as the result of easy lending practices of the past few years, I personally used to worry about my children having to meet these debts. Now I have begun to worry about my grandchildren paying the debts.

And another comment, from a banker in a major developing country, on the destructive and distorting effect of lending that is insufficiently policed:

> In the last ten years, much of the borrowing by developing countries has been for projects, not all of which made economic sense. More important, and more distressing from an economic point of view, a great deal of that borrowing went into financing capital flight, because developing countries maintained overvalued currencies.

The thrust of such jointly imposed conditionality must be the channeling of funds into sound, productive enterprise. This may mean that ingredients of conditionality should be: (a) the active encouragement of a local stock market; (b) ground rules that provide a favorable climate for private investors, both domestic and foreign; and (c) loans for infrastructure projects such as roads, dams, or even education, to be made not to governments but to the institutions and organizations that actually do the work or provide the service.

Finally, a comment on the subject of conditionality from an executive in the retail sector in Europe with a fundamental, if perhaps impractically drastic point of view:

When they make loans to developing countries, the big commercial banks have to set conditions that make productive sense. Specifically, I mean that the banks should ask: Just what is this loan for? If it is for a nuclear plant, or for armaments, they should not make the loan. If it is for productive enterprises—necessary infrastructure, useful capital goods, needed consumer goods, food production—they should.

Banks already pursue this kind of policy when they deal with companies. For example, if I go to a bank and say that I want to build a wonderful new head office, no bank, given present economic conditions, will give me the money. At least, no sensible bank will. But if I go to the same bank and say I want to set up a new store, and here are the projected sales from that store, I will get the money. I think the banks should act the same when, for example, they make a loan to Chad.

People will raise the bugaboo of sovereignty. Well, as a retailer, my sovereign rights are also infringed. For example, I can't sell a bottle of whiskey to a kid. By the same token, it makes no sense to sell the most sophisticated weapons to the big kids who run some governments. What, for example, was the point of selling an atomic reactor to Iraq? It was done because we think short term instead of long term. France wanted the oil of Iraq, and the sale helped the balance of payments. But if I sell my whiskey to a kid and the kid gets drunk and smashes my store windows, I have no right to complain, do I? More to the point still, I have no recourse.

Some business leaders came up with ideas and observations that stretch the mind far beyond conventional approaches.

1. Quintupling IMF Resources

An industrialist in India:

I believe . . . that IMF resources should be increased five times. Not, of course, immediately but over a reasonable period of time. The funds should contain some reasonable constraints. These need to be discussed. They have to be geared to individual countries, resources and absorptive capacity. But these constraints should also be imaginative. The money should, for example, not be applied only to projects. It must also be applied to what I think of as the raw material of projects, by which I mean, among many other components, people. This means that the funds must be applied to education in every sense of the word, but preferably and primarily to job-related education.

I know that thinking of increasing IMF resources five times sounds impossible. And it appears at first glance as if the idea would make a major demand for sacrifice on the industrial countries. But I believe this is not an accurate perception. It seems to me to be the most evident self-interest. Not only will it create the markets that the industrial countries need, but there is the even more fundamental question: What is the alternative?

2. Harmonizing Fiscal and Monetary Policy Worldwide

A banker-statesman in Egypt:

If it were possible to harmonize the policies of the major countries that are market economies, I believe that would be a very important contribution to the economic welfare of the world. It cannot be done through the UN or any existing UN institution. I believe market economies should create an institution of their own that can tackle the problem.

3. Making SDRs the World Reserve Currency

A financial statesman known for his cutting-edge thinking:

The role of the SDR should be enhanced so that it becomes the world reserve currency. This would not only make sense for the world economy, but would also solve some of the problems of the U.S. dollar, which is now both a national currency and the effective world currency, a complex and difficult role. I know, of course, that making the SDR the currency for world reserves is not a matter that can be tackled immediately, but I do think it can and should be done over a period of twenty to thirty years.

Meanwhile, there is broad concurrence among industrial statesmen—with some exceptions—that the present volatile, sometimes distorting and often disruptive seesaw of exchange rates should be reorganized. A system should be devised which, to the maximum possible extent, permits exchange rates to be determined by the normal forces of supply and demand, but which also makes some provision to prevent the extremes in fluctuation that are caused by factors extraneous to fundamental economic reality.

Two observations:

1. The arms expenditures of LDCs currently total about $600 billion. This is roughly the equivalent of their outstanding financial obligations.
2. Liquidity of OPEC countries stands at about the same figure. In the past, these funds were invested almost entirely in short-term and medium-term instruments, overwhelmingly unproductive ones. If this liquidity were channeled into productive investment, in the OPEC countries themselves or in other developing countries, a constructive bridge could be built from the present problems of debt-ridden developing nations to a sound, long-range solution.

3. TECHNOLOGY AND MANKIND

Technology is a response to need. For example, the technology of robotics is a response to the fact that, increasingly, human beings are long-lived, healthy and educated, and therefore in need of work that does not include spending long, demanding hours at boring and repetitive tasks far beneath their mental and creative capabilities.

Technology does bring in its wake new and different problems that have to be solved. It always has, and always will. The challenge is to address these problems intelligently, which, in the present context of resources available to mankind, means both practically and humanely. What needs to be done from a practical point of view must be balanced with what should be done from a human point of view. The basic relationship between technology and mankind is not an adversary one; it is a complementary one. Technology, creatively devised and logically implemented, supports mankind and enhances the life of the human race.

The main problems connected with technology at this time appear to be:

- Unemployment caused by technology.
- Training and/or retraining of both the workforce and the general public to cope with technology.
- The transfer of technology from the technology "haves" to the technology "have-nots," which tend to run parallel to the sociopolitical North–South axis but are not synonymous with it.
- Technology and energy.
- Technology and population.

On technology and unemployment, an industrial leader in France comments:

> I see only one perspective. You cannot unscramble the proverbial egg. Technology exists. Technology inevitably means fewer workers in factories, and more in service and study. I think this is a desirable development. It is undoubtedly true that overall there will be fewer people working. But I look at what has happened in the past hundred years both on the farm and in the city. A hundred years ago, farmers worked from sunup to sundown, never had a vacation, hardly ever had any time they could call their own. Now farmers, certainly here in France, work less than the man in the factory. In less than a hundred years, work time for the average farmer has halved. The same is true in the factories. A hundred years ago the average work week was around eighty hours; now it is about forty hours. I have no doubt that within less than a hundred years, the average work week for people with the worst jobs will be down to twenty hours. I consider that a good thing.
>
> People with good jobs, by which I mean jobs that

> interest and challenge them, in whatever field, will always want to work longer. Their interest in work is not only money, but the excitement, the personal challenge and the social utility of what they do. But for people who work for a living, technology is a boon.

An industrial leader in Spain discusses the global aspect of technology and the implications for unemployment:

> It is clear that you cannot stop technology. . . . In my own sector, electronics and communications, there have been discussions with unions who wanted us to introduce technology gradually. If Spain were an island living independently of the rest of the world, this might be possible, if not necessarily desirable. But Spain is part of the world and our industry must be competitive and be able to export. To do that, technology is a priority that must be applied. You cannot control employment by controlling technology. . . .
>
> I do not know how much looking back at history and the two previous industrial revolutions really teaches us. When we look back, it is indeed true that each industrial revolution has created more jobs than existed before it happened. Whether this will be true again, I do not know. Therefore I worry about it.

On training and retraining, industrialists in all sectors of the economy—sunrise or sunset—agree that there is cause for concern. A senior executive in the United States, with top-level experience in both the public and the private sectors, delineates the problem unvarnished.

> There is no doubt that robots will increasingly take the place of humans on dead-end jobs. One would have to concede that this is fundamentally a good thing. Good or bad, however, it will certainly happen.
>
> The question then becomes, What can be done to retrain the people who did the jobs that the robots will do better? If they are young enough or adaptable enough to be retrained, that of course needs to be done. And in that effort, the private sector must take on a large

share of responsibility, if only because it will be better at the task.

> But we also have to face the fact that there will be segments of the population that cannot be retrained for the jobs that are available. For them we have to create safety nets. Some of these safety nets can consist of interim jobs that are not themselves highly skilled. For example, I can see no reason why steelworkers who are no longer needed in the production of steel cannot be trained to build bridges, railroads and other infrastructure ingredients that are clearly needed. But, in a fundamental way, a major period of transition is unavoidable.

And from another senior U.S. executive who is deeply enmeshed in the excitement of the sunrise service sector, a parallel thought:

> I see in the service industry a brilliant future which will both replace and create jobs. But it is true that people who must relocate and be retrained from the smokestack industries to services will often find this a very painful experience. This is true for many people in the short term. For some, who are too intractable, won't move, won't respond to retraining opportunities, it may well be a long road. But there are a great many who can be retrained and can respond to opportunities where the jobs are created. For those who cannot respond to the necessary restructuring of the economy, we need the safety net that the government can provide; indeed, must provide. I consider that, along with defense, the government's primary responsibility.
>
> The people who will need the safety net are people who are now in their forties and early fifties. This also means that, within twenty years, we will see the end of this particular problem. There will be no problem for the young ones. They will have grown up in the new era of computers, information, communications, and all the other services that characterize our particular period of history.

The problem, and the task, is not confined to the developed world. The newly industrialized countries, and indeed the still industrializing countries, share it.

From a Brazilian industrialist and former Planning Minister, this observation:

> There has to be a strong elementary and high school system at the public level, plus selected higher education that focuses on concrete professional needs. There is a clear and evident need in all societies for recycling education and for retraining people to keep up with the economic requirements of their societies. This has been true for the last three centuries, and is true most emphatically now. Increasingly, people have to be retrained throughout life.
>
> I see it here in Brazil. Engineers who do not understand computers can command a salary . . . of $750 a month. If they understand computers and know how to work with them, to all intents and purposes the sky is the limit to what they can earn. This kind of continued and continual reeducation has to be done both by the private sector and the public sector. In Brazil, universities have special courses that are given in the evening after working hours for retraining, and a number of private organizations exist that also have evening courses running from 6 to 8 p.m. for executives and professionals. . . .
>
> Everywhere in the world we need networks of these kinds of approaches and institutions.

On technology transfer, the most result-oriented minds in the developing world, and certainly the most responsible actors on the economic scene, concur that the best way to transfer technology is in the private sector, focused on concrete projects.

A banker in Egypt who heads a Pan-Arabian financial institution specializing in direct investment in productive enterprises spells out this approach.

> I am convinced that the best way to transfer technology is through direct venture projects in which there is participation by foreign and domestic capital. In such an

enterprise, the transfer of technology is directed by equity or licensing or management arrangements that are focused concretely on a concrete project, where both the recipient of the technology and the provider of the technology have a direct stake in what happens. The best governments can do to promote technology transfer is to encourage such projects with incentives and the necessary legal and regulatory adjustments.

As in any other economic endeavor, price is a consideration. But price and desirable cost-benefit ratios are not synonymous. As another Egyptian industrialist points out:

> I am convinced that technology is needed all over the world, in both the industrial and the developing countries. I also believe it is available. The only problem I see is that sometimes the price is more than the developing country, or the entrepreneur in the developing country, can afford.
>
> For example, I wanted to buy some technology on raising fish. I shopped around in the developed countries where the technology exists. But the price was too high. I finally got it, at a rate I believe we can afford, from the Chinese. And it seems to be working fine.
>
> Of course, the developing country, or the importer of technology wherever he is, must also know what to do with the technology he imports. Being able to absorb the technology in a productive way is even more important than the price.

Addressing the question from a national rather than a personal point of view, an industrialist in the Philippines adds:

> It is important for developing countries to be selective in the type of technology they import. I must make sense in local terms. In the Philippines, for instance, I believe there is no place for advanced technology except where we have a clear comparative advantage or really cannot do without.
>
> We do not need advanced technology that we cannot put to sensible and profitable use, just because it is the fashionable thing to have.

> I am not against the most advanced technology available. I just want to make certain that it makes sound economic sense in local terms.

A hands-on demonstration of how technology transfer works best also comes from the Philippines, from an industrialist who calls on direct experience to make his point.

> First, we experimented with sending people abroad to become technologically educated. We found when they came back home that they understood certain basics, but could not translate these basics into concrete application as it was needed. This led me to the conclusion that we do not get the optimum transfer of technology in this manner.
>
> What we are doing instead is to import experts for either medium-term stints of three to five years, or as career opportunities. These experts then provide systems and procedures and we encourage them to bring in other experts as needed from wherever.
>
> But—and this is a vital point, indeed the secret of the entire process—every one of these imported experts has Filipinos as the second-in-command and as the third-in-command, who get trained on the job. This, I believe, is the most effective way of transferring technology, certainly in the area of management.

From the other side of the technological divide, a group of German industrialists has come up with a three-ply suggestion:

- Public subsidies for the training of technicians and managers from developing countries in German industrial undertakings.
- Subsidies for German technicians and managers in the private sector engaged in technology transfers to developing countries.
- Government guarantees for returns on investment via the licensing route that match existing guarantees for capital investment in developing countries.

Swirling around the promise and problems of technology is the issue of energy, particularly nuclear energy, which technology makes possible and human fear and ignorance obstructs.

In this context, industrial statesmen feel that a couple of truths deserve restating and a few myths need to be put to rest.

It is true that the industrial world had developed profligate habits in its energy use and had neglected, indeed all but ignored, the development of "soft" energy sources.

It is not true that the world is running out of nonrenewable energy sources in the foreseeable future.

As one leading industrialist, for whom energy is a basic raw material, puts it:

> I see no really pressing problem there. The fact is that there is enough coal, for example, in the world right now to provide all the energy we need for two hundred years. This is not to say that it will not be difficult to find, to dig out, to process, and that we should be stupid in the use of energy, as we have been. We should pay attention to the use of natural resources, and we should conserve. But I think there is enough energy on the planet for as far out as I can see not to require a reduction in the standard of living by anyone.

The heart of the technology–energy issue, however, is nuclear energy. A German industrialist analyzes the problem in its many-faceted aspects:

> Everywhere in the world, in the developed as well as the developing countries, we need better education for better technology. Not only investors but other members of society must at least understand the basics of the inventions and the technology that is being developed. We cannot live in two different worlds.
>
> At present, for example, in Europe we suffer from people who make judgments about inventions and technologies without understanding, or even trying to understand, what is really involved. The paramount example of what is happening . . . is nuclear energy. Public debate on the desirability or otherwise of nuclear energy is conducted largely in slogans. The slogans claim that there is something naturally evil about nuclear energy; that it is incurably harmful to the en-

vironment; that the pollution it produces is infinitely worse than the pollution produced by other energy sources such as coal and oil. But this is simply not true. Coal and oil produce their own forms of pollution. [You just have to look at the Acropolis to see it. And gas as an energy source contains sulfur dioxide as a waste, which must be treated or we get sulfuric acid and the notorious acid rain. The point is that every form of energy has problems, including pollution problems, that have to be solved. The solution with gas, for example, is to make certain that either there is no sulfur in the fuel or the sulfur is removed from the waste. That is a very expensive proposition. Other forms of energy, such as coal and oil, have equally obvious costs, and I mean not only direct costs but costs for the environment.]

The truth is that the best solution from an environmental point of view is nuclear energy. For example, very few people in the current climate of sloganeering on nuclear energy know that less radioactivity is produced by a nuclear plant than is produced by a coal plant. Also, if we look at the real world, we see that if we add up the accidents, and the damage to the environment done by coal plants, and include accidents in mines, more people have died in one year from coal production than in all nuclear plants that exist. The truth, in fact, is that not a single person has actually died as a result of accidents at a nuclear plant. . . .

One of the problems with atomic energy is that . . . it is mixed up in the demagogy, and therefore politically, with atomic war. But when you think it through, the existence in Germany, for example, of a number of nuclear plants is meaningless in terms of danger to individuals when compared with the Russian nuclear missiles that are already, in fact, targeted on German cities. One touch of the button in Moscow will obviously create infinitely more nuclear havoc than human error could possibly create in nuclear energy plants.

I believe that energy will play a major role in the future development of the world, including the developing countries. . . . Energy is vital to the developing countries and to the nutrition of the increasing populations that all of them have. The only possibility to provide the cheap energy that is needed, with minimal environmental problems, is through nuclear energy.

Underpinning, surrounding, and finally transcending the issue of technology is the problem of population. Fashionable wisdom holds that the planet is overpopulated now, certainly will be by the year 2000, and that its resources will not sustain a human population increasing in geometric proportion. Although any or all of these assertions may well be true, their focus is too narrow to deal with current reality and the approach too simplistic to address the future.

A broad-gauged perspective of current reality would reveal as the real problem the care and feeding of the young in the developing countries and the care and feeding of the old in the industrial countries. While in the developing world too many of the young suffer from lack of opportunity that spans a wide spectrum, including such basics as adequate nourishment, housing and health care, the developed world is aging rapidly and the proportion of the young whose work has to sustain the old is becoming increasingly skewed.

Global experience has demonstrated that the most effective contraceptive is a higher living standard. As one developing country industrialist put it, "Anyone can understand a cost-benefit analysis of having children." When economic conditions in a society no longer make children the only social security and old age protection available to parents, population growth dwindles at a rapid rate.

Also, there is no direct relationship between population density and hunger. Belgians are well fed, while there are countries in Africa with very low population density that are rife with malnutrition, undernourishment and actual starvation.

And the world's agricultural resources are still untapped in many areas. If existing technology were applied, there would be no problem feeding the present population of the world, or even the 6 billion who are expected to populate the planet by the end of the century.

A Spanish banker sums up the currently *un*fashionable approach to this question:

> The world has teetered toward a negative attitude on the subject of population. Fundamentally, I believe that

> reproduction is a matter of individual freedom and that countries can pursue policies that make for more growth, or policies that make for less growth, in which this individual freedom is exercised. At present, the old countries have become pessimistic. Europe, for example, cannot replace its present generation, with the result that the population is aging. This, in turn, produces an ever greater burden for the young and more need for state intervention.
>
> Personally, I believe that the young are an investment. What I see happening is that in societies where, from an economic point of view, the population battle is not necessary, it is being fought. In developing countries, the argument is that there are not enough resources. But the image that comes to my mind is if, say, you have a dance and sixteen boys have arrived but only ten girls, there are two solutions. You can either send away some of the boys, or invite more girls. I am in favor of the second solution. I believe there are enough resources in the world. The real problem is to find them and find the best way to use them. Overall, I think the reasonable solution is to move toward policies that produce a younger population rather than an older population worldwide, and then learn how to manage the planet's resources. Technology is the tool.

And from Egypt, where the population pressure on economic resources is very real, a similar sentiment:

> I am convinced that the problems that technology creates, technology can solve. The problems created by technology now are short term. In the long run, any technology adds more global wealth than it requires in expense.

A last word on the topic from an astronaut:

> I saw earth from the moon. That vision taught me that technology and commitment can overcome any challenge.

III. GOVERNMENT AND THE PRIVATE SECTOR: THE VITAL BALANCE

Everywhere in the world today, governments have become economic as well as social institutions, and companies have become social as well as economic organisms. The important question therefore—and it is a question in the First, Second and Third Worlds—is: What is the best balance between government and the private sector?

1. THE FIRST WORLD

There is consensus in the First World among industrial leaders, with some constraints and provisos, that that government governs best that governs least. This viewpoint is in part a reaction to counterproductive restrictions that obstruct the efforts of private sector managers to meet the world's evident need for productive economic enterprise. But the viewpoint is fashioned primarily by a deeply held conviction that freedom is a fundamental value for mankind and that it is indivisible.

Two industrial leaders, with painful personal experience in their own nations to draw on, put it this way.

In Spain: "Our values depend on freedom, and free enterprise is an integral part of freedom."

In Italy: "Free enterprise is fundamental for democracy. If we fail to realize this, as we did in Italy for some time, we end up in a very dark night. It was free enterprise that kept the nation going in its darkest days."

Still, all freedom has constraints, and the difference between freedom and license includes limits that are understood, acknowledged and practiced.

As a third European industrialist notes:

> The question being posed these days is: Even given the fact that no alternative system has turned out to be either more efficient or more humane, are there not limits to the market system? Should there be limits?
>
> The critics of capitalism today base most of their criticism on the past, on the early days of capitalism when some of the methods were understandably primitive. Today we live in a considerably more socially minded market, and in a market economy that tries to find ways to limit the social failures and human costs of the early days of capitalism. It is true that the market, and society overall, do have noneconomic components that must be recognized and attended. But it is important to meet these concerns with as little interference as possible. And when I look around the world at countries that are more or less economically successful, I see a direct correlation between the amount of interference and the amount of economic success. The less there is of the former, the more there is of the latter.

The same industrial statesman provides an addendum:

> The big problem in Europe at present is that there is too much regulation and, perhaps even more important, that the regulation comes from people who actually detest the free market. They believe in regulation not so much to meet social requirements, but because their personal bias against the free market prompts them into designing regulation to control it.

And another European industrialist gives a neat summary of how an optimum balance between government and the private sector can be designed: "The best role that the state can play in the economic system is to provide efficient legal and regulatory structures that work well and are administered by high-quality personnel."

There is consensus as well that one area in which legal structures are desirable—preferably on a global basis, or to begin with for all OECD countries—is the area of environmental protection. While companies are willing to internalize constraints to safeguard the environment, legislation that will make these constraints equitable (instead of providing a competitive advantage to polluters) is a better way.

Industrial leaders propose two provisos for such legislation. One is that laws and regulations be based on a rigorous cost-benefit analysis that makes economic as well as social sense. The other is that lawmakers be honest with their citizens in explaining that the cost of environmental protection will inevitably show up in the price they pay for the product.

From an industrialist in Canada, in a sector deeply involved in this issue, a note of optimism: "Some years ago, this seemed to be a major and very intractable problem. But I am optimistic about it now. I see the poles coming together and solutions being devised that make sense for all."

In the European segment of the First World there is a body of opinion, including industrial leaders, which argues that basic utilities such as energy, water supply and some aspects of transportation and communications should have public sector participation. Those who hold this view reason that if the public sector holds substantial but minority equity and is represented on the board but stays out of management, a balance can be achieved between efficiency and other valid public concerns. Germany's VEBA, a public sector owned energy company, is cited as a case in point.

From France comes a somewhat testy explanation of why constraints on the public sector are important in the area of economic endeavor:

> The main argument against governments in business is that they are no good at it. When they do get involved in economic operations, governments do not create businesses. They create lumbering dinosaurs that are economic losers. They also create monopolies. Take the example of railroads here in France. Having created a government monopoly on railroads, the government then inevitably moved to eliminate competition such as, for example, competition from trucks. The economic and social cost is that once a government is in a monopoly situation, it does not need to make a real profit. It can always stack the deck so a profit will appear, not as the result of good management or of providing a good product or service, but as the result of a lack of competition. . . .

> And if a government-owned company is in trouble, it can always count on the Treasury to provide the cash it needs. In France, we have the example of the car industry. If Renault, which is government-owned, needs extra money, it gets it, in effect from the taxpayers, who are not involved in any decisions made at Renault itself, or even in a decision of whether they want to give their money to Renault. Citroën, on the other hand, which is a private sector company, has to look for shareholders who are willing to risk their money on the company, and who have at least some say over how the company is managed. The fundamental difference is that, in the Renault case, the people who contribute the money have no choice, and in the Citroën case, they do.

From Australia, a comparable argument and another concrete illustration.

> In Australia, as in many other countries, both industrialized and developing, the government is operating businesses in which it has no justifiable place. It is simply wrong for government to run these. All it does is to enlarge the bureaucracy and centralize power.
>
> Take, for example, the railways in our country. They are run by government because, the argument goes, they provide a public service. In effect, this is not so. The railways are costing the citizens money. They also make it difficult for competing systems of transportation to get a fair crack at the market, which would give better service to the consumer. What is actually happening is that the population is being taxed without having a voice in how these taxes are spent.

A spokesman from Japan sees a somewhat different perspective, which dovetails in principle but differs in detail:

> If a project is extremely large and has a very long-range payback and the ROI [return on investment] is too far off; or if private sector involvement would lead to too much duplication of productive facilities; or if the project is fundamentally of a public nature, then there is

no reason why government should not undertake such a project.

However, this is true only in these three categories. Otherwise the public sector tends not to have the efficiency and effectiveness of private initiative, or the incentive for human activity and inspiration that the private sector offers.

The problem with any economy run by the public sector, or any enterprise run by the public sector, is that it tends to be dull.

The other problem is that whatever monies and energies go into the public sector are not available, by definition, for the energy and dynamic of the private sector, which is, generally speaking, more productive for society as a whole.

Two systemic problems bedevil the assessment of the optimum government–private sector balance. One of these concerns time, the other measurement.

A European industrialist focuses on the time element.

> The main problem with government thinking is that it is tied to time terms of reference that are politically determined but have no necessary relationship to the problems that need to be solved. The time frame that is needed to address some of the major problems mankind faces is longer than the time frame that is available to most political and governmental systems. . . .

The problem of measurement is equally challenging. The competence and effectiveness, indeed the productivity, of the Tertiary (service) Sector is difficult to measure even in the private sector. But in the private sector, the basic economic yardsticks that constitute the proverbial bottom line apply. In the public sector, they do not. As an Australian industrialist notes:

> One of the problems with government enterprises is that there exists no measurement for the success or failure of a public entity. For example, government corporations can cite the jobs they create and the capital they employ, but there is no way to quantify the social ob-

> jectives they intend to fulfill. What governments tend to do, therefore, is to simply define the input and the money they have borrowed as output, and leave it at that. No disciplined measurement is involved. Indeed, none exists.

Another Australian industrialist gives a colorful illustration of the waste that seems to be congenital in government economic activity: "The Lord's Prayer, which lays down some very fundamental codes of behavior, has 56 words. The Gettysburg Address, which states basic political convictions and defines important political processes, has 240 words. A U.S. law and accompanying regulations relating to the distribution of cabbages runs to 35,000 words." The same man also has an intriguing suggestion as to how the governmental process could be trimmed down, at least in the legislative branch: "One of the problems with legislation is that politicians never review past legislation. I think it would be a very good idea to have a session of the legislature at regular intervals devoted to the elimination of unnecessary legislation."

2. THE SECOND WORLD

Orthodox totalitarian and monopolistic concepts of economic planning and activity are crumbling in the Second World. They are crumbling because more than half a century of experience in Russia and more than a quarter of a century of experience in Eastern Europe and China have demonstrated beyond argument that the system does not work. It simply does not deliver the goods. As a U.K. industrialist who is the head of a chemical company with an important pharmaceutical division points out:

> Centrally planned economies seem to require at least three times the resources that private enterprise requires for the same production. I know, for example, that in the Soviet Union the creation of certain pharmaceutical products has in fact required three times the resources, in time, work and raw materials, to produce

drugs comparable to those created by private enterprise in a free economy.

The gap is even more horrendous in the transfer of technology. An example of what happens when technology is under government command is that the cost-effectiveness of technology is in the ratio of about 20 to 1 to the cost-effectiveness of technology in private sector economies. And even that 20 to 1 ratio is achieved with the help of theft and espionage.

Hungary and Yugoslavia are today the "point economies" in the Second World, experimenting with new balances between government and a nascent private sector, and ways of introducing private sector disciplines into at least some government economic activities.

In Hungary, where there is a flourishing underground private sector economy, the government is increasingly legalizing that "second economy," for two reasons: It meets consumer needs that the official, state-run economy does not meet; and, when legalized, it furnishes the state with tax revenues, always a desirable outcome from a government point of view.

A Hungarian planner-industrialist who is involved in this process of economic evolution points out that the Hungarian economy is still hamstrung by lumbering state monopolies in a number of sectors, although the government has, in recent years, dismembered some of its more disastrous dinosaurs into smaller units, where at least an attempt can be made at measuring profitability.

Two other significant steps taken in Hungary during the past couple of years have enhanced the economic evolution process: A pricing mechanism that forces companies to price their products to be competitive by world market standards; and the innovation that directors and managers of economic enterprises, even in public sector entities, are no longer appointed by the government. They must compete for their jobs.

In the other "point economy" of the Second World, Yugoslavia, an industrialist who heads a capital goods company with international activities emphasizes the need for competition: "Without it we will not develop." He, too, urges the importance of market-determined prices. He cites the peculiar but nevertheless revealing comment of a Yugoslav government theoretician who has proclaimed: "When all countries go socialist, we must save one capitalist country to determine prices!"

In the Yugoslav system, workers are actively involved in setting profit targets and making investment decisions that directly affect their pay and living standards. The same industrialist notes that workers in the enterprise he manages understand and accept economic necessities such as plant closings or investment in research and development from which their personal returns will be long term. He argues that it would be fair, and would stimulate more creative investment, if workers were paid the equivalent of dividends, although a different label would have to be found for such payments.

3. THE THIRD WORLD

There appears to be a general conviction that the best government–private sector balance differs somewhat from the optimum in the First World.

An industrialist in the Philippines sets out a viewpoint shared by many:

> I believe it is the prerogative of the private sector to be the principal vehicle for development. In some countries, and under some conditions, I do believe it is necessary for the government to set the framework and even to make direct allocations of resources to priority areas; but even where that is necessary, it is a very delicate balance. If the government exercises undue influence, you very quickly get distortion and disagreement, not development.
>
> The legitimate government role, I believe, is to set direction and provide the private sector with the incentives and support to pursue those directions. The government should nurture an environment where the private sector can respond.

An Egyptian industrialist has a more specific prescription:

> In the developing countries, the first priority for government should be to survey the country's resources.

> Then it should fix priorities for development, and thereafter it should concentrate on infrastructure and leave the rest of economic activity to the private sector.
>
> The only exceptions to this are, perhaps, strategic sectors and projects that are so big that the private sector cannot tackle them. I am convinced, however, that governments should leave the absolute maximum possible to the private sector.
>
> In this kind of logical development, financial institutions have an important role. Financial institutions can conduct credible feasibility studies. They can promote projects and put packages together. And they can be responsible for start-up. They can be pioneers. Thereafter, they can sell the equity they have acquired back to the private sector on as broad a basis as possible.

Concurrence and an additional comment from an investment banker in Egypt are particularly interesting given the source:

> The best role for government is to set policy, to establish ground rules, but to stay out of projects on a practical basis. I believe it is vital for an investment to be established with purely economic criteria and I believe it is also necessary for dividends to be higher than interest rates.

A Canadian industrialist whose company operates in more than 125 countries, including scores of countries in the Third World, poses a pertinent question:

> The real question in that context, in both developing and developed countries, is, Where is the economic dividing line at which infrastructure stops? Take a system of communication satellites. Is putting up a satellite system part of an infrastructure that government is responsible for? And if it is, do the operations that are made possible by the existence of such a system require government participation, or intervention in any form? The line is difficult to define, and perhaps it varies by stage of development and therefore by place and time. What I do know, and have seen over and over again in

both developed and developing countries, is that government intervention, indeed government activity of any kind, that steps over the line is almost invariably and demonstratively anti-productive.

An insight from Brazil:

> In certain developing countries, the government gets involved in entrepreneurial activity mainly because the capital market is not strong enough to make it possible for an effective private sector to develop and work. The answer to that problem, however, is not government intervention, but the enhancement and strengthening of capital markets.

From India comes a policy directive with examples by sector of what works and what does not work.

The directive:

> If I sum up my conviction in a country such as India, and I do believe this goes for a number of other countries, what we need is more business in government and less government in business.

The examples:

> There is one sector where we really did it right. . . . That sector is agriculture. The government set a framework that was an incentive framework. It provided support prices . . . credit, . . . research and development in the form of seeds and other inputs; and it provided irrigation. It then left the rest of it—that is, the actual production effort—to the farmers. And the farmers responded magnificently. India no longer imports food. . . .
>
> In industry, the ideal would be for the government to provide such basic infrastructure as roads, railways, power and a school system. And after that, leave the private sector alone. . . .
>
> Our company, for example, produces jeeps and at present I want to change the engines we use. I found

> the best engine for the purpose and am quite ready to pay the price for it, but the government tells me I can't do that. My question is: How do they know?
>
> If they tell me that because of the oil shortage in India and the balance of payments and price constraints involved with petroleum, they want me to make diesel engines instead of petroleum gasoline engines, I would understand. That kind of direction I would consider a legitimate role for the government in a country like India. But in the question of choosing the engine that would be best for the product, our knowledge is obviously superior to theirs. But they make the decision. I consider that absurd.

But an industrialist in Malaysia sounds an important note of caution here: "In the government–private sector relationship, a minimum of government control is possible only when there is a maximum of internalized control in the private sector."

Finally, a word from successful but probably sui generis Singapore:

> Planning is only as effective as its implementation. In Singapore the private sector has prodded the government to do some things, while the government has prodded the private sector to do others. But this only works because both sides are receptive to the ideas of the other.
>
> Senior government leaders in Singapore have a sensitivity for and an understanding of the private sector because of their active role in managing state corporations, or because they have private sector backgrounds. For example, the Permanent Secretary in the Ministry of Finance, who is responsible for taxation, is not isolated from a business view of the implications of tax policy, because he also sits on the boards of government corporations that have rigorous bottom-line disciplines. He therefore understands the impact a tax decision will have on profit, growth and investment. This dynamic is at work at various levels within government administration, so that most people in the executive branch realize that the private sector

must create wealth in order to provide the resource base, i.e., the taxes, that the government needs to meet its objectives.

4. THE SOE/MNC NEXUS

While there is increasing disenchantment with state-operated enterprises (SOEs) in both developed and developing countries, there is no doubt that they will continue to exist for the foreseeable future. The operative question therefore is: How can private sector companies, and in particular multinational corporations (MNCs), compete against or cooperate with SOEs?

There is a clear North–South consensus on what the ground rules have to be. One industrialist in the Philippines puts it well:

> There should be no state enterprises that cannot be viably created and sustained. If a state enterprise cannot do that, it has no valid economic or social role.
>
> To create state enterprises with the purpose of providing jobs is short-sighted if the enterprise does not produce something that is required and competitive in either the domestic or the international market. If you don't have that, you have, in effect, finally nothing. If state-operated enterprises are not economically competitive on a world scale and, I would add very quickly, profitable, they are really just a burden on the taxpayer and a clear example of taxation without representation.

An industrialist in the United Kingdom who both competes against and occasionally cooperates with SOEs around the world comments that

> SOEs are not quite as they are represented in popular fiction, that is, benevolent and beneficient social institutions. The truth is that they are shielded in two ways: One, most of the time, SOEs have a monopoly of production and that is pernicious per se. The second unfair and socially undesirable advantage they have, at least in the short term, is that they cannot go bankrupt be-

> cause they are shielded against bankruptcy by the state, which in effect means the taxpayer. But there is a penalty built into that protection, at least in democratic countries and, over the long term, probably everywhere. Taxpayers will not forever bear the burden of an inefficient enterprise just because it is owned by the state. So, sooner or later, they must become efficient and economically sound.

Another U.K. industrialist adds a list of specific complaints that involve union monopolies acting in concert with state-owned industrial and service monopolies.

> In the United Kingdom, union monopoly power is related to and connected with the state monopolies. State-owned enterprises are the most heavily unionized and, in effect, unions are part of the state sector. The result is twofold: State-owned enterprises themselves, being heavily unionized by monopoly unions, suffer debilitating effects on their own efficiency, costs and productivity. In turn, this makes the product or service they provide to private sector companies in Britain both costly and inefficient. For example, British companies in the private sector, which have to rely on state-owned enterprises in such vital inputs as energy and transport, cannot compete with American firms that get efficient services.
>
> The second result of this combination of state and labor monopolies is that the unions, through their bastion in the state sector, exercise undue influence in the private sector regarding wages, restrictive practices and other union-imposed conditions that are inimical to productivity. If there were not this bastion of state sector/union monopoly, private enterprise could negotiate effectively with the unions based on their own needs and the realities of their business.

How then can SOEs be made more efficient and/or more fairly competitive?

One idea comes from Italy, devised by an industrialist in the private sector who believes in SOE/MNC competition:

> When international tenders are put out, if there is the same transparency of operation for state-owned enterprises and for multinational corporations, a transparency that is governed by global rules, the two will be legitimate competitors. What is wrong with state-owned enterprises now—and therefore with the terms of competition between SOEs and MNCs—is that there is no transparency in SOE operations. This applies to SOEs in the command economies as well as in the market economies.

What should these global rules be? A Spanish industrialist believes that "SOEs should have no discriminatory privileges and MNCs should have no discriminatory obligations. There should be a code that would provide for SOEs and MNCs the same obligations, the same privileges—and no demagogy to justify discrimination."

For their part, MNCs could make an important contribution if they became truly multinational, not only in their operations but in their ownership. A U.K. industrialist notes:

> Multinational corporations claim to be international, but in the overwhelming majority of MNCs the shareholders are all—or almost all—nationals of the home country. The capital base is domestic. To be sure, the shares of some MNCs are quoted in stock markets outside the home country, but somehow the stock always seems to flow back. This is the major deterrent to true international thinking, and therefore behavior, of MNCs. As capitalists, we should be able to solve this problem. It is important that we do.

Some industrial leaders (a minority in both North and South) argue that what really matters is not who owns the enterprise but who manages it. An observation here from Canada:

> The real danger to an economy is inertia. What makes the difference between an economy that suffers from inertia and one that does not is the supply of executives who have grown up in the hard world facing the challenges of the private sector. If there are enough of those, even if they enter the public sector—in govern-

> ment, in the bureaucracy of state-owned enterprise, on the boards of state-owned enterprises—I am not too deeply worried about just what segment of the economy is run as public sector and what segment is run as private sector.
>
> The fundamental difference is whether the managing of enterprises is, or is not, done by people who are willing and able to stick their necks out, and not by people who can, and want to, hide in the morass of bureaucracy.

And a similar sentiment, with an extra dimension both practical and philosophical, from Brazil:

> It is a mistake to divide the world into bureaucrats and entrepreneurs. I think it would be ideal to design a method to get in and out of both systems. By this I mean a system that would make it possible for entrepreneurs to work in government and for bureaucrats to work in private enterprise. Individuals should not think of one or the other as a one-time career for all their lives. They should think of society as a whole, of which private enterprise is a part.
>
> Closer interaction between bureaucrats and entrepreneurs, and the in-and-out system I propose, would also enlighten bureaucrats on the true function of profit. It would change the present level of ignorance, or even antagonism, by bureaucrats about entrepreneurs, and by entrepreneurs about bureaucrats, into a system in which each would enlarge the horizons of the other for social good.

5. THE BOTTOM LINE

A senior executive who is also a scientist in one of the most innovative and technologically advanced U.S.-based multinational corporations assays a bottom line:

> The great advantages of free enterprise for all economies, whether developed or developing, are three:

1. It is an efficient resource allocation mechanism.
2. It is the best form of social organization extant for productive collaborative work. It is, for example, a clearly more successful system than either an army or a bureaucracy.
3. It is an institution, and a structure, designed for innovation, adaptation and flexibility—all of this in a context of social change.

The emphasis on the role of private enterprise within each country and each culture must be that it meets the realities of the country and its culture and is appropriate as well to the most advantageous form of economic organization possible within that culture.

Everywhere, government is essentially responsible for a strategy of alleviating social stress, while free enterprise is responsible for the efficient allocation of resources.

In this context, companies must be very careful not to lose the element of risk-taking, which is a basic necessity for any creative environment. Private enterprise is in a position where failure very quickly becomes evident and where accountability for that failure is clear, absolute and unavoidable. It is this risk of failure, and the clear responsibility for it, that prompts change and adaptation.

IV. THE CREATION OF WEALTH

Industrial statesmen everywhere share four specific convictions on what it takes to create wealth.

The first of these is that the basic resources of humanity are—and always have been—imagination, knowledge and creativity.

The second is that wealth is produced by people. And while sharing wealth is an ethical imperative as well as a paramount political and social concern, the emphasis must be, in the first instance, on creating it. Distributing poverty, however equitably, is not a desirable solution to the problems of any culture, any country, or any person.

The third conviction is that the profit-disciplined segment of the private sector has the institutions best designed to adapt to change, and to create it. The simplest reason for that, as one industrialist put it, is that "if something is to be changed, one must actually do it." Business does it.

The fourth conviction is more complex. It holds that the task at hand is not so much the maximization of wealth as its optimization, and that this optimization cannot be measured in quantitative terms alone. It must be measured in human terms.

Two practical conclusions derive from these convictions. One, in the blunt words of an Indian industrialist, is that "all economic activity—whether it is in agriculture, industry, services or infrastructure—must create wealth or the country will go down the drain."

The other is that freedom and wealth, the two most important ingredients of the good life, are as a European businessman sees it, "not a complete prescription either. The first phase of the industrial revolution did have both of these, but fell down on its social concerns. The robber barons, wherever they operated, created enormous wealth, but they also created, or at least had no concern about, social misery. This is not possible anymore. Social factors, social responsibilities, must now be factored into the creation of wealth."

1. THE SOCIAL RESPONSIBILITY OF CORPORATIONS

While there is concurrence on the challenge that social responsibility presents for corporations today, there are differences on definition: Just what is the social responsibility of corporations at this point in human history?

A Spanish banker-industrialist offers a classic definition:

> Companies do have a social responsibility, of course. It has two aspects: a responsibility to internal constituen-

cies, and a responsibility to external constituencies. Among the former I count stockholders, employees and management. A company has to give each of these what they expect to the maximum extent possible. That means dividends to stockholders, salaries to employees, and appropriate compensation to management. It can do this only if it creates wealth. That is its nature and main social responsibility. If it is saddled with too many other social activities and asked to provide too many other social benefits, it may not be able to meet its basic objectives. That, I repeat, is to create wealth.

A company also has external constituencies. These are its suppliers and its customers. In a bank, for example, the suppliers are depositors. And a bank's job is not only to give these depositors their proper reward, but also to create an institution that is safe and sound on which these depositors can depend for the long haul.

The responsibility to customers is clear. It is to provide them with a product or service they want, at a price they can afford to pay.

There are broader social requirements as well. Attention to ecology is one of them. I think of these not so much as responsibilities, but as constraints in the creation of wealth that must be honored.

A more nuanced notion comes from an industrialist in India:

> There is a legitimate question of just where corporations should draw the line in terms of their social activity, their social involvement and, perhaps above all, the allocation of profit resources to social ends. I would say it probably depends on the society in which they operate. I would argue that corporate responsibility needs to have some kind of relationship to its own activity. And I would emphasize that this relationship needs to be defined consciously, sensitively and imaginatively, and will undoubtedly vary from place to place and from time to time.
>
> In our own company, for example, here in India, we provide free education for the children of all our employees. Clearly this improves employee morale in a

> major way. It also fits in with my conviction that the solution to the problems that face India today—population growth and poverty—can be met in only two ways: education and fast economic growth. Contributing to these two solutions as effectively as possible is what I consider to be the major social responsibility of corporations like my own, in India, today.

A businessman from Singapore states the specific social contribution that multinational corporations can, and in fact do make to developing countries:

> The social contribution of multinational companies can take many forms. But the most important is to maximize the development of talented people by providing the training, creative environment and challenges from which local leaders—for both the private and the public sector—will emerge. MNCs have a unique ability to recognize talent and put it to work.

A senior executive in the United States, who has a background in both science and government, offers a comprehensive, calibrated comment here.

> Government is essentially responsible for a strategy of alleviating social stress, while free enterprise is responsible for the efficient allocation of resources. I do believe that companies can and should internalize some social stress within their own enterprises if it does not interfere too drastically with economic efficiency. Doing this constitutes in fact a form of hidden taxation and is dangerous if it goes too far. It is dangerous because there is no overt accountability. Just as the welfare state is dangerous when it gets out of hand, this kind of internalization of the assumption of social responsibility by private companies can be dangerous if it gets out of hand. Since there is, after all, no free lunch, the cost of private enterprise assuming social obligations must reflect itself sooner or later in the cost of the product. And that then leaves the question: Who elected corporate officials to make social decisions?

In an appropriate government, by which I mean a democratic, reasonably effective government, citizens decide how they want to pay the price to take care of the basic needs of people whom the private sector cannot absorb. This is a legitimate government function. Private enterprise cannot compensate for the inadequacies and inequities of the social system.

If this does not work, the answer is not for private enterprise to pick up and pursue this responsibility, but for people in private enterprise to play an active role in the political system and fix that system so it will fulfill its role properly and efficiently.

And an Australian speaks with comparable conviction, suggesting three specific guidelines:

I do not believe that companies have a social role other than the role which is built into their own operations. That is comprehensive in itself. In our company, for example, we have three criteria for the kind of social action we will take.

(1) It has to relate to our company's geographic or business area.

(2) We will not do things that the government does.

(3) We will support people or projects that are clearly demonstrative of enterprise and initiative.

From Venezuela comes a different viewpoint, calling for a broader, more visionary interplay between companies and society.

Management is a complex force. As I see it, it consists of four elements: Generation, which results in motivating people. Integration, which produces organizing principles and structures. Channeling, which provides goals. And, finally, energizing, which means tapping the ingredient of human energy at all levels.

Being this kind of powerful force, the private sector and its management have an enormous influence on people and on the societies in which they function. They must understand this and use it wisely.

> For example, I believe that private sector management must, at least in developing countries, lend its expertise to the nonprofit sector of the economy, in socially contributive ways. This includes government, labor, and groups and organizations devoted to other aspects of social progress. For example, here in Venezuela, we have an organization that does this, called quite appropriately "Dividends for the Community." This brings together some two hundred companies who contribute both a percentage of their profits (ranging from 2 to 5 percent) and their management skills to social programs.

Discussing another important aspect of his concept of social responsibility, the same industrial statesman raises the issue of the specific responsibilities of family-owned companies.

> There are really three families in a family-owned company: the core family; the extended core family; and the senior executives of the company who become in fact part of the corporate family. What they must do, together, is to determine in a systematic way what the role of professional management should be. This, I believe, includes professional training for members of the core and extended family and access to ownership by the non-family members of management. It also requires coordinated consultation on how to cope with the problem of succession in a way that is most conducive to the success of the company and the welfare of society.

Finally, a very different assessment from the chairman of an organization that is unique in its structure and outlook. It is an Israeli conglomerate, which operates as a collection of private sector companies in terms of bottom-line orientation, but is owned by the trade union movement. This, as the chairman notes, gives it "a particular bifocal approach," which leads him to the conviction that "private enterprise in profit-oriented market economies will have to include in its planning and its target-setting the fact that social problems do exist and have to be solved, and must be figured into a bottom-line oriented solution."

He illustrates his thesis with his company's approach to the problems of unemployment:

We start with the fact that our companies cannot, at any time, make a product that does not have a market. We cannot do this because we simply cannot close factories and create unemployment. What we do therefore is to invest heavily in new technologies to anticipate the market. We also do extensive long-term planning in order to avoid boom-and-bust cycles within our industries. This does create constraints. We cannot, for example, take advantage of a short-lived boom in a particular industrial or agricultural sector, hire employees and then fire them when the boom has collapsed. The essence of our strategic planning therefore is not for maximum output all the time, but for long-term strategic considerations designed to create products that always total somewhat less than market demand.

Example: cement production. The market for cement depends on the building industry, which is almost by definition an industry with tight boom-and-bust cycles. Our planning calls for enough output to meet the basic need of the industry, allowing in boom times for imports if necessary. Our output is enough to guarantee a market even during recessions.

What this means is that an enterprise needs strategic plans and capital to finance technological investment, output and inventory in a socially responsible way—but in a socially responsible way that makes sense and meets the needs of a market economy. Our planning horizon, for example, is the year 2000. This planning includes the training of our labor force at every level, including the recasting of their mental abilities, so they can keep up with the technological demands that we know will be made on them between now and the year 2000.

I am firmly convinced that the private sector—and I mean the global private sector—should find methods to include social goals in its strategic planning.

2. THE ROLE OF PROFIT

The problem, one industrialist notes, is that there does not now exist an economic theory that puts the human being first and demonstrates that efficiency and ethics are co-determinant. For companies, that is a daily reality, and profit is the lifeblood of that reality.

Profit, its meaning and its role, is probably the least understood and most maligned concept extant. In popular mythology it is a phantom that knows no frontiers and haunts both North and South. Addressing one manifestation of the apparition, an industrialist in a developing country notes:

> In an uninformed society which is also poor, propaganda against profit is a good political tactic. What we in the private sector need to explain is, "profit to whom?" Most people who are opposed to profit on emotional grounds are not opposed to the kind of money a typist makes in a corporation. Their problem is with the sums of money they believe managers, and especially owners, get. What they must be made to understand is that the profit of a public corporation goes to thousands of shareholders and that successful enterprises create wealth and income on a very broad basis.

The specter appears in much the same guise in the developed world. As an industrialist in Italy comments:

> There is a feeling that profit in private enterprise should not have a personal value for the owner of the enterprise, but should have a collective social value. I think it is important to improve the image of private enterprise and to make clear the valuable role that industry plays in making products and rendering services that contribute to everyone's life and well-being.
>
> The tendency in the private sector is to pride itself on making profit per se. But if profit is to be not only understood but accepted by the general community, it must be portrayed as what it is, a means to produce goods and services, not an end in itself.

It serves an additional function which can also be explained to the general public. It is an instrument of measuring and getting efficiency. It is also a tool that provides stimulus and incentive.

The risk at present is that public opinion sees profit only as personal enrichment.

Next, some suggestions on how the mistrust and misconceptions swirling around profit in the minds of millions can be corrected.

First, from Australia, a thumbnail sketch of the role of profit that is brief, realistic, clear and irrefutable:

> Unless an enterprise is profitable, it does not create wealth. This means it cannot grow. It cannot create jobs. It cannot create the kind of excitement that gives people a sense of accomplishment. In short, a dynamic organization needs profit to create opportunities.

Then, from the Philippines, a more comprehensive conception:

> Profit is what makes the world go round. It is the incentive for investment and development. Whenever governments have taxed profits excessively, you get capital flight and people flight. This happens not only in developing countries. I would cite as classic examples in the industrialized world the U.K. and Sweden.
>
> I believe that the role of profit is understood by the silent majority everywhere. That majority actually knows, even if it cannot articulate in its own mind or in public, that profit constitutes both incentive and reward for the individual's investment of time, money and effort. I believe that silent majority also understands that it is unrealistic to expect individuals, groups or societies to invest time, money and effort without a reward.
>
> What perhaps we need to explain better is that there must be a healthy level of profit to sustain growth. By growth I mean in the first instance the growth of the enterprise, which, however, is not possible without the concurrent growth of the individuals within the enterprise. I believe growth, of both the enterprise and the

people in it, to be the first priority of business. I would add that the growth of an enterprise is difficult, if not impossible, without growth of the national economy as well. It seems clear to me that enterprises within a national economy are as interdependent as are the economies of nations in today's interdependent world. Interdependence is a logical progression from enterprise, to nation, to the world. And no component of that progression is possible without profit.

From Australia comes a suggestion as to how the concept of profit can be communicated effectively:

> I am convinced that common consequences make for cohesion. What we need then, to define profit for the general public, is to create an awareness of the shared consequences, both positive and negative, that profit, and the absence of profit, produces for all.

And from Japan, a particular emphasis:

> Profit is not a goal or a mission. It is a tool. The goal is service to society. Service to society consists essentially of supplying goods and services that society wants and needs, and profit is a return for this social contribution. The fundamental fact is that without profit there is no reserve for research, there is no growth, and there are no taxes for social purposes.
>
> Profit is required for survival. With more profit, you can do more. Profit exists of course in command economies as well. In Communist countries it is simply called by a different name. And to the extent to which it does not exist, in any economy, the economy stagnates. There is no money and there are no resources to do anything.

Finally, from France, a definition and a metaphor:

> People must be made to understand that profit is needed to keep a business in good health, so that it can do what a healthy business does, i.e., hire the best employees, get the best machinery, find the best market for its

products. These are the real uses of money in business. This is the fundamental role of profit.

Profit is not an aim. It is a necessity to keep a business alive. It is comparable to breathing for a human being. We do not live to breathe, but we do have to breathe to live. In the same way, a business is not designed to make profit, but it must have profit to exist.

3. THE MAGIC OF ENTREPRENEURSHIP

While profit is the inescapable necessity that makes economic activity possible, in market or command economies, entrepreneurship is the magic ingredient that makes economies bubble and grow.

Can such magic be dissected and fostered? Can entrepreneurship be analyzed and enhanced? The answer seems to be a tentative and limited yes.

An Egyptian industrialist puts it this way:

> I believe that entrepreneurship is a talent, and it is rare. Perhaps between 1 and 3 percent of the population anywhere has it. But, like all other talents, it can be either developed or stifled. Society and the political system can encourage entrepreneurship, or kill it. In a society where production is appreciated and the entrepreneur given opportunity, entrepreneurship will flourish. In a society where these elements are missing, entrepreneurship will wither and either flee or die.

There does appear to be a unanimity on the components of entrepreneurial talent that spans cultures, countries and stages of economic development. The profile that emerges is a combination of character traits—courage, imagination and foresight—with a honed perception of opportunity and the willingness and ability to accept both failure and reward.

There is consensus as well on what motivates entrepreneurs, which stands in complete contradiction to the popular stereotype. The prime motivation for an entrepreneur anywhere, this consensus holds, is, as it is for talented individuals in any walk of life, the challenge and charm of making the most of one's gift. Beyond that, the propelling force is not a personal passion for money or property, but a desire to contribute to the common stock of well-being through the creation of goods or services for society, jobs for people, wealth for nations and advancement for mankind.

A U.K. industrialist proffers a final, inspiring thought on the magic of entrepreneurship. He holds that a spark of entrepreneurship exists in almost every individual and, given appropriate management and motivation, can be lit, with tangible and intangible rewards to both the individual and the enterprise:

> The truth is that there is no conflict whatsoever between ethical, socially concerned behavior and the drive for efficiency and accomplishment. On the contrary, people work harder and better, and with more psychic satisfaction, when they know that what they are doing is good in the basic moral sense of that term—good for other people and good for society as a whole. In my experience, this, not financial considerations, is the greatest incentive.

V. VALUES

1. TOMORROW'S WORK PLACE

If there is one certainty about the work place of tomorrow, it is that it will be different. There will be more machines—robots and computers—doing most of the repetitive, dirty and boring work, and taking on some tasks that require mental speed and agility. People in the work place, certainly in the industrialized countries, will be increasingly educated, skilled and affluent. And they will bring to both work and life a different sense of values.

This will have practical consequences for the way the work place is organized; for the relationship between labor and management; and probably for patterns of ownership.

From a U.K. industrialist, a vision of what may be ahead for corporate organizations:

> The most exciting prospect I see for the future holds opportunities for change in the way business is done that are made possible by the new technologies at our disposal. I see the possibility, indeed the likelihood, of a "Swiss Army" type of company, where there is only a very small core of full-time professionals at corporate headquarters, while the rest of the work is done by people who are essentially self-employed and who make their contributions in their own time, in their own way, by using computers to communicate. The corporate core will provide a stimulating and rewarding center, but the real spur to work will be individuals who are self-motivated, which will increase their productivity and intensify their satisfaction.
>
> I also believe that the new possibilities in automation, i.e., robotics and allied technologies, can, and indeed should be used, not to create larger assembly lines, which are mind-deadening and make boring products, but to create greater flexibility. Since robotics can be constantly reprogrammed, robots can be used to make a greater variety of products and require a greater variety of tasks from human beings.

The company this industrialist heads, a large multinational enterprise in the chemical sector, is already making moves in that direction.

> We are working on plants that are small but cost-competitive, by which I mean, for example, plants that do not turn out 500,000 tons of a chemical, but 50,000 tons, and achieve their competitiveness by advanced technology and by being closer to the customer. This has social as well as commercial advantages, because closer local relationships are established. The product and its relationship to the market, the enterprise and its relationship to the community—indeed the size of the enterprise itself—all suddenly assume more human, more manageable and nevertheless cost-competitive dimensions.

There are additional advantages to such a network of small plants. They are less vulnerable to disruptions through technical failure or through human intervention, which can range anywhere from strikes to terrorism. This makes the enterprise more flexible in every way. It also lessens the investment risk.

Another advantage is that we can make investments every year, somewhere around the world, instead of having to do long-range strategic planning to make a mammoth investment only once every ten years. We have found that this approach is possible with available technology. What it takes is a new engineering philosophy and, of course, a new managerial approach.

A U.S. industrialist describes another aspect of the organization of tomorrow's work place. He notes that the new communications technologies "make it possible for large organizations to communicate not only from the top down, as is traditional, but also from the bottom up and horizontally."

He points out that in his own organization, which has 800 companies in 127 countries, "a network of interface on the horizontal level is now possible in a way that has not been possible before. This creates the opportunity for a fascinating combination of decentralization and integration. It is an amalgam that could never have occurred before. It has major organizational and psychological implications."

The major psychological implication, by broad-gauged consent, is that participation is the strongest motivation, and that there will be increasing participation of the workforce, at every level, in the productive enterprise.

Another industrialist "dots the i": "Participation in design, in planning and in decision making."

Just what forms this participation will take, and how it will be organized and implemented, is still a matter of debate as well as experimentation. There are the generic experiments of the supervisory boards of German companies, with direct labor participation. There is the equally generic but more amorphous *ringi* system of Japanese industry. And there are the experiments of individual companies, primarily in the United States and Canada, which range from flextime, job-sharing and job-enrichment programs to quality circles and a seat on the board.

One example of experimentation comes from Canada, described by the industrialist who designed and implemented it:

> I believe that it is important to give workers more management decision power in the area where they are most competent and where they are directly involved. In manufacturing, this means primarily the factory floor.
>
> Example: We have a plant that is unionized in which we have eighty-four job classifications. We have a comparable plant where we had worker participation and cooperation in devising job classifications. The result is six broad categories of work and salaries geared to the ability of the worker to perform in these categories. The more categories he can perform in, the more money he gets. With this basic system in place, we let the labor force work out job allocation. The result is impressive. Productivity is much higher than in the unionized plant with its carefully delineated, and very rigid, eighty-four job classifications.

And the same industrialist has an experimental suggestion:

> One of the most overlooked reasons for industrial action, i.e., strikes and slowdowns, is, I believe, boredom. Blue collar workers in our time are educated, healthy, earn a very respectable amount of money and are, in effect, junior capitalists. I am all in favor of this, but one of the results is that you simply cannot ask people like this to do the same dreary task year in and year out and expect them to be content with it. Therefore, I think it would be a good idea for blue collar workers to have a sabbatical of, say, three to six months, every three years. This could be financed by deducting some small percentage from their wages and putting it into a sabbatical fund that the company could match. I believe it would make a significant contribution to better labor-management relations.

Underlining the productive importance of better labor-management relations, a U.K. industrialist points out that

Most human beings, most employees in large companies particularly, in fact produce between 30 to 40 percent of their potential. If their human needs were met more imaginatively they would respond to this care with more self-motivation and more creativity. The result would be that their productivity would increase from the present 30–40 to, say, 50 percent. If you had superb leadership, you could probably get it up to 55 percent. Just imagine what difference that would make for everybody.

Tomorrow's work place will also require different approaches and skills from management. As an Israeli industrialist points out:

> We are, amongst other activities, involved in the metal production industry. Not so long ago, metal production consisted of, say, 100 people operating 100 lathes, each of which was worth around $15,000. Today, the same production comes from one machine costing $3 million. That machine is run by one man. Therefore the motivation and competence of that man has unprecedented value. One man operating a $3 million machine being ill or badly motivated one day can make a significant difference to production. On the other hand, if the man is properly motivated, he can make a considerable contribution to profit.
>
> In a different context, think of a biochemist who has the major thrust of a company's research in his head That head can determine the future of the company So you cannot deal with these productive and creative people in the same old way. And the trend is for more and more employees to be in this vital, valuable category. An effective manager, therefore, will have to manage not, say, 200 people who are skilled laborers or technicians, but instead he will have to manage 10 creative geniuses. That is a very different kind of management and neither conventional theories of management, nor conventional education in business administration deals with it.

He also maintains that this trend will bring with it a change in ownership patterns.

> Creative people in the work place of tomorrow will want, need and deserve a piece of the action. They will also want to play a different role in management. What I see therefore are enterprises that are increasingly owned by employees, and these employees will also become part of a new kind of participatory management. As a result, the difference between employees, owners, and managers will increasingly disappear.

A less drastic view from the United States points in the same direction:

> Participation of labor in management is evolving everywhere, but taking different forms. In the United States, where neither labor nor management believes that labor representation on the board is a good thing, the manifestation I see, and I see it increasingly, is ownership participation in the form of stock options or profit-sharing plans, not just for managers but for employees at every level of the company.

The concept is echoed in the developing world, with an extra dimension. One industrialist from Egypt says:

> It is very important to have good relationships between owners, managers and workers. The best systems to achieve this have to be designed in response to the local culture. What is important everywhere is that the more friction can be minimized, the better off both labor and management will be; and, of course, the enterprise itself.
>
> In the developing countries, perhaps a system of profit-sharing would be a good idea, primarily because it will broaden stock ownership. And a broadened stock ownership is the best bulwark against both government intrusion and communism.

2. THE FUTURE OF LEISURE

One inevitable result of the changes in the work place is that these will provide more leisure for most members of society and that both the content and meaning of leisure will have to be rethought.

An assessment of this topic comes from Japan:

> In Japan we have the tripartite labor/government/industry council. It consists of fifteen members only and it meets every month, so real discussion is possible and does indeed take place. At a recent meeting, we discussed industrial robots. The labor members raised the problem that robots could become the enemy of labor. I pointed out that, on the contrary, the robot was the best friend labor ever had. It will do all the nasty, mean jobs that men never liked to do and indeed should not be doing. At the same time robots will increase productivity, and the fruits of that increased productivity can be shared with workers in the form of more leisure time. The real question we need to address in the age of the robot is the question of sharing the work that is left for the benefit of the human spirit. We must design the work place of the future in such a way that everyone gets a crack at working, and that some do not hog work while others are left unemployed. Finding the solution to this problem will, in effect, be the ultimate fruit of what science and knowledge in the nuclear age have provided in the way of opportunities. And the greatest of these opportunities is the time that will be available, not for leisure—I don't want to call it that, because it has all kinds of connotations, both desirable and undesirable—but for human development.

And a prescription for required action, also from Japan:

> The fundamental fact is that in the world, especially in the advanced countries, we will need increasingly fewer people to do the work that society requires. If the economic pie is big enough, we can accommodate the change. We will have room for people who will do the

work that needs to be done to provide goods and services and we will have a leisure service industry that will respond to the growing needs of people with more time to develop themselves.

It is very important to educate people for this new society, to make sure that leisure becomes, not an incentive to make people lazy and wasteful, but an opportunity for people to develop themselves intellectually, artistically, and in every other area of human potential.

Personally, I believe that our universities need to address this problem as soon as possible. They should create faculties for citizens, not just faculties for students.

This new scope of leisure involves a new value dimension. It troubles an industrialist in Malaysia, who points out that

> In the developing world also, in the long term, we may well have to look at the possibility of creating a work week of only three days in order to give employment to all the people who need it. The problem is to maintain a work ethic within those three days and also not to destroy social values and virtues.
>
> We may have to devise new forms of education, both to keep skills up to scratch as they are needed, and to provide values for leisure time.
>
> The Greeks knew that the mark of civilized man is his use of leisure. We must find our own ways of using leisure in socially desirable ways.

What might these socially desirable ways be? The Malaysian industrialist suggests a form of national service that would have people serve, not in the military, but in such occupations as fire fighting, police, nursing or an international peace corps.

The idea of an international peace corps is endorsed in the United Kingdom and Japan, where industrialists argue that it would give the idealistic young a constructive outlet for their energy and their idealism.

From Australia comes another version of putting leisure to use to solve local problems:

> Social problems of all kinds are addressed most effectively at the local level, where government, business and

voluntary agencies can cooperate for optimum results. If we could turn welfare into workfare to meet local social needs, or even inspire the young to use their leisure for social action at the local level, a great many problems that now plague us could be solved.

3. PLURALISM: OLD AND NEW

Religion probably represents the oldest form of pluralism on the planet, and mankind's record in dealing with this manifestation of pluralism is not inspiring. There does seem to be a deeply felt need for religion everywhere. The problem remains, as it has always been, how to strip faith of its fanaticism and allow pluralism to prosper.

Commenting on the need for religion in the modern world, an industrialist in Japan notes:

> We should develop a more fundamental concern for the values that religion teaches us. In Japan, for example, Buddhism for most of us is just a matter of observing some ceremonies. But the meaning of religion should be not just ceremonies for special occasions or, as it is in many cases, teaching us how to die. The true meaning of religion should be to teach us how to live. I therefore believe it is important for a religion, whatever it is, to become active again so that it lends meaning and perspective to our lives, and to our culture.

A Moslem industrialist assesses the same need, and the dangers connected with it:

> In many Moslem countries we now have a return to basic religious principles. These include a return to fundamental values. Some of these are evidently desirable; but we have to find a way whereby the return to sound principles and values is not associated with other, less desirable ways and ideas. For example, we have to make sure that a return to family values does not also result in holding back the development of women. Extremism is undesirable in any ideological framework, in any society.

Another thought on the topic comes from India:

> Most religions are tolerant in principle but not in practice. Perhaps this is due to the fact that, historically, religions were used to govern. Today, the motivation for religious fanaticism is either political or economic. In that context, religion is still used as a tool. In the final analysis, religions are an ideology, a set of values, and what really matters is how the ideology is shaped and, above all, how it is applied.

And Spain, too, has had its own historic experience with the soaring inspiration and the searing fanaticism of religious ideology:

> Our planet is now a small society and like all small societies it needs tolerance. We do not want to have a plurality of ideas, but it is also logical, normal and good for people to defend their ideas and even to defend them with passion. This is true about ideas in the religious realm, in the political realm, in the economic realm, even in the arts and in sports. The key is that this defense, however passionate, must be exercised with respect for the liberty of others.
>
> I believe it is vital for individuals to adhere to a principle. It is equally vital for them to respect the freedom of others not to adhere to the same principle. We need a free market not only in the economic realm. We also need a free marketplace of ideas.
>
> On a small planet, where human beings live with all their genius, all their inspiration, all their ideas and convictions, there should be freedom for the expression and development of all these. But, however strongly and passionately a belief is held, in any aspect of life, the limit must be the freedom of others not to believe the same thing. Neither truth nor right are achieved by violence or compulsion.

A more recent form of pluralism, but intensely pervasive at present, is nationalism.

One young industrialist, in Brazil, analyzes the paradox of nationalism in the world of today:

> One fundamental fact of the present is that we have transnationalism not only in economics, but also in ideas, values, information and communication. There exists a transnational logic and rationality and it is increasing. But increasing in parallel fashion are the irrational forces of nationalism. As the rational need for internationalism becomes apparent, people seem to feel a more urgent need for community to balance this recognition.
>
> It is strange, because the original argument for the nation state was that it would provide security. Now the nation state can only reach for nuclear warfare, which makes the argument for security nonsensical.
>
> There are three images to describe the state in which we find ourselves. One is the image of a fly in a bottle, trying to get out. And we are told there are sages who could show the fly the only way to get out.
>
> The second image is that we are like fishes in a net. The fisherman will get most of us and many of the rest will die. Only a few will be able to find their way back into the water and survive.
>
> The third image is that we are in a labyrinth and there is a way to get out. It is true that some paths lead nowhere, and some lead back to the beginning. But there are paths that will lead us out of the labyrinth into the light. This is the image I hold to be true. The way out of the labyrinth is through dialogue and experiment, trial and error, and reason. Nobody knows the only way. We can only decide what is ideal and do what is possible.

Dialogue, trial and error, reason—and the exasperation and limitations contained in the necessary process. A U.S. executive in the service sector, who is actively involved in several facets of the process, comments:

> The first and most important thing is that we continue to talk, however much we are fed up with the process. And we should continue to talk at many levels: through research centers, think tanks, international organizations, artistic organizations. All of these create topics of mutual interest that can be discussed, and they do solve some problems.

In these discussions, in which I sometimes participate in my sector as well as in my civic activities, it is true that my patience does occasionally give out. Nevertheless, we need these forums if we are going to learn to live together with the differences in attitudes and values that we still have.

When you think about it, it really boggles the mind that on this planet we still have religious wars when we have already landed a man on the moon. The fact is that we have made enormous scientific and technical progress but our emotional development has not kept pace. It appears that emotional maturity has to be relearned for each lifetime. I believe multinational corporations make a very important contribution to the creation of worldwide networks of shared values and experience, but whether there is a shortcut through this process of bringing our emotional maturity up to par with our scientific and technological abilities I do not know. It may well be the most fundamental question of our time.

A Japanese industrialist takes a practical approach:

People say that the world today is in some ways more diversified than it has ever been and is worse off than it has ever been. The problem is how this diversification can be converted into communication; how the dissension between societies can be bridged and dissolved into harmonies. I believe the answer to this is education, communications and trade. When societies exist in isolation—and we in Japan know about this—there is no tension, but there is also no progress. Tension has creative aspects. The problem lies in preventing tension from becoming explosion.

From Canada come both affirmation and puzzlement:

I believe pluralism is marvelous. It makes life interesting. What puzzles me is why all of us tend to feel good about geographic diversity but seem considerably less enchanted with cultural diversity. When we encounter

> diversity in nature, we love it. When we encounter it culturally, we tend to freeze. Why?

As an Egyptian industrialist puts it: "We must learn not only to accept, but to enjoy the differences between us."

Finally, from Japan, a neat summary of this complex, age-old issue:

> The most important value we need to learn is that we are all human beings on a very small planet. We can share scientific knowledge and create new development but at the same time we need to recognize each other's individuality, including the values that are contained in every person's individuality.
>
> I believe that real equality consists of recognizing differences, honoring them, and, if possible, appreciating and enjoying them.

4. CHANGE AND CONTINUITY

Coping with change and continuity, and the historic flux that ineluctably contains both, has been the lot and challenge of mankind throughout history. But the last quarter of the twentieth century and the first quarter of the twenty-first may well be a period of change unprecedented in both scope and speed.

A U.S. executive outlines some of the implications:

> I see the quality of life being changed in major ways by three factors: technology, genetic engineering and the service economy. These three will fundamentally affect, if not dominate, both the accumulation and the distribution of wealth. They will also provide the framework for the workplace specifically, and for society in general. Therefore I believe the most important requirement for any society today is a psychological readiness for change.
>
> In the technological area, the laser, power generation through nonfossil fuels, and the possibility of engineering changes of matter, including human matter, will create changes and challenges of almost excruciat-

ing magnitude. In services, transportation, communication and information will create a very different working environment. What will increasingly matter, and what will make the fundamental difference between countries and between individuals, is the factor of brain-value-added. Among many other aspects, this makes the old division between North and South increasingly irrelevant. Countries can make the leap into this new era, whether they have been traditionally developed and industrialized or not. Because now what will matter is not the brawn power that was needed in the early days for the successful development of agriculture; not the machines that were required for the development of industrial societies; but brainpower; and that exists anywhere and everywhere.

The required leap will depend to an unprecedented degree on individuals. That in turn will create unprecedented stress because both individuals and societies can no longer blame their lack of development on givens, such as land and territory, or achievements that have capital-intensive requirements such as machinery, or even on such old sociopolitical arguments as colonial exploitation and unfair terms of trade. What will be required to function in this new society is simply individual excellence, the optimum use of individual brainpower.

We will have, indeed we already have to a large extent, the knowledge. What is needed now is the courage, the commitment, the discipline. In a very real sense it will no longer be possible for any society, or for that matter for any individual to say, "They didn't let me; they impeded me; they exploited me. They wouldn't let me do it." In this new society every individual really has the opportunity to use his or her individual talent, and to demonstrate achievement. Individuals and nations will be measured by the reality of their achievement.

There is of course a reverse side to this coin. Failure will be punished more drastically, for both individuals and nations. For countries, the most important factor will be whether society can be organized to make it possible for individuals to succeed. The successful societies will be those that are the most flexible, the most open to change, the societies best designed to let individuals identify opportunity and pursue the opportunities they see.

Looked at from this perspective, some countries that now seem very strong, such as Japan, may well turn out not to be strong, because they are socially too rigid. While other countries, such as for example Brazil, which are now still relatively weak, will be able to make the required leap because they are basically open societies, geared to flexibility, change and risk-taking.

From Brazil comes a passionate advocacy of involving the young in the change that is both needed and inevitable.

One reason why young people now seem to be disillusioned and in revolt against materialistic values, against what they see as artificial rules, standards, conventions that are meaningless, is that they see around them a world in which there is still enormous misery and great injustice which, given the tools our society has, make no sense. From the viewpoint of the young, the older generation did not arrange the world well. What is needed is to get these idealistic young, who are our greatest treasure, into a dialogue of reason. They need to be convinced that violence is destructive, not creative, and will not result in a better world.

There are many forms of violence. Violence can be disguised as dictatorship or other forms of brutal imposition. Sometimes it is even disguised as apparent wisdom and the voice of experience. But progress and improvement happen only if things are discussed and understood. Only when issues are discussed and understood does desirable, effective and lasting change take place.

A U.S. scientist-executive believes that one of the changes that must happen, and is in fact happening already, is a change in our sense of community.

Historically, a sense of community was based on geography. Now, and increasingly, I believe the sense of community will be based on shared interests. These can

> be economic interests, such as the ownership of oil, or the growing of coffee as a major crop. It can be based on age. It seems to me, for example, that young people in many cultures today share a sense of community and some values that are different from those of their parents. Scientists worldwide tend to share a sense of values, an approach to life, that gives them a sense of community. In a different way so do artists.
>
> Supporting these new communities of interests, indeed both making them possible and intensifying them, are the new electronic media of communication. Our technology makes it possible, for the first time in human history, for people sharing the same interests to work together wherever they are and worldwide.

Another American, an industrialist with extensive experience in high-level government, offers a vision of what the knowledge we have, and the technology available to disseminate it, may mean socially and politically:

> We have an enormous amount of knowledge at our disposal now. The challenge, the effort required of this generation, is to apply globally what we know. We need to funnel the knowledge we have; circulate it below, above, around; feed it into the political process, into international institutions, into public consciousness everywhere. We have to make people realize throughout the world that we do have the knowledge which, if applied—intelligently, properly, freely—can make for a better life for everyone.
>
> As a practical matter, when that consciousness takes hold, it will lead to a substantial conversion of the current global expenditures on arms to other, economically more productive, uses. The resources that would be freed when we no longer need to spend them on armaments, should go, in my opinion, in the first instance into education and, secondly, into health. I also believe that it is vital to spread knowledge, and particularly management techniques, in agriculture. This would solve basic problems not only in terms of feeding people adequately but also in creating a saner bal-

ance between town and country, between rural and urban segments of society.

As I see it, a spread of the knowledge we already have can solve problems by economic means and at the same time will make possible a system under which sound political decisions can be made from the bottom up. I know this is a slow process, but I am convinced that it can be done. I am also convinced that, given broad-based knowledge, the advantages of free societies will become crystal clear and will become the global choice.

To do what can be done will take, as it always has, inspiration. An Italian industrialist suggests one source of that inspiration:

> What we need, particularly in the industrial world, is new inspiration to do our best. We need to discover a new element, a new relationship between our life and what we do with it. We have to design a new philosophy, a philosophic unified field theory, that will enable us to look at the core of problems, not at their periphery.

Agreement comes from Canada, illuminated by a different metaphor:

> The world is in need of an ideology that can serve to lead it out of its current morass of political rivalries and economic destructiveness and incompetence. What we need is a Christ or a Buddha in the economic sense, a charismatic prophet who can preach economic ideals that will make sense to everyone in the world, and who can inspire people to follow.

But follow where?

A very senior Japanese industrialist—senior in standing, age and experience—suggests that the need is "to search for a universal truth which can be commonly held by all the people around the world. That is to say that beyond all existing nations, races, religions, ideologies and all other kinds of obstacles, a universal ideology should be established, based upon the human principles common to all." Underpinning this notion, a Canadian industrialist proposes a slogan: "There is nothing like an earthling."

This leaves the final question of whether such a vision, proposed and shared by reality-focused industrialists in East and West, North and South, represents the proverbial pie in the sky, or whether it is a plausible course of action for mankind.

From the Philippines, a sober assessment:

> We could use more idealism, more altruism, more concern for the next person, ultimately on a planetary basis. But it must start with the individual. If the individual does not have this idealism, altruism and concern for the next person, then the family won't have it, the society won't have it, the nation won't have it. It has to start with the individual, at home, and spread out from there. I do, however, think we are capable of it as a race.

From Australia, some sage counsel and a caution:

> We must educate people for change and make them aware of the benefits of change. We must make them aware also of the alternatives to change and the consequences of these alternatives. Perhaps if we add to change, continuity as a value, people would be more willing to accept the value of change.

And a realistic final note from another industrialist Down Under:

> I am a great believer in the human mind. People are great solvers of problems. In solving problems, however, they create new problems as a by-product. Then, they have to apply again man's ingenuity to find ways around these new problems. And there is, I hope and trust, no end to this process.

The Conversations

Australia

ON COMPETITION

Ralph Ward-Ambler
Managing Director
McPherson's Ltd.

Competition is a complex phenomenon. It seems to me that it must be looked at on different levels, because it exists on different levels.

There is individual competition. There is the competition of collective enterprises such as business or, in another area, sports organizations. There is the competition of subgroups of society. These include industries, ethnic subgroups, religious subgroups, geographic subgroups. Then there is national competition, i.e., competition between nation-states. And finally, there is regional competition, as illustrated by such organizations as the European Economic Community (EEC), the Latin American Free Trade Association (LAFTA) or the Organization of Petroleum Exporting Countries (OPEC). At each level of competition, the competitive freedom of the elements within the level is reduced. For example, regional competition reduces the freedom of national competition.

It is also important to realize that competition exists in its pure form only if the competitors are allowed to suffer the consequences. There are various ways of structuring the risk/reward balance. I believe that where the reward is high, the consequences of failure or success should be uncontrolled. But there are situations where both reward and consequences are controlled. And there are situations where the penalties are controlled. Finally, there are situations where penalties are uncontrolled. In all instances I believe that it is the risk/reward ratio that really matters.

The Time Frame of Competition

There is also a matter of time frame in competition, and the risk/reward ratios that are implied by that time frame. I divide these time-related risk/reward ratios into primary, likely and possible. For the individual, I would say "primary" is survival; "likely" involves a time span of 0–10 years and relates to such matters as housing or education; and "possible," in individual terms, would cover lifetime risks and rewards.

For an enterprise, the primary risk/reward equation revolves around the budget year and, in many unfortunate cases, the myopia of quarterly returns. The "likely" ratio is 0–5 years, which is about as far as most corporate planning extends; the "possible" ratio is 25–40 years.

For subgroups of society, the "primary" time span is 0–2 years; the "likely" time span, given political considerations, at least in democracies, is 0–4 years; the "possible" one, of course, is 0–infinity.

In national competition, the "primary" time frame is the remaining tenure of the current government which, in this case, is the same as the "likely" time frame. The "possible" time frame is new tenure and the continuation of new tenure; that can be a time frame ranging from 0 to 20 years.

For regional organizations, the "primary" time frame is 2–5 years, during which they can address such issues as tariffs; the "likely" time frame is 5–20 years, during which international agreements can be constructed. The "possible" time frame can be anything.

Competition in Democracies

The real problem I see with competition in democratic countries is that governments plan in order *not* to compete. A working enterprise must compete but doesn't have the freedom to do so. Let me illustrate. In Australia, for example, much of the price of labor is determined by government through such mechanisms as the minimum wage. That clearly makes it impossible for us to compete on an equal level with a country, for example, like Czechoslovakia.

This is not to say that government in a democracy does not have a legitimate and important economic role. For example, I believe that government should set ecological and environmental standards to which all economic enterprises must adhere. I can even see a hands-on role for government in laying the foundation for some economic enterprises by providing subsidies or research in areas of development which are important to society, but for which there is no feasible market.

This trend of thought leads to a consideration of the economic soundness of government enterprises. As I see it, the main problem is that there is no measure for the success or failure of a public entity. Government corporations can, of course, cite the jobs they create and the capital they employ, but there is not a way to quantify the social objectives that they intend to fulfill. What governments tend to do is simply define the input and the money they have to borrow as output, and leave it at that. There is no disciplined measurement involved.

I believe that the proper economic role of government, in addition to the two functions I have already cited, is to structure policy priorities and to create and apply constancy in the economic environment in which companies can then operate.

Competition in the North–South Context

The relationship between the North and the South in the global context is usually regarded from either a political or a philanthropic perspective. But there is a competitive aspect to that relationship as well. I believe, for example, that multinational corporations, wherever based, should be given the maximum freedom to compete anywhere in the world, and perhaps, in turn, be levied with a supertax on profit that could be put into a capital fund designed for investment in developing countries. But harnessing a capital base is not enough; you also have to get people to use it. It seems clear to me that multinational corporations are demonstrably the most competent at using such a capital base.

However, the question of creating industries in the developing countries is not simple. We must face the fact that what we, in the North, do in the process is to create effective competition for ourselves. In many developing countries today, for instance, some industries have the best and most modern equipment, designed and capitalized by the developed countries, which also provide technology and management. I am thinking here of a Motorola microchip facility in the Philippines. That's a very sophisticated operation by any standard, and perfectly capable of world competition. As we all know, so are steel facilities in Brazil and Korea, and—a bit down the line, but then in major proportions—the petrochemical facilities of Saudi Arabia.

The question arises whether, in a world of diminishing resources, stagflation, unemployment and high interest rates, the concept of an open, integrated world economy, characterized by the free movement of products and resources, is still plausible and/or necessary. My answer is that it is highly desirable, but perhaps unrealistically altruistic given present realities. I would equate it to Christianity and its ethics and demands, which I consider equally desirable but which, I rather think, will take a long time to implement fully.

I am convinced that structuring an optimum system of economic relationships in the global arena will require a lot more than conviction, political rhetoric and philanthropic impulse. I believe that the dynamics of competition will successfully bridge the gap that political rhetoric has defined and distorted. My proposition is that, if the constraints on both risks and rewards are removed, or at least minimized, the competitive dynamic will do the job. Conversely, I am convinced that the greater the constraints imposed, the longer it will take for the North–South gap to disappear.

Profit and Entrepreneurship

It is important, in this context, to address two other concepts that are often misunderstood, misinterpreted, or indeed deliberately distorted. The concepts are profit and entrepreneurship.

First, on profit: One of my more fundamental convictions is that common consequences make for cohesion. To achieve an understanding by the general public, anywhere, of profit and its function, what we need to do is create an awareness of the shared consequences, both positive and negative, that profit produces for every segment of society.

Entrepreneurship is a less simple proposition. The basic ingredients of entrepreneurship are courage and imagination, plus a talent for the perception of opportunity, and the willingness to accept both failure and reward. Outside social influences do have a bearing. They can inhibit entrepreneurship, and they can spur it. I would have to say, for example, that hardship, deprivation and ambition are probably major spurs. But do I want to recommend these as a desirable social environment? That is a very important question. Therefore, what shapes and encourages entrepreneurship, in terms of outside influences, constitutes a very delicate balance.

But if the growing body of opinion triumphs, which holds that the competitive free enterprise system is no longer viable, what we will get is an atrophy of private enterprise and managerial freedom that will restrict production and wealth worldwide. At the same time, pluralism and political freedom will undoubtedly be eroded.

Competition and Social Responsibility

I do not maintain that entrepreneurship as a value system does not have a social component. I believe business does have very specific responsibilities to society.

These work at three levels:

The first is personal, where the responsibilities are dictated by religion, morals and mores.

The second is organizational, where a collection of people, in effect, set the rules and regulations of their own constraints.

The third is a response to external constraints that society imposes on both individuals and organizations. These outside constraints play an important role. They can constrain enterprise and they can encourage it. The balance is as delicate as it is important to the shape a society assumes.

Competition and Values

In the final analysis, that shape is defined within a context of values—in which education plays a major role. For example, I believe that we, in the industrial societies, have made a major mistake in the past two decades in our educational approaches. Generally speaking, we educated the young to focus only, or at least primarily, on macroproblems, not on microproblems. Our business schools have been at the cutting edge of this trend. Their approach has been to educate every student to become the president of a company, instead of turning out graduates who can become the competent supervisors who really make the system work.

This educational approach has the additional danger of leading almost inevitably to quick disillusionment, given the unavoidable contrast of expectation and reality. I believe it is important to give individuals an objective that they can really do something about. If they focus only on objectives which are out of their hands, and to which they can contribute nothing, this not only breeds disillusionment but actively encourages both arrogance and negativism.

There is, however, another side to this coin. We must educate people for change. This includes making them aware of the alternatives to change and the consequences of these alternatives. I am convinced, as well, that we must not focus too much—as I believe we do today—on the problems of change. People have coped with change throughout history. Look at how they have coped with the absolutely phenomenal change of the past fifty years. It does prove that we can do it.

And that brings me to my final point: What do I mean by "we"? I mean mankind on this planet. It seems to me that small, successful societies have developed as a result of isolation. The only way we can replicate, on a planetary basis, the experience of successful island communities is to make clear what the alternatives are. To put it differently, we have to become aware that our planet is, in itself, a small, isolated island in the universe.

With this awareness, we can make use of existing knowledge to resolve global crises and improve the human condition, because the awareness will lead to a common objective, a recognition of shared priorities which, given our knowledge, we can then appropriately apply and adequately manage.

Brazil

A BRAZILIAN PERSPECTIVE

José Mindlin
Chairman, Metal Leve SA
Vice President
Federation of Industries
of the State of São Paolo

I travel a great deal and, in the process, come into contact with the economic, social and political realities of both developed and developing countries. To me it seems crystal clear that global interdependence is a pervasive fact of life, and that therefore the problems of developing countries are not *only* problems of developing countries. They are the problems of the industrial nations as well.

I am surprised—in many places and on many occasions—at how little this is recognized. It seems to me so obvious that the solution to the world crises, both the present crisis and future crises, can be found only if industrial countries realize that the crises of the developing world are also theirs.

Take, for example, the problems of the current financial

crisis. One way or another, the debts of the developing countries will have to be renegotiated. Countries don't go bankrupt. But if the rules that the IMF enforces, and the advice it gives, do not pay attention to existing social problems, these rules and this advice, however desirable from an economic point of view, can constitute a danger to the international world order.

A New Design

I am convinced that the world requires a new monetary system in which global issues can be realistically discussed. At present, the IMF has too few resources. Also there are political problems. Perhaps we should change the IMF's weighted voting to a relative voting proportionate to the economic power of the country. From that point of view the IMF pattern as it exists now seems outdated. There is need for a new design. For example, present interest rates worldwide are such that no productive activity can afford them. This makes no sense for the industrialized nations or the developing countries.

The United States was superbly creative after World War II in designing an international order; but that order, it seems to me, has now run its course. It was essentially established by the developed countries and, in a way, dictated to the developing world. It was not reached by consensus. Economically, it was based on the developing countries producing raw materials and the industrial countries producing manufactured goods. This is no longer possible.

Technology: Know-How and Know-Why

I am considered, and indeed I am, a practical man. But I am also a dreamer. I look around me and I see that most of today's realities were yesterday's dreams. And so I dream today of technology becoming an instrument for a better life for all, not a private asset. In that context, the question that occurs to me is: How can we change the world to provide open access to technology? I am convinced that one ingredient of this is that technological agreements must be based not only on know-how but also on know-why. By this I mean a method of technological cooperation that provides open access to research and mutual exchange of results.

One example that comes to mind is the resources of the deep sea and the draft of the law of the sea. What is clearly needed somewhere along the line is for the countries and the companies in the United States and Germany that have the know-how to transfer, by licensing, their know-how to the developing countries. Because the resources of the sea that technology now makes available really must, one way or another, be made available to all.

I speak here from direct experience. In my organization we started with licensing, which worked fine until we became competitors in the world market. Then we began having problems. We proceeded to set up R&D of our own. Now we are an originating factor, however small, in the world market. I believe that is the pattern that must be followed globally.

The Touch of Midas

An important tool for development is joint ventures by industrial country companies with developing country companies. This includes joint ventures in which local entrepreneurs have majority equity. In this kind of an arrangement, money becomes not an end in itself but a tool for development. Right now we are in the situation, not only here in Brazil but largely worldwide, where the financial sector attracts resources that should be going into productive use. At the extreme end, we then get wealthy countries accumulating additional wealth, while there are others that have nothing to eat or to wear. It is the classic touch of Midas. What is needed for economic growth is a different fiscal treatment of financial investment and productive investment in order to attract resources into productive investment. At present it works the other way around. Savings should be lured into productive investment, not into financial speculation.

A Personal Stake for Employees

Let me give you a concrete example here in Brazil. We have a social integration fund designed to meet some of the social needs of employees. The money is administered by a government agency, which lends it to the private sector; the private sector repays the money as a loan. I think it would be better if the fund instead took equity in the enterprises so that the employees get a real personal stake in the enterprise. This way, industry employees become investors in a productive entity instead of, in their own way, being once again speculators in money. This should happen particularly in small- and medium-sized enterprises. It would strengthen the smaller companies and give them the opportunity to invest in technology and in administrative and managerial experience. It would also create new markets. At present, in Brazil, we have a population of 120 million people, but only 50 million consumers.

Democracy as a Functional Tool . . .

Functionally I believe that what we should do in Brazil today is to have an organized interchange of interest groups with the government. The government should be compelled by law to consult with a range of representative groups. In the sixties and seventies we had a fair amount of sectoral interaction with the government, that is, each sector presented its own cause and its own needs to the government and was quite often listened to. However, nobody represented the global needs even of the industrial sector, let alone the whole complex interaction of interests that makes up a wholesome economy.

I am convinced that, to deal effectively and realistically with the problems we face in Brazil today, governments cannot decide in a closed room what should be done and then inform the people of their decision. What is needed is the broadest possible participation in the decision-making process. It is not that any one of us has the answers, but the more that participation takes place by representative groups, the bigger the chances are of finding solutions. Certainly such a process is more liable to produce solutions than government working on its own.

. . . and a Balance Wheel

I do, of course, have ideas on what the optimum relationship could be between the public and the private sector. I firmly believe that private enterprise is best designed to give consumers the options they deserve through the mechanism of the market. But sometimes the private sector goes too far one way or the other, and then perhaps government competition is necessary to complete the cycle. In Brazil, some state-operated enterprises also went too far. They went into vertical integration, far beyond the initial basic production, into producing consumer goods, engineering enterprises, other services. But I believe there is something healthy about an interaction of government and private enterprises within a democratic system that allows freedom and change.

As for the allocation of resources, and indeed income distribution as well, I believe it is not a question of whether it should be done by government or the market. Or rather, it is not a technical question; it is a political question. Government and the private sector essentially live in different worlds, except perhaps in Japan, and what is needed is more participation by the private sector in government.

Bureaucrats and Entrepreneurs

It is an indulgence and a mistake to divide the world into bureaucrats and entrepreneurs. I think it would be ideal to design a system in which there would be a way of getting in and out for both. By this I mean for entrepreneurs to work in government, and for bureaucrats to work in private enterprise. Individuals should not think of one or the other as a one-time career for all their lives. They should think of society as a whole, of which private enterprise is a part. It is not a separate entity.

Profit, for example, is not an end in itself. It is a tool for social development and growth. The focus of discussion should be not so much on what profit is or is not, but on what can be done with it. At present, bureaucrats everywhere tend to believe that profit is bad and it is their privilege, indeed duty, to tax it. Closer interaction between bureaucrats and entrepreneurs, and the in-and-out system I have described, would enlighten bureaucrats on the true function of profit. Such an interchange would also transform the present level of ignorance, or even antagonism, by bureaucrats about entrepreneurs, and by entrepreneurs about bureaucrats, into a system in which each would enlarge the other's horizons for the social good.

This process of broadening horizons should be reinforced through education. I believe, for example, that graduate schools of engineering and business have to teach their students how to be good professionals and managers. But that is not enough. They must also be taught how important it is to be good citizens, and that everything is everybody's concern. I know that such a process will be a gradual one. All important change is gradual, and here we are dealing with a fundamental mindcast, a sense of values, a sense of what is really important in life.

Rebellion or Change?

One reason why young people everywhere seem to be disillusioned and in revolt against materialistic values, against what they perceive as artificial rules and standards that are meaningless, is that they see around them a world in which there is enormous misery and great injustice which, given the tools our society has, make no sense. From their viewpoint, the older generation did not arrange the world well. The best program, I believe, is to get these idealistic young people into a dialogue of reason. They need to be convinced that violence is destructive and not creative, and will not result in a better world. There are, of course, many forms of violence. Violence can be disguised as dictatorship or other forms of brutal imposition; sometimes it is even disguised as apparent wisdom and the voice of experience. But progress and improvement happen only if things are discussed and understood. Only when issues are discussed and understood does effective and lasting change take place.

FIXING THE FINANCIAL SYSTEM

Mario Henrique Simonsen
Vice Chairman
Brazilian Institute of Economics
Former Minister of Finance

The storm cloud of international indebtedness hanging over the world's economic climate is almost as much a topic of conversation—at least everywhere I go—as the weather. Since I suppose I have as much right to be a weatherman as most other people who are doing forecasts nowadays, here are my thoughts, my predictions and, I trust most useful, some ideas for what we can do to change the atmosphere. Because the storm threatens us all.

In the Short Term

In the short term, the most important problem the world faces is stagflation, and the role of stagflation in relationship to growth. For this, worldwide, the role of the policy mix in the United States is crucial. In the seventies we believed that freeing exchange rates would almost automatically take care of the problem. But this theory has now been challenged by the facts. At present, unless we can get in the United States a policy mix that calls for tighter fiscal policy and a less tight monetary policy, the results will be bankruptcies and waves of rescheduling of outstanding debts—not only in all of the Americas but also in the European countries.

Until now, the commercial banking system has been successful in rescheduling commercial loans and in recycling the world's money. But this may no longer be feasible. The possibility exists that, sooner or later, there will be panic, and a rush on the banks, leading to a worldwide depression. We must therefore reexamine and probably strengthen the roles of the IMF, the World Bank and international institutions such as GATT.

One approach to the problem would be a policy mix that would call for exchange rates that are not fixed, but are tied to the economic core rates of each country and call for devaluation by the core rates of inflation with occasional adjustments. This would have to be policed and, in a sense, enforced by the IMF.

Strengthen the IMF

At present, the role of the international organizations such as the IMF is much too weak. For example, the IMF can hand out advice but it cannot furnish sufficient money. Specifically, the IMF should now activate its substitution account and increase quotas over time. There should also be much closer co-operation between the IMF and the commercial banking system worldwide. This can be done by the commercial banks buying IMF long-term bonds.

I believe it is vital for the IMF to increase its base and become a major part of the recycling process. The commercial banks have done a tremendous job, and indeed can assist in continuing to do so; but since there is no central bank for the world, there exists at present no opportunity for commercial banks to monitor, even less to put conditionalities on their loans. Only the IMF can do that.

To illustrate this: In the last ten years, much of the borrowing by developing countries has been for projects not all of which made economic sense. More important, however, and more distressing from an economic point of view, a great deal of it went into financing capital flight because the less developed countries (LDCs) maintained overvalued currencies.

Three Steps

Three steps are required to tackle the present problem:

One, the commercial banks should lend money to the IMF.

Two, there should be a substantial increase in IMF quotas, and I am thinking of as much as 100 percent. This is not possible, of course, at the moment. But we could gradually increase quotas over a period of perhaps five years.

Three, the role of the SDR should be enhanced so that it becomes the world reserve currency. This would not only make sense for the world economy but would also solve some of the problems of the U.S. dollar, which is now both a national currency and the world reserve currency, a complex and difficult role. I know, of course, that making the SDR the currency for world reserve is not a matter that can be tackled immediately, but I do think it can and should be done over a period of twenty to thirty years.

Greed and Fear

The major motivations for people's actions are unfortunately greed and fear. The first major recycling in the world system was essentially a matter of greed. Now we are dealing with a need for recycling that is prompted by fear. To make the process less dangerous, we need coordination and intermediation. Both can be accomplished through effective international organizations.

Shore Up Other International Institutions

Not only the IMF but other international institutions—institutions that we already have in place, yet either do not appreciate or do not use as much as we should—also need to be shored up so they can serve more effectively the purpose for which they were designed. For example, the GATT should be strengthened to make it impossible for any country to impose tariff barriers or nontariff barriers. Enforcement should be strong, calling for penalties on the offending countries, not only by the country that has been hurt but by all other countries in the GATT, who would then automatically introduce countervailing tariffs.

Another more complex and far-reaching example is the United Nations. At present, we have a situation in which the UN is important when the problem is unimportant, but the UN is marginal, at best, when the problem is important. The only way I can see to strengthen the UN and give it more power for enforcement is for the UN to have its own armed force. This, of course, would still not make it effective when the issues at stake are between the superpowers, but it would make it possible for the UN to tackle other problems. At the moment the UN, which is, after all, the only effective international organization that we have, is at the border of demoralization.

The Proper Role of Government

Speaking of institutions also raises the question of the role of government, and specifically government intervention in the economy. I think we need to face the fact that government intervention of some kind, in some areas, cannot be avoided. What we should try to do is contain it within the limits of a number of externalities wherein the government is probably, if not the most effective, the only conceivable instrument. In such areas as pollution, for example, or the management of nonrenewable resources, we need cooperation and therefore we need a central authority. Government should concentrate on these sectors and not move into sectors that can be tackled better by the private sector.

Government has a legitimate role, obviously, in such areas as defense, or firefighting, as well as in pollution and the control of energy consumption. In the last case, it can exercise its role by regulation and also by price signaling, but it should not get involved in production. To sum up, the government's legitimate role is regulatory where regulation is required, but not entrepreneurial.

In certain developing countries, the government gets involved in entrepreneurial activity mainly because the capital market is not strong enough to make it possible for an effective private sector to develop and work. The answer to that problem, however, is not government intervention but the enhancement of capital markets.

I would make it an absolute rule for government not to subsidize its own operations. Where they exist, they should be allowed to compete freely and fairly in the marketplace. The results would be an interesting exercise.

Sometimes government enterprises can be efficient. In Brazil, for example, we have a good generation of technocrats who went to work for the government and did a very credible job with government enterprises. On the other hand, we are finding that big companies are becoming increasingly bureaucratized and are also managed by professional managers, not by owners. If the state wants its own enterprises, run not by political appointees but by competent technocrats who are good managers, then, in principle, who owns an enterprise should not matter. The most important difference between government and private enterprise in our day is not so much the ownership but the capital market structure. When there is no strong capital market structure, enterprises are, in effect, owned either by the government or by a family. Family ownership is all right in terms of efficiency in small- and medium-sized enterprises, but it does not work in larger undertakings. Failure in family-owned enterprises, once they go beyond a certain size, seems to come almost inevitably after two generations.

It is interesting, and I believe illustrative, that the three strongest and most effective economies, and certainly the three economies where the private sector plays the most effective role, are those of the United States, Japan and Switzerland, which have the world's most developed capital markets. If you have a strong capital market, you tend to have widespread private ownership, which strengthens not only the economic structure of a country but its political structure as well.

In running state-owned enterprises, what makes the difference, as I have noted, is whether they have in management—and derived from that, all management—people who are political appointees or people who are professionals. The difference is illustrated by Mexico, where top managers in government enterprises tend to be political appointees and the enterprises are largely mismanaged, and Brazil, where top appointees are largely professional and the enterprises are therefore well managed.

The world needs an integrated economy. Indeed it already has an economy that is integrated in many ways. What is required now is a strengthening of international institutions which can develop the global regulations that will enhance the most desirable development. Among them are such institutions as the World Bank and the Regional Development Banks. My concern is not so much with change—we need change and we will have change—as with opacity and accountability. The comparison is with the layer of ozone that may create climactic changes. I want to be sure that government activity does not become an ozone layer.

Take the problem of agriculture. This is clearly a question of technology and education. I believe the role of the government can and should be, for example, to establish an experimental farm that can show neighboring farmers the uses of technology. But it should then leave the farmers alone to do what they can and to develop as they can with their own entrepreneurial instinct and their own deep knowledge. To set up such experimental farms throughout the country would be a very good role for the Minister of Agriculture.

Let me illustrate the appropriate role of government in another way. It is clear that we should shift from nonrenewable to renewable sources of energy. To do this should clearly be the role of the private sector. However, the government should create price signals—for example, through taxation—to discourage the development of nonrenewable sources of energy, and offer subsidies to encourage the development of renewable resources. Also, something must be done to prevent a repetition of 1973 and 1979 when oil prices went sky-high, essentially by the fiat of a combination of countries and a market that could not deal with this fiat because it had no alternative sources. I believe there must be tax policies on oil to encourage the development of synthetics. A reason for government intervention of this kind is that only government can effectively have the longer vision that it takes to make this kind of policy.

In energy, we do need government regulation for allocation. Market allocation in this area seems to be too short-sighted. Look at what is happening to synfuels in the United States. The market cannot set a price for exhaustible resources.

The Vital Link: Education

For the long term, I am convinced, the central problem is education: not only in terms of knowledge and practical application but also education in values. The two fundamental values that I see as requisite are tolerance and the conviction that freedom is reciprocal.

Focusing on specifics, I believe there has to be a strong elementary and high school system at the public level, plus selected higher education that focuses on concrete professional needs. There is a clear and evident need in all societies for recycling education and for retraining people to keep up with the economic requirements of their societies. This has been true for the last three centuries, and is true most emphatically now. Increasingly, people have to be retrained throughout life.

I see it here in Brazil. Engineers who do not understand computers can command a salary that is the equivalent of $750 a month. If they understand computers and know how to work with them, the sky is the limit. This kind of continual reeducation has to be done both by the private and the public sector. In Brazil, universities have special courses that are given in the evening after working hours for retraining, and a number of private organizations exist that also have evening courses running from 6 to 8 p.m. for executives and professionals.

In my opinion, education is also the vital link in two other social and economic issues on which global debate has so far shed more heat than light. One of these is population control. I believe such control is necessary, but it cannot be done through forced sterilization. What needs to be taught, in the simplest terms, is the cost-benefit analysis of having children. Almost anyone can understand that, and will act accordingly.

The other area in which education must replace rhetoric if the real problem is to be addressed is the transfer of technology.

Technology consists of three stages. One, you dismantle a watch; two, you put it together; three, you innovate on it. At present, the form in which technology is transferred is wrong. There is no point in transferring the metaphorical "black box" if no one can use it. If a country has good engineers, it can discover what is in the black box. But most of the countries that need the transfer of technology do not now have such engineers. What this adds up to is that, in the transfer of technology, the most important problem is to educate the recipient countries (a) to be able to understand what it is they need, and (b) to be able to work with it.

Forecasting the Year 2000

Finally, I am convinced that what happens in the year 2000 depends on what happens in the 1980s. I have never seen a period when forecasts were so hard to make because the variables are so unpredictable. I believe that the fifties and sixties were an extraordinary period and one can't extrapolate from them. They did produce the clear failure of socialism to achieve its goals, and they also produced a more humane left that seems to be at odds with productivity. It appears that socialism can manage a basic industrialization but does not work thereafter in consumer or industrial goods, and is even worse in services. But just where the demonstrated failure of socialism leads us, I do not know.

Canada

OBSERVATIONS OF A FLEXIBLE ACTIVIST

Thomas Bata
Chairman
Bata Ltd.

The current economic state of the world is, of course, distressing, but I hope and believe there is a floor under the economic contraction that the world has experienced in recent years. I have watched depressions before, as well as changing values. I recall only a decade and a half ago or so a distinguished statesman telling me that the time of the private international company had come to an end. He predicted then that there would inevitably be more government planning around the world, and that the public sector would overwhelm and finally absorb the private sector everywhere. Clearly, that has not happened. I also remember predictions by highly respected people like Howard Perlmutter about twenty years ago that by the end of the century the entire economic activity of the world would be controlled by three hundred multinational companies. That too, obviously, is unlikely to happen.

There are cycles in people's attitudes and values, and the pendulum does swing. But while it is true that the pendulum swings, the world, at the same time, moves, and when the pendulum swings back, the whole clock is not in the same position as it was before. One should therefore not take anything for granted, but be a flexible activist. Which is what I consider myself to be.

As such, I have watched the developing countries, as well as and including countries espousing Marxist doctrines, change from an almost unmitigated animosity toward private enterprise and multinational corporations to an interest in collaboration. State-operated enterprises—particularly in countries with centrally controlled economies, which in the past really wanted to kill the private sector—are now more interested in working with multinational corporations than in eliminating them. Also, I see in many countries, including the USA, a change in labor attitudes. Labor has become much more pro private enterprise than it was in the days of prosperity. This is understandable because self-interest dictates it. Workers see the need for job creation and know that only a prospering private sector can really create jobs, especially jobs that are worth having. Hopefully, this attitude will survive a return to prosperity.

Whither Sovereignty?

Speaking of evolving attitudes and how they effect a desirable global harmonization of fiscal, monetary and, finally, overall economic policy, I see a long-term trend away from absolute national sovereignty toward economic collaboration between states. In the medium term, the trend in the developing countries is toward regionalism rather than globalism. This is true particularly in Africa, where artificial political boundaries that were essentially drawn during the colonial period clearly make no economic sense. Regional collaboration is therefore needed to achieve economic and social progress. I believe that an emerging regionalism will have economic structures and an economic base rather than a political one. At least initially, this evolution is needed in Latin America as well as in Africa and Asia.

In Asia, ASEAN is an example of what is happening, and indeed what should be happening, although it is moving more slowly than it should. But then it took Europe centuries to move toward its own integration based on rational economic criteria. One of the retarding factors is that the current structure of the United Nations helps create political rigidity and an environment in which political factors play *against* the development of economic structures that would really help the developing world go where it needs to go. There will be, no doubt, people of goodwill who will want to change this, and this change might give the UN a great mission of a positive kind.

Regional Coalescence

In some functional areas, sovereignty is already being surrendered to achieve reasonable objectives. I think here of such areas as aviation, conservation, anti-pollution measures, and weather observations. It seems that nations can work together where there are realistic objectives and where what needs to be done does not touch political pride. And it is possible that there will be increasing recognition of the need for more of this kind of cooperation for purposes that are clearly beneficial to all.

It is not that I see heaven on earth arriving in the foreseeable future, but there is the example of the United States and, in a different way, Canada and Europe, to illustrate what is possible and to function as trend-setters for the rest of the world. Each one of these regions, the USA, Canada and the EEC—and they are regions in the true sense of the word—has managed to achieve a rational customs union as well as economic policies that tie together large and culturally diverse populations. There are, of course, within and amongst each of these groupings great problems that tend to receive disproportionate attention from the media, and create the impression that less progress is being made than is actually the case.

What I hope will happen soon is a regional, if not global, approach to monetary rules. I have seen the advantages of this kind of regional monetary approach. An example is the French franc, which serves a regional role in much of the Francophone part of Africa, and has been very effective even under terrible conditions of drought in the Sahel.

Such currencies probably cannot have the name of any of the existing currencies. That would be too political. But names can be found that protect political pride and make economic and financial sense. Europe is experimenting with the European Currency Unit (ECU), and the experiment seems to be working out.

Needed: An Economic Seer

Human evolution seems to require inspiration, and I believe that the world today is in need of an economic ideology that will serve to lead it out of this current morass of political rivalries and economic destructiveness and incompetence. In addition to an ideology that makes economic sense on a global basis, we probably also need a charismatic prophet, who can preach economic ideals that will make sense to everyone in the world and who can inspire people to follow. This is not as unrealistic as it may sound. I remember, in my own lifetime, when the first "prophets" began talking about the possibility of a united Europe in the 1920s. I remember, too, the politicians and the bureaucrats who opposed the notion in each country, and predicted it would never happen. Well, in Europe the fact is that much *has* happened, and it happened primarily because Europe did have, at the right time, leaders with vision. If the dream can come true, or at least be in the process of coming true, in Europe, where age-old rivalries are often violent and irrational, I believe it can also happen on a global level.

Government and Private Enterprise

An economic ideology must define the relationship between government and private enterprise. I believe that the role of government in the economic area needs to be voluntarily limited. The government does have a role. The metaphor that comes to mind is that the government should not have a foot on the brake of the automobile, but rather keep a hand on the clutch just to make certain that when there is a real need for the shifting of gears, that shifting is made easier.

One of the most important areas of necessary government activity is, of course, the creation and maintenance of infrastructure, without which investment anywhere is hardly possible. The difficult question is to decide where infrastructure starts and where it stops. Take a system of satellites: Is putting up a satellite part of an infrastructure that government is responsible for? If it is, do the operations that make possible the economic existence of satellites require government participation or intervention in any form? So the real question becomes: Where is the economic dividing line at which infrastructure stops? Because government intervention—indeed, government activity—that steps over the line is almost invariably and demonstrably counterproductive. In many countries, governments have unnecessarily entered wide areas of economic activity while neglecting the creation of infrastructure, and particularly its maintenance. One can see the difference in the whole economic activity in a country where the government has provided and maintained a good infrastructure and concentrated on service to its economic entrepreneurs.

This leads to the troublesome area of governmental inefficiency and corruption. Corruption should be eradicated, but I know that progress in this direction will be slow and patchy. However, I have observed around the world that progress in many countries is not so much hampered by corruption as by inertia and incompetence. What makes the difference between an economy that suffers from inertia and one that does not is the supply of educated administrators and managers and, in the economic field especially, executives who have grown up in the hard world of facing the challenges of the private sector. If there are enough of these, even if they manage state-owned enterprises or are on the boards of state-owned enterprises, these enterprises can prosper. But such executives will only be available if the private sector is big and the state sector is small.

Global Problems

The number one problem facing the world today seems to me to be population explosion. It can carry the seed of destruction for the entire planet, and it should be feared as much as nuclear weapons. I would feel desperate about this had I not, in my own lifetime, seen serious turnarounds and some very real successes. I remember, for example, in Mexico fifteen years ago, the subject of family planning—and certainly the more concrete subject of population control—was taboo. It was taboo in the political community, and in polite society as well. Then, some time ago, I heard the man who is now President openly discuss the problem, and face the issue. There has been comparable movement in India and even in Brazil, not to mention China. I am therefore optimistic that humanity will resolve this problem, but it is not going to be easy.

If I were to define what I believe the world needs fundamentally, I would say: (1) control of the population explosion; and (2) cultural pluralism combined with racial tolerance. By this I do not mean only elimination of oppression in white-ruled countries, but a worldwide openness. I know it can be done. Canada is one example of changing attitudes.

Some time ago, I would have argued for Canada to be an all-out melting pot. Now I think that the maintenance of multiethnicity can make an important contribution. It can be a risky road, but I believe it is worth taking. The example in my mind is an event that we organize in Toronto every year in June—it is known as the Toronto Caravan. In this event, each cultural group in Toronto, which is now very much a multi-ethnic city, prepares a pavilion of its own in which it can display its cultural and ethnic uniqueness. There are over forty of these, ranging from Korean and Pakistani to Swiss. Each group organizes cultural events of various kinds, including art displays and food specialties. More than a million people visit the pavilions during the ten-day event, and get a better understanding of their fellow citizens. All of this is a voluntary effort, engaging each ethnic group, and especially its youth, in positive and constructive activities which are also an economic success. So I have come to think that if there is a large number of ethnic and cultural groups, none will dominate, and you will get harmony through an interplay of differences. I would like to see the spirit of the Toronto Caravan translated into a global system.

Global Investment

Bata has production and marketing facilities in scores of countries around the world. Even at this stage of economic uncertainty, we are planning new plants in Bangladesh, Indonesia, Kenya, Brazil and several other countries. It is true that under current economic conditions we do see a drying up of profits, and that forces us to be more careful about where we risk money and management effort. Our natural tendency then is to put money where there are larger regional and national markets. Except for those with specific natural resources, the small countries will not attract investment, nor will they be able to produce local entrepreneurs of sufficient stature to make real economic progress. On the contrary, when there are contractions in world trading, a good many of the small enterprises existing in those countries disappear. Formation of larger economic groupings, supported by strong political ties promising continuity, is the answer. In today's world of rapid communications, the countries involved in such arrangements do not even need to be geographically contiguous. What is important is that they should form a unit for free trading in which export to industrialized countries should be a calculated factor. But it should be subordinated to intra-group trade. South to South trade is being talked about, but there is still the erroneous belief that South to North exports are the panacea.

Another important ingredient of economic progress worldwide is the free movement not only of capital, technology and know-how but also of people. In Canada, we have found an interesting approach to that problem. Within limits of absorption capacity, we welcome new people of all races. Once an approved immigrant arrives, he has security of residence, freedom to select his activity and a hope of early citizenship. That brings in many people with excellent skills who, because they have come on a permanent basis, use their abilities much more effectively than a temporary adviser could. This is one of the main reasons for Canada's great progress in recent years in the fields of technology, industry and culture.

Most developing countries deny themselves such benefits by closing their borders even to their neighbors, let alone people of other races. The EEC is a good example of intra-community movement; other groupings of countries need to take similar steps.

I am convinced that future prosperity for everyone on the globe depends on getting the developing countries on their way economically. Intergovernmental aid is essential, but I do not think aid alone will achieve the desired result. What is needed is to help the developing countries help them themselves. That this is entirely possible is illustrated by the growing number of newly industrialized countries (NICs) and by other countries approaching that status. Most of them welcomed direct investment and the work of multinational corporations, and several of them have developed multinational companies of their own.

How Bata Does It

In the remaining developing countries, many of which are in Africa, those interested in development face the most difficult problem. As I look around the world, it seems very clear that multinational corporations are the only ones that can make a real and speedy impact. I have the example of our own company in Kenya. We were one of the first industries to set up in that country when we put in a shoe-manufacturing, tanning and retailing facility. Now there are several locally owned shoe-manufacturing enterprises, as well as a number of supply industries of materials, components and services. Most of them were started by former employees of the Bata Company. We are pleased to see this, and we encourage it. We buy from these facilities, and use their products in our factories and stores. I am happy to report that most of these enterprises are flourishing. No doubt, members of a future generation coming from these enterprises are getting ready to strike out on their own and become entrepreneurs again, which will result in a future forward economic push. What this illustrates is that expertise and sound economic growth must be started by practical example. We in Bata showed a number of countries that it can be done and, perhaps more importantly, how it can be done. We educated in the true sense of the word: We transferred knowledge and management skills beyond our own enterprise. Many other multinational companies have done and are doing the same, and more should be encouraged to do so.

Of course, the picture is different in different industries and different countries; but the Bata experience is one example of how results can be achieved in all developing countries where governments create an environment to encourage enterprise. This is how we can help developing countries. It is in our interest to do so, for it is the raising of living standards of the Third World's people that is likely to be the engine generating long-term prosperity of the industrialized world as well.

CAPITALISM: CHARMS AND CHALLENGES

David M. Culver
President and Chief Executive Officer
Alcan Aluminum Ltd.

It would seem self-evident that if you truly believe in liberal values and individual freedom, you have to believe in the capitalist system. In the socialist system, the problem with "From each according to his ability, to each according to his need" is that it is a splendid idea, but no one will agree on what each should give and each should get. Therefore, only Big Brother can decide, and that is the end of freedom.

One of the things that capitalism must make clear is that its purpose is not simply the maximization of profit. *Profit is a minimum requirement, but not the objective.*

The real objectives of free enterprise are: (1) to give economic freedom and responsibility to the individual to choose, and to enjoy the consequences of his choice: and (2) to use the minimum requirement of profit for sustained job creation, for sustained creation of challenges and, above all, for the sustained growth of people.

The free enterprise system succeeds only when you allow people to grow by giving them responsibility, as early as possible and as much as possible, for their own decisions. The state centrally planned economy does not provide opportunity for individual growth. Only when individuals can create as much as possible, on their own schedules, are they optimally alive and productive. I imagine you've noticed that, whenever you find yourself on a guided tour, you get drowsy very quickly, while when you make your own plans and follow them, you have a lot more energy. If I were to use one phrase to sum up, the maximum objective of free enterprise is to provide opportunities for people to grow quickly and fully.

What Makes Economic Planning Work

When the history of the current macroeconomic system is written, together with the planning that was meant to guide it, it will become clear that what went wrong was that the planners overlooked one important factor. Economic planning is practiced by highly trained, logical people dealing with quantitative probabilities and assessments that leave out the emotions and value systems that really move people. Motivation is a word that is in all the textbooks, but it really is at the heart of getting things done. It draws on emotions—what turns people on, and why—and requires a set of values that are the hallmark of the enterprise.

Many Japanese companies know this, and use it extraordinarily well. A very good example is the extent of productivity turnaround achieved when Japanese companies have taken over failing U.S. plants, using the existing equipment and workforce. In some cases, quality and productivity increases have been remarkable. These achievements have usually been based upon awakening emotional commitment to a clear set of values, which are often very simply expressed. Here—and I believe anywhere—you get excellence when people know what the values are all about, and are committed to them.

Public Understanding

Business, particularly big business, is very disappointing when it comes to explaining itself—it does not do a good job of getting its message across. It does not know when, where and how to fight. Its critics deal in slogans and ideologies, while it responds with facts and figures. Certainly, facts and figures may be necessary to puncture myths, but business also needs to proclaim its values, and with a message that is persuasive and convincing.

For purposes of analysis and understanding, I would like to divide the range of concerns that companies in a capitalistic society need to address between those that are intrinsic to the enterprise and those that are external but nevertheless of vital importance.

Intrinsic Concerns: Allocation of Funds

Let me begin with the allocation of funds. There is nothing wrong with competition, nor with profit, provided that is regarded as a minimum requirement and not a maximum goal. However, we business leaders in the Western world have a tendency to shoot ourselves in the foot by concentrating on short-term profits. What we need is an end to the tyranny of the quarterly financial statement, both inside and outside a company. Internally, we need to avoid "Stop–Go" politics which waste resources and frustrate those who have to carry them out, particularly in capital expenditure and R&D programs. We must learn to build more continuity into company management, without, however, losing flexibility—a tricky balance.

I believe that there are signs that we are heading in that direction. I notice, for example, that the stock market seems to ignore the quarterly financial statement, and pays more attention to the fundamental economic realities in a corporation. This is healthy and encouraging.

Technology

Another concern with important internal, as well as external, dimensions is technology. The public has been led to an expectation that technology can solve all problems, and particularly in North America it often expects more than business can deliver. Putting technology to use requires very large allocations of capital, know-how and manpower over a continuous period; the time scale may run to ten or twenty years. It is often not possible for companies to bring to commercial reality (which is what the public sees) all the technological developments that are open to it. Technology must be kept focused and relevant. The questions that technology *can* answer are virtually without limit. The questions that technology *should* answer are particular to each business, and it is vital that management ask the right questions in the first place.

In that connection, it strikes me that one of the problems managers—and perhaps even mankind—face is that we have an information overload. We have too much information and too little knowledge. We need to turn off the tape occasionally to think through what we know and decide how it can best be applied.

Management and Labor

A third—and perhaps the most important—intrinsic concern for companies is the relationship between workers and management. One of the most overlooked reasons for industrial actions is, in my experience, boredom. Blue collar workers in our time are educated, healthy, reasonably paid, and are really budding capitalists. I am, of course, all in favor of this, but one of the results is that you cannot ask people like this to do the same dreary task and expect them to be content with it.

I believe that it is important to give workers more influence in the area where they are most competent and where they are directly involved. This means primarily the job floor. For instance, there are considerable benefits to be gained from having worker cooperation and participation in devising job classifications. This can lead to a significant reduction in the number of job classifications, greater flexibility, higher productivity and a greater variety of work for the worker himself.

I do not believe that workers should be represented on boards of management. Because of the mandated responsibility of company directors to represent the interests of all shareholders, there is an almost inescapable conflict of interest, and the contribution workers can make at the board level is not going to be very great. I do, on the other hand, believe in giving workers the maximum information one can, and involving them in decision making as much as possible. I also believe in doing everything one can to help make workers partners in capitalism. At Alcan, we have an employee savings plan in Canada to which nonunion employees can contribute 1 to 4 percent of their pay. We invest the monies in one of four funds: a common stock fund, a bond participation fund, a guaranteed interest fund or an Alcan common share fund. The company matches the investment up to 70 percent, depending on length of service. We found, interestingly enough, that more than 70 percent of our eligible employees invest their savings, and the fund most of them choose is the Alcan fund.

The fundamental aspect of desirable labor-management

relations is to demonstrate mutual respect. I believe, for example, and have publicly said—even when we were in a situation of industrial strife—that we have the best workers in the world. This does not mean that we do not sometimes have our differences. It is the same in any good relationship. But all differences can eventually be worked out on the basis of mutual respect.

External Concerns: Inflation and Disinflation

External concerns that have impact on companies in a capitalistic society sometimes seem to be legion. Let me concentrate on a few.

It is easy to blame politicians and central bankers for having given too much credit too freely, thereby creating inflation, and then for keeping money too tight and creating disinflation. The process of managing the world's economies is highly complex, and is likely to give rise to bouts of inflation and disinflation as politicians and bankers try to grapple with it. Wise company management allows for these trends, and plans for them—and around them.

Free Trade

Everyone is in favor of free trade until it comes to the goring of their own particular ox. While this is understandable, it makes no sense. Business should push politicians to go as far as they can in the direction of free trade, while recognizing that there really are limits: for example, the protection of an infant industry if it is a sound long-term prospect for the country. Pushing for free trade brings short-term costs as well as long-term benefits. In pushing for it, business should recognize, but try to counteract, the natural reluctance of politicians to see the loss of jobs that may be entailed in their own constituencies. It takes political courage to recognize and act upon economic facts, and to organize a framework, not of rescue, but of change, so that people and assets are retrained and redeployed.

International Trade and Investment

International institutions can and must provide an improved framework for world trade. The GATT is an important organization, and has carried out well its original task in the area of tariff reduction. Its role now needs to be expanded to include trade in services and to continue work on nontariff barriers.

In the United Nations, there is a need for agreement on rules for global investment that will establish the reciprocal rights and obligations for both the investing company and the host country. I also believe that the World Bank, and the Regional Development Banks associated with it, have a significant role. Business should cooperate with them, and on a proactive basis. An example of what I mean is a major study on aluminum worldwide done by the World Bank. We cooperated with this study by providing information, commenting on drafts of the report and reviewing the final product. In this way, we hope that a more realistic view of the global situation is achieved. This, in turn, means that the World Bank can make loans for sound economic development that make sense for everybody.

State-Owned Enterprises

Despite their best efforts to remain independent commercial undertakings, the reality is that all state-owned enterprises in the free world sooner or later succumb to political influence, and allow this political influence to distort their behavior as an economic enterprise.

First, there is their absolute performance. The fact of the matter is that, on average, a dollar of investment in the private sector produces several times the output of the same investment in the public sector.

Second, the government, having drawn up the ground rules of the economic game and administered them as the referee, then enters the game as a player. This, quite understandably, discourages the other players, and discourages further investment.

This is not to say that a society can be totally run from the private sector. Apart from administering the ground rules, there are social needs, such as law and order, education, medical services and the provision of the physical infrastructure of society, which are clearly legitimate roles for government. But except in very special cases, I would not count direct participation in business among these legitimate roles.

The Environment

That one seemed to be a major and intractable problem. But I'm optimistic about it now. I feel the trade-off between environmental regulation and economic growth is becoming understood. I see the extreme positions coming closer together and solutions being devised that make sense for all. At Alcan, for example, we are cooperating with UNEP, the global organization that monitors the environment, and are participating with it in the preparations for the forthcoming World Conference on Environmental Management.

No Soft Options

I distinguish between hammering out a compromise that is creative and meaningful and choosing the easy way out, the soft option. I believe 1981 was a watershed year in the economies of the West. From the early thirties to the early eighties we had a world that could afford, and did indeed take, soft options whenever it came to a fork in the road. In the past, for example, strikes were prohibited in Canada for public sector workers. Somewhere in the soft option period the question was raised about the public sector workers' right to strike. The argument was that since everyone had the right to strike, why should not public workers have it too? This ignored the fact that public workers have security that workers in the private sector do not have. Anyhow, the soft option was to let the public workers strike, with rather devastating results.

I think we are now entering a period in which we will once again address and choose the hard options rather than the soft ones. For instance, students who are in the universities today realize that they have to work hard to get good grades, to acquire professional competence, because when they get out, it will be hard to find a job. They are being trained for the hard options. I find this encouraging because history seems to show that societies that do take the soft options for any length of time are eventually overrun by societies that live by the hard options.

Addressing one such hard choice—perhaps the quintessential one—I would like to say a word on the allocation of resources. The fact is that the present uneven allocation and development of resources in the world means a wide range of wealth and poverty. The sad truth is that there is no quick fix for poverty. There are slow and steady solutions, and companies can contribute to them—mainly by creating jobs and fostering people's growth as quickly as possible. Multinational companies, in particular, can train local people in developing countries, both directly for their own employment and indirectly in the community that grows up around their operations. All of this takes time. But it is the only thing that really works.

Another area of choice that we all deal with at work and at home, socially and individually, has to do with cultural diversity. When we encounter diversity in nature, we love it. When we encounter it culturally, we tend to freeze. Why is that? I leave you with that question.

Egypt

ISLAM AND ECONOMIC ORDER

Dr. A. M. Hegazy
Chairman, Chloride Egypt; Chairman, Islamic Council for Trade

There are principles in Islam that delineate economic order and offer dynamic guidelines to development. The first of these is faith in the fact that God created wealth for man to develop and to get the benefit thereof. This means that it is incumbent on a good Moslem to make better use of the resources God has provided. This applies both to natural resources and to human resources.

The second principle, deriving from this faith, is that whoever develops wealth is not really an owner; he is simply an administrator of the wealth God has given. The proof of this is that at death, nobody can take his wealth with him.

The third application of Islamic principle to economic order illuminates the relationship between the private and public sectors. It makes clear that government should rely essentially on the private administration of wealth, and interfere only when interference is warranted in terms of the strategic interests of the broad masses of the population.

I believe that government, especially in developing countries, does have a valid role in overall, indicative planning. It can set parameters. But then it should get out of the way and let the private enterprise sector develop. At present, many developing countries with intrusive government planning are working on projects that are really unnecessary, projects that, in terms of real goals for society, are a total waste. Governments also make mistakes because they do not have the time or the inclination to look at long-term alternatives. They tend to address problems on a crisis basis, which may be politically necessary, but does not make for the soundest economic or social decisions.

Here and now, we need to design a system that is best suited to motivate people to work and compete. This means that government should be limited to strategic sectors of the economy, and private institutions should be developed that can get people together on a common interest. I would add the observation that the world seems to have developed a habit of waiting for government to do things, and I think that is a very bad habit indeed. We must get rid of it.

The Specter of Fanaticism

When one proposes a religious perspective on economics, one is almost always challenged in terms of tolerance and the tendency toward fanaticism that a religious perspective seems to carry in its train. I am convinced that these concerns, while understandable, are not necessarily warranted. Fanaticism arises only when government deliberately fosters it for either economic or political reasons. It is obstacles and frustrations, and primarily economic obstacles and frustrations, that inveigle people to revolt against society and become fanatics in the process.

There are two weapons against fanaticism. One is the teaching of tolerance through education, culture and trade. The other is education in religion itself—the true meaning of religion. Both are enhanced by providing role models in society that can demonstrate through their own personalities and their own way of life how true faith can be practiced without fanaticism and intolerance.

Multinational Corporations as Role Models

Speaking of role models, in the economic sphere multinationals can provide such a model. I believe in joint ventures with multinational corporations. The most important contribution multinational corporations can make to such ventures are their managerial skills. And it is managerial skills, or rather the lack thereof, that are the main obstacles to development. In this context, I am convinced that the major obstacle to the effective transmission of technology in the world today is that the developing countries do not have the capacity to absorb it. And that situation, too, can be corrected by managerial expertise.

I am aware of the fact that this will take both time and training. I am certain, in my own mind, that the kind of tripartite joint ventures in which I am involved, i.e., joint ventures intended to combine the know-how—especially the managerial know-how—the technology of multinational corporations, the capital of Arab countries, and the opportunities that exist for productive enterprise in a country such as Egypt, are the ideal solutions. That is real development.

The more international ties we can create, the better off everyone will be. In the process, and for the process, we need to get rid of "isms"—all "isms," ideological, political, economic, religious or whatever. We live in a world in which "isms" have no relationship to the realities of society and human development. And human development is what is needed.

The Importance of Merit

Instead of "isms," what we need for human development is the criterion of merit. This applies to economic undertakings, to educational institutions, and it applies also to international institutions such as, for example, the International Monetary Fund. The IMF cannot have, and should not have, one formula that applies to all countries. Countries differ in their needs, their structure, their abilities and their requirements. Organizations like the IMF should have a set of principles, but then adjust those principles to local realities, using merit, in its broadest, most imaginative sense, as a standard.

The Concept of Sufficiency

The Islamic objective in economic development is to achieve "sufficiency." This is different from subsistence. It includes not only food, clothing and housing but also transportation, education, health, and even helpers, relative to the level of income. Those in society who have not achieved sufficiency must be taken care of by society through the tax route.

There is the Islamic concept of *zakat,* which is a voluntary tax on both production and capital that is used to take care of all the needy in a community. And taking care of the needy begins with the family, then extends to community, then extends to the nation. *Zakat* should be applied not only on production and capital but also, and particularly, on unused funds. Such a tax would motivate investment. Islam is opposed to unproductive money—and it believes in participation of both risk and benefit. That is why an Islamic bank will not pay interest on purely financial papers. It is an equity participation institution.

The same Islamic reasoning also leads to giving labor the opportunity to participate in the results of the enterprise. This means profit-sharing for the workforce.

The Function of *Zakat*

The basic principle is that wealth is to be applied to investment, and that *zakat* meets the social needs of the community. If, in Egypt, we collected *zakat* as Islam requires, the Treasury would get more money than it gets now. And it would be contributed from, and with a sense of, responsibility.

Another economic principle of Islam is efficiency. Islam is opposed to using wealth in a manner that is wasteful or corrupt; it teaches that people with wealth should be neither extravagant nor tight in their use of wealth. It proposes that if you acquire and spend economically, based on ethical and moral values, then God is with you, and social and economic action become not only socially acceptable but morally and ethically rewarding.

I believe the most important short-term problem the world faces is what I have described before as sufficiency for all. This applies to people in both the industrial countries and the developing countries. Both North and South should concentrate on solving that problem with whatever it takes in terms of transfer of technology and financial resources.

A very important ingredient of this process, I believe, is a system of education that is job-related, that is, related to the tasks that have to be done on the farms and in the factories in the countries in which they have to be done. Perhaps we should think of a global system of some minimal taxation that would be comparable to the Islamic principle of *zakat,* which would be levied on all the developed countries for use in creating in the developing countries a minimum living standard. Introducing and applying such a tax could prevent social problems that might otherwise come to haunt us all.

FREE ENTERPRISE IN DEVELOPING COUNTRIES: THE CASE OF EGYPT

Dr. Mostafa Khalil
Chairman of the Board
Arab International Bank
Prime Minister (1978–80)

In developing countries, the role of free enterprise is different from the role free enterprise plays in developed countries. All developing countries have certain characteristics and face certain basic problems, among them a low GNP, low savings, and governments under pressure to deliver infrastructure and social welfare. All of us in the developing countries also have the common problem of people wanting improved living standards in societies that are characterized by a lack of entrepreneurship and, indeed, an absence of entrepreneurs. Most developing countries, after liberation, embraced socialist ideas of one stripe or another. Egypt is a classic case in point. In Egypt this immediate post-liberation period was characterized by nationalism, and in the economy, by extensive nationalization.

What Went Wrong

Egypt started private industry in the 1920s, but during the revolution of 1952 banking was nationalized, and in 1961 the private sector was nationalized. Government took over and was the only real entrepreneur left in the country. All other entrepreneurs left for other countries where they had the opportunity to exercise their imaginations and their talents. Then, President Sadat launched the Open Door Policy, which was designed to encourage the private sector, both domestic and foreign. But the private sector, now lacking the experience and the financial ability to identify economically viable investment projects, only invests in projects that have a swift payout. The reaction is understandable though not necessarily desirable. Entrepreneurs, responding to the Open Door Policy, concentrated on trade, not investment. This created a general climate of opinion that private enterprise is interested only in making a profit, and that there is no concern with the country's interests or the people's interests. In addition, investors faced the obstacle of an enormous and obstructive bureaucracy. Finally, in recent years, with interest rates as high as they were, people deposited money into financial instruments, not into investment. What happened, in effect, is that savings exceeded consumption.

An Effective Stock Market Is Fundamental

For effective investment, investment that is led by entrepreneurs, an effective stock market is required. People who invest must have the foresight to plan for at least four to five years. They also need sound feasibility studies that can offer some guarantee that their investment is sound. And perhaps above all there is a need for confidence in the political and economic system.

In Egypt, I believe the situation is promising. What happened is that the financial institutions became entrepreneurs. They made feasibility studies. They financed, on an equity or a loan basis, investments that seemed sound. They were able to take the risk, and their reputation for both expertise and probity made it possible for them to sell their shares in a new enterprise once the project became profitable. That is a sensible system for a country such as Egypt

The Role of Government

The best role for the government is to set policy, to establish ground rules, but to stay out of the project on a practical basis except for projects that the government determines to undertake for compelling national reasons. I believe it is vital for an investment to be established with purely economic criteria; it is also necessary for dividends to be attractive to investors.

In a country such as Egypt, it is important for the equity/loan ratio to be high at the beginning. We need to start the way Germany and Japan started after World War II. The banks must get involved in a major way in new enterprises. Once an enterprise is really going, the banks can sell their shares to the general public; in that way they recycle deposits and broaden the base of ownership. And I am convinced that the best way, from a social point of view, to fight communism and its ideas is to broaden the base of ownership.

Planning

It is vital for developing countries *not* to have a rigid planned economy. Instead, what developing countries need is a national plan that is elastic and indicative. The reason developing countries must have such a plan is that infrastructure projects that are essential to industry must be undertaken by the government, and it is important for industry to know just when and how these infrastructure projects will be tackled. I am speaking of such areas as transportation, communications, harbors, and such social infrastructure projects as education and training. Industry needs these infrastructure projects and only the government can undertake them.

The International Dimension

It would also be very desirable indeed to achieve harmonization of fiscal and monetary policy throughout the world.

We have all seen how important the fiscal and monetary policies of the United States are to the rest of the world. If it were possible to harmonize the policies of the major countries that are market economies, such harmonization would constitute a significant contribution to the economic welfare of the world. I do not think that, at this stage, this can be done through the United Nations or any existing UN institutions. The private sector economies should create an institution of their own that can tackle this problem. It is perhaps possible to use the IMF as a base. The problem of such harmonization is, as I see it, whether the major powers will pay the necessary attention to the problems of the smaller, weaker, developing countries. I believe it is important, even in existing institutions, for the international institutions to pay more attention to the smaller, weaker economies that do believe in private enterprise.

One practical approach is to create more co-financing with financial institutions in the countries themselves. There should be more co-financing with such institutions as the International Finance Corporation. And it would be a good idea if the World Bank had a separate institution, a separate fund, for feasibility studies. The same is true for the Agency for International Development. Finally, at present the interest rates of the World Bank and of the regional banks are too high. The spread between their loans and those of the commercial banks is too little.

Consumption and Investment

And that leads to the important, socially complex and politically delicate question of what is the optimum ration between consumption and investment? The answer is never simple. A great deal depends on the state of the economy of the country concerned. I believe it is important to have projects with quick yields before a country can start with a long-term project. But then, of course, there are the political questions and pressures to consider. Fundamentally, investment is tied to savings and therefore the question really becomes: What is the best way to encourage savings? One ingredient of that, it seems clear to me, is to watch inflation and to keep it under control. But one must never forget that governments are by definition political and social structures, not economic ones. On the other hand, I am totally convinced that you cannot have private investment, effective private investment, unless you have a free democratic system. Any other political system will want to control the economic system, sooner or later, in one way or another. Therefore the immediate political problem is to strengthen democratic institutions, because only with strong democratic institutions can you have a free, effective private sector.

Socially, it is vital to strengthen the income level of the lowest economic income groups. This is an economic necessity as well because they provide the broad-based market. One aspect of this, in a country such as Egypt, is that in agriculture we need to encourage land ownership rather than tenancy. In industry, it means that we need to have a minimum wage. In education, it means that we need to design education to be more job-directed, more shaped toward vocational education, more designed for problem-solving than the rote system.

Power, Competence . . .

Another complex and delicate balance, both of power and competence, must be calibrated in the relationship between the economic activities in the public sector and the private sector. Government-owned corporations can be efficient if the right people are represented in the general assembly of stockholders and then on the board that chooses the management. The problem with state-run enterprises now—this is true in command economies and in mixed economies such as Egypt—is that they are not run by management boards, not by expert managers, but are, in effect, run by the respective ministries. And if you get a minister running a company, he does not run it as an economic unit making economic decisions. He runs it as a political institution and makes his decision on a political, and possibly a social, basis. The need for state-owned enterprises is to separate management from political control.

One solution, or at least an approach I see here in Egypt, is that financial institutions that are owned by government should represent government on the boards of public policy enterprises. That way at least you get economic decisions, not political ones. I see this as a bridge mechanism until we get a class of managers who can run enterprises, whether they are owned by the state or by the private sector.

. . . and the Transfer of Technology

Which brings me to another much-debated subject, where I think the optimum solution is really quite simple. I refer to the transfer of technology. I am convinced that the best, most efficient, most creative and most rewarding way for the developing countries is to transfer technology through direct venture projects in which there is participation by foreign and domestic capital. In such an enterprise the transfer of technology is directed by equity, or by a licensing or management arrangement that is focused concretely on a concrete project, where both the recipient of the technology and the provider of the technology have a direct stake in what is happening. Governments should encourage such projects with incentives and the necessary legal and regulatory adjustments.

The Importance of Values

All economic development is embedded in a sense of values, and I would like to address three areas in which values and perceptions play a major role in contributing to—or detracting from—development.

Let me begin with values as an overarching and underlying concept. In the developing countries, the pressing problem of young people today is that they are separated from the economic system. They cannot participate in it because there are not enough jobs for them. And they cannot make decisions. In a country like Egypt, the problem with our educated young is that they cannot get jobs commensurate with their education. Part of that is the fault of the education system, which is not sufficiently job-focused.

Another problem is that value systems differ. Education and progress can change them. What is needed most, I believe, is more emphasis on the value and dignity of work. Right now what is happening in the developing countries is that the highly educated people, especially the ones who are specialized and have marketable skills, leave their countries. These men and women should be kept at home by offering them better pay; better promotions; above all, promotion by merit and ability and not by seniority; and a situation in the structure where they can be offered opportunities and challenge.

In Labor-Management Relations

This leads me directly to another area where values are fundamental, namely, the relationship between management and labor. It is very important to have good relationships between owners, managers and workers. I believe such unions as United Auto Workers in the United States are beginning to understand this. The Japanese have their own system for creating this kind of harmony. I do not believe it is necessary to have workers on the boards of companies, but they can be represented by committees under the board. These kinds of systems need to be designed in response to the local culture. What is important everywhere is that the more friction can be minimized, the better off both labor and management will be. And, of course, the better off the enterprise will be.

In the developing countries, perhaps a system of profit-sharing would be a good idea, primarily because it will broaden stock ownership. A broadened stock ownership is the best bulwark against both government intervention and communism. Broadened ownership will provide political weight against government intrusion and left-wing ideology, and it will function as well in terms of public relations, by which I mean the relationship of the enterprise with all the publics it serves.

Why Profit Arouses Suspicion

The third area in which perceptions play an important role has to do with the function of profit. A great deal of ignorance and antagonism beclouds that word. Perhaps we should simply rename the concept and call it "return on investment." Or define it as the margin between sales and expense. Today, "profit" is, in many minds, a word that arouses suspicion. It needs redefining.

I also believe that overt acts with social goals by private enterprise are very important. For example, in our bank we set aside 3 percent of pre-tax profits for contributions to society. These have a very wide range: they run from charitable contributions to the war wounded and the blind to cultural, social and religious institutions. They include scholarships for students. The important thing, especially in countries such as ours where there is a serious bias against the private sector, is both to make these contributions and to publicize them.

Not by Bread Alone

Still, as we all know, man does not live by bread alone, and there are noneconomic demands, perhaps especially in developing countries, that contribute to peace and harmony. I see two important areas of contribution that can be made to meet these noneconomic demands. One has to do with human dignity, and that requires that there must not be discrimination on racial, religious or any other grounds. Colonialism has come to an end, and this is as true for Russian colonialism as it is for the South African variety. It would also be desirable if we could eliminate the fear of war which nowadays derives largely from the struggle between the United States and the USSR. We must learn not only to accept but to enjoy the differences between us. In practical terms, the important thing is to devise systems of cooperation in every area and at all levels. We need institutions such as the UN, but we also need additional, and perhaps even parallel, institutions in the multiple facets of life.

The Real Role of Religion

The other aspect of meeting the noneconomic needs of human beings has to do with faith—in an ideology or a religion. In that context, the most important thing for people to learn and understand is the true meaning of religions as moral and ethical institutions, i.e., institutions that teach a system of values. In that sense, religions can achieve harmony and not become means of strengthening differences.

The problem is not religion but the political use of religion. We can overcome fanaticism only by teaching that fanaticism does not solve problems, and that can be taught only when people see something tangible. Fanaticism becomes a problem if there is a minority, and if that minority is discriminated against in one way or another. Therefore, if governments truly respect human rights, and do not use religion for political purposes, there is no reason why religion cannot also be tolerant.

The second problem with religion is that each religion seems to harbor extremists within it. The only solution to that is education: teaching these extremists that they must respect human rights. Until that is learned, what government can do is simply not tolerate the use of force by fanatics.

Vulnerability, Change and the Human Potential

Fanaticism—wherever it exists—is an expression of a psychic vulnerability. But the most important vulnerability shared by all of us, by which I mean mankind on planet earth, is our vulnerability to nuclear destruction. What is needed, therefore, is disarmament and an agreement to abide by international law. We also need to develop international laws to protect the environment, and we need to find ways of enforcing these kinds of international agreements.

I know this is a tall order, and it will take time, ingenuity and effort to achieve. But I believe it can be done. What gives me this faith is the conviction that there are no limits to growth, either technological or in the human mind.

France

TAX AS A DEVELOPMENT TOOL

Denis Defforey
Chairman
Carrefour

The main problem around the world, with the exception only of the United States and Switzerland, is that government does not play its proper role in the economic system. I believe that government's role is not to produce, but to give orientation to production. It can provide that orientation through the tax system. Such orientation is needed. It is possible for an individual producer to think that what he produces is important, and that is not always necessarily so from a national, or an international, point of view. There are cases also where what someone produces is useful but not necessary, and there are conditions under which it is more important to have necessary production. The problem with systems of taxation as they exist today is that governments tax profit, not usefulness. A good tax system would provide incentive for useful production by taxing such production to a lesser extent than production that is less useful.

One of the important issues is how taxation can be used to help the developing countries. What happens now is that governments transfer taxpayers' money in government-to-government aid, and nothing changes. Take the most extreme example: government aid for disaster relief in Africa. Disaster is temporarily, and not very effectively, alleviated; but the basic problems remain and it is only a question of time before disaster strikes again. If a government used only part of that relief money to allow a large tax deduction to a food company going into the disaster-ridden country and attacking the problem at the fundamental level, it would be much better for everyone. Because, unlike government, that company's aim is to do the job well, permanently. That is where its success lies—as well as that of the country in which it contributes to the solution of a basic problem.

A less drastic but equally relevant case: Say a company invests in Brazil. It is a huge market, but it is not easy to get started there, and it is difficult to get money back for some time. So an investment shows up in the balance sheet as a loss for many years. If the investment could be depreciated, if it became tax-deductible, a lot more investment would go into countries where it is needed, with everyone benefiting.

Really large investments, and especially large-scale investment by many companies, would also reduce political risk. Right now, for example, companies in France, particularly medium-sized companies, might invest in Latin America if they see a payout in a five- to ten-year period; they will not invest in a project that stretches over fifty years. But if there were more investment in Latin America, particularly by big companies, smaller and medium-sized firms would consider their own investments to be safer. This investment depreciation schedule I have in mind should be tied to the political risk the country represents for an investor. If we don't do something like this and do it soon, everyone will want to invest in the United States, which is politically safe. But in terms of world economics, that makes no sense.

Look at it from the vantage point of my industry. In recent months the Germans have bought the A&P; the United Kingdom has acquired Grand Union. But the United States does not need any more supermarkets or superstores. On the other hand, a country like Argentina does need such stores. Buenos Aires, with a population of 12 million in greater Buenos Aires, has only two superstores, with a total area of 250,000 square feet. So that, in terms of world economic logic, is where investors in my industry should move.

Government: Right and Wrong

It is wrong for governments to protect domestic prices. For example, beef production in the United States and France is very costly. Argentina, let us say, or Uruguay, could produce beef at a much lower price. And it is important for consumers throughout the world to have beef at the lowest possible price. I think a reasonable economic yardstick would be: Where can a product be produced at the best price for the consumer, and at the lowest cost for the company?

Take one area of production about which I know a good deal. In the United States, and for that matter in some countries in Europe, we have been producing fruit and vegetables with imported workers and subsidized prices. Would it not be better if we produced the food in the countries from which the workers come, without subsidies?

Fundamentally, I believe there are really only two games: the government game and the market game. Mixing the two is almost always disastrous. Nevertheless, the reality in the world today is that most of the systems that exist are mixtures. It is part of the reason that we are in such an economic mess worldwide.

Government does have certain tasks in an economic system, even if the system is, as I believe it should be, a free market system. There are certain long-term investments, with social utility, that only a government can undertake. Let me give you an example. When it is decided that it is desirable to have a green belt around an industrial community, only a government can undertake that kind of venture. Or assume that it is decided that it is a good idea for a society to fight alcoholism or drugs. This can only be done by government. Or take the question of transportation. Everybody would like to use their own car, but we really can't do that, if only because, as in Paris, we would create increasingly impossible traffic jams. Therefore, we have to have the subway or buses. But neither the subway nor the buses necessarily have to be *operated* by the government.

In sum, I believe government should set the ground rules but not get involved in the economic game.

Horizons, Near and Far

It is also important that the rules are not changed too often. Business needs dependable rules in order to plan and operate. The real problem, it seems to me, is that business horizons are long, while the horizons of politics are short. What happens is that the ground rules are laid from a political perspective instead of from a business perspective.

The Pioneering Role of MNCs

I frankly fail to understand the fashionable attack on the big multinational corporations. I have seen big companies in developing countries make efforts at economic development that the governments of these countries never would undertake. I think, for example, of Nestlé in Brazil. Nestlé went into Brazil in 1925, and ever since has helped farmers to produce quality cattle, to produce quality milk, to transport that milk in refrigerated containers, to give the farmer and the consumer economic opportunities neither one has had before. It was a very long-term undertaking. To the best of my knowledge, Nestlé has not yet brought any money home from Brazil: it has invested all its earnings in Brazil. What I am saying is that, in more than fifty years, Nestlé has not changed its policy in Brazil. Is there any government that has not changed its policies in Brazil over the term of its own regime, let alone a period of fifty years?

The fact is that international companies have done more for LDCs than the LCDs' own governments. This is true even in the industrialized nations. Take the computer. The American "invasion" of France brought IBM. IBM in turn brought France the best technology, good jobs, exports, an important contribution to the country's balance of payments. Today, IBM is one of the ten most important exporters in France.

Profit and Breathing

I would have to concede, however, that there is a difference between financial business and industrial business. What is happening right now is that money is being made on money instead of on investment. The present situation prevents people from creating businesses that provide jobs for workers, new products and services to consumers. I believe businesses are created to grow. But in order to grow, they need money for reinvestment. What most people don't understand is that profit is needed to keep a business in good health, to make it possible for a business to hire the best employees, get the best machinery, find the best location. These are the real uses of money in business. This is the fundamental role of profit. Profit is not a target, not an aim: it is a necessity for keeping a business alive. It is comparable to breathing for human beings. We do not live to breathe, but we do have to breathe to live. In the same way, a business is not designed to make profit, but it must have profit in order to live. In fact, in order to exist.

The reason I am against governments in business is because they are no good at it. When they do pursue operations, governments do not create businesses; at best, they create monopolies. Take the example of railroads. Having once created a government monopoly on railroads, the government then inevitably moves to eliminate competition, such as, for instance, competition from trucks. We've seen that here in France. Once a government is in a monopoly situation, it does not need to make a real profit. It can always stack the deck so that profit will result, not as the result of good management, or of providing a good product or service, but as the result of lack of competition. And if a government-owned company is in trouble, it can always count on the Treasury to provide the cash it needs.

In France, you have the example, in the car industry, of Renault, on the one hand, which is government-owned, and Citroën, which is a private company. If Renault needs extra money, it gets that money, in effect, from the taxpayers, who are not involved in any decision made at Renault itself, nor even in a decision on whether they want to give their money to Renault or not. Citroën, on the other hand, has to look for shareholders who are willing to risk their money on the company, and who do have at least some say over how it is managed. The fundamental difference is that, in the Renault case, the people who contribute the money have no choice, and in the Citroën case, they do.

Technology: The Human Equation

A truly gut-wrenching issue of our time is technology and unemployment and the relationship between them. The issue deserves thoughtful concentrated attention both from government and the private sector. But, basically, I can conceive of only one sane perspective. You cannot unscramble the proverbial egg. Technology exists. Technology inevitably means fewer workers in factories, and more in services and study. I think this is a desirable development. It is undoubtedly true that overall there will be fewer people working. But I look at what has happened in the past hundred years both on the farm and in the city. A hundred years ago, farmers worked from sunup to sundown, never had a vacation, hardly ever had any time they could call their own; now farmers, certainly here in France, work less than the man in the factory. In a hundred years, work time for the average farmer has at least halved. The same is really true in factories. A hundred years ago the average work week was around eighty hours; now it is about forty hours. I have no doubt that within less than a hundred years, the average work week for people with the worst jobs will be down to twenty hours. I consider that a good thing.

People with good jobs, I mean jobs that interest and challenge them, will always want to work longer. Their interest in work is not only money, but the excitement, the personal challenge and the social utility of what they do.

As I look around me, and this is true everywhere in the world, there are really two kinds of people: people who live in good conditions, by which I mean they live in a nice place; they have a happy home; they have interests in the home, such as music, or reading, or working in the garden. These people have no problem with how to use their spare time. Working shorter hours is no deprivation for them. Then there are people who live in what I think of as bad conditions. They live in a bad apartment, in a bad district, their homes are unattractive and filled with tension and discord. There are aspects to that kind of bad living that can be changed by intelligent planning.

Addressing the more specific challenge of training or retraining people for the jobs of the present and the future, I would have to concede that it is badly done now. When I encounter a boy of, say, twenty-five who is looking for work, and he tells me what schools and universities he has attended, that may be all right. But when a man of forty-five comes to me looking for work appropriate to his abilities, and what he presents is the same academic nonsense, then I know something is wrong with our system. At that age, it should be experience that counts.

I see an analogy here to military service. If someone has served in the military for one or two years of conscription, twenty years later whatever he has learned will be totally out of date and meaningless. He won't know how to use a machine gun anymore, let alone what to do with the weapons that have evolved since the time he had his training. It would make much more sense to have a man get military training for a couple of weeks each year to keep a working relationship between the man and the job he has to do. The most effective military services in the world today, those of Israel and Switzerland, do precisely that.

I believe the same approach holds for industry. There has to be continuous training, probably throughout a man's working life. This training has to be provided by industry itself, by the private sector, and by public schools and institutes of higher education.

North and South

You cannot today talk about any aspect of economics or development without addressing what, for want of a better formulation, we call the North–South conflict and/or cooperation. Looking at it from a European perspective, I recall that for decades there was a continental version of this that went under the heading of class warfare. Now, some people in Europe still talk about class warfare, especially Communists, but to most people this idea makes no sense anymore. What we are seeing now around the world is not class warfare within countries but a kind of class warfare between countries, like, for example, the economic and social tensions that exist between Mexico and Texas; or, in Europe, between Northern and Southern Europe; or, in more acute form, between Europe and

North Africa. This will get worse as the baby boom in the southern countries faces an increasingly aging population in the northern countries.

And that leads me by, I believe, logical extension, to one of the burning problems of the day, the financial predicament of developing countries. Once again, I see a corporate analogy. If a country feels that it must have a car factory, and if that factory gets into trouble, it gets help, a government bailout of one kind or another, like Chrysler or Renault. If worst comes to worst, a company can declare bankruptcy, pay 10¢ on the dollar and reorganize. Now countries are in the same position. I believe what has to be done for countries like Poland or Mexico is much the same thing that we would do if these were bankrupt companies: write off and reorganize. The big commercial banks have to depreciate some of these loans and set conditions when they make new loans—conditions that make productive sense. Specifically, I mean that the banks should ask: Just what is this loan for? If it is for a nuclear plant, or for armaments, they should not make the loan. If it is for productive enterprises—necessary infrastructure, useful capital goods, needed consumer goods, needed food production—they should.

Banks already pursue these kinds of policies when they deal with companies. For example, if I go to a bank and say that I want to build a wonderful new head office, no bank, given present economic conditions, will give me the money. At least no sensible bank will. But if I go to the same bank and say I want to set up a new store, and here are the projected sales from that store, I will get the money. I think the banks should think and act the same way when, for example, they make a loan to Chad.

People will raise the bugaboo of sovereignty. Well, as a retailer my sovereign rights are also infringed. For example, I can't sell a bottle of whiskey to a kid. By the same token, it makes no sense to sell the most sophisticated weapons to the big kids who run some governments. What, for example, was the point of selling an atomic reactor to Iraq? It was done because people think short term instead of long term. France wanted the oil, and the sale helped the balance of payments. But if I sell my whiskey to a kid and the kid gets drunk and smashes my store windows, I have no right to complain, do I? More to the point still: I have no recourse.

Germany

THE MAGIC OF THE MARKETPLACE

*Dr. Rolf Sammet**
Former Chairman
Hoechst A.G.

What is the best relationship between investment and consumption? I believe the market should decide consumption. The market reflects everyone's desires, and changes with people's needs. It provides the freedom to express these needs and desires. Companies have to analyze the market and respond with investment. This sounds elementary but it is vital; if they don't do it, they will suffer losses and will not remain alive. There can be no success for a company or a product without a market. I am convinced that if we move away from the market system, the results we get will be worse, not better. This is true both for a company and for society in general. If we look at other experiments that have been made and are being made,

*Dr. Sammet was chairman of Hoechst at the time this conversation took place.

for example, in the Communist countries, which try to plan consumption and investment, what we see is a picture that is neither more humane nor more efficient. Leaving aside all political convictions, I believe there is now throughout the world an increasing recognition of this. There is, of course, a very good reason why the market system is more efficient. It provides constant feedback and direction.

The question being posed these days is: Are there limits to the market system? Should there be limits? The critics of laissez-faire, and of capitalism generally, base most of their criticism on the past, on the early days of capitalism when some of the methods were understandably primitive. Today we live in a considerably more socially minded market, and in a market economy that tries to find ways to limit the failures of the early days of capitalism—both the failures and their costs.

A very good example of this is the United States and the early days of monopoly control. Society, in order to defend the market system, reacted to the abuses of monopolies by creating anti-trust laws and regulations, the assumption being that the best protection against the excesses of one enterprise is to create another enterprise. I myself, if there were only one organization making a product in a particular market, would worry about whether that enterprise receives the needed direction from the market. I would argue that Rockefeller, in his very earliest days as an oil monopoly, did not get the kind of market direction that he should have received. Given competition, however, I believe there should be as little interference as possible in the working of the market.

It is true that the market, and society itself, does have social components that must be recognized and attended. But I think it is important to meet these social concerns with as little interference as possible.

Variations on the Theme

It is also true that different countries, at different stages of their development, have different possibilities. Not every country is capable of practicing a free market economy to the same extent. It is, for example, okay today for Germany to have no tariff, but this is not necessarily true for all other countries. For example, less developed countries would, without duty protection, ruin their agriculture. And there is no doubt that industrial plants with small capacities geared to domestic requirements would not always be competitive without protection against products from large capacities on world markets. Also, consumers will not necessarily benefit from the advantages of free competition in terms of lower prices if that competition is not functioning at the trading level. Chile provides us with a typical illustration of this reality.

The Problem in Europe

Europe is suffering at present from high unemployment and industrial overcapacities, and there is a widespread view that governments could and should tackle these problems by interfering in the free market system with protective measures and subsidies. Many countries have experienced the negative results of such policies, but very few seem to have learned their lessons from them.

I do not believe that we should approach the problem by forcing investments. In Europe at the moment we have a great deal of unused capacity, and what we need is not more investment to create jobs, but more demand. Demand cannot be compelled. It is tied to such intangibles as trust, faith and hope.

It is our experience, at least in Germany, that a tangible rise in demand will not come from higher income or lower taxes alone. It is a general mood of confidence that will make people spend more. If the future looks uncertain, they will put their money into savings.

A further problem is the high volume of foreign debts in many countries. We have to reverse this trend slowly. There is no quick-fix solution. I am certain that citizens throughout Europe realize that their states cannot keep piling up debt, that if they do so, this will sooner or later lead to bankruptcy. So the longer we keep piling up social costs that add to the deficit, the more we undermine the citizen's faith in the system. And if people have no faith in the system, they do not spend money.

The North–South Dialogue: Asking the Right Questions

The developing countries, in their current attitude toward the world economy, speak about the allocation or reallocation of resources. What they really mean is: How do we get the riches of those who worked for these riches? But this is a destructive question for all concerned. The redistribution of the world's riches won't make the poor rich. It just means that, deprived of incentives, the producers will no longer produce; there will be considerable waste; and the poor will remain as poor as ever. What we need to do is to try to teach the developing countries how to produce, and to make them understand that there is no future in policies that proceed on the assumption that others sow and you reap. This is not a solution to an economic problem.

It is human nature for everyone to want to be rich. The Communists, in their system, manage to make everyone equally poor. But in the end, under a market system, while not all are equally rich, more people are better off than they are in a Communist system.

If we look at the world today and observe what mentality and attitudes have contributed to creating the kinds of countries in which people want to live, then the United States is certainly the most instructive example. People went to the United States because they believed that in the United States you can start as a dishwasher, work hard and get rich—not by robbing banks and getting other people's money, but by planning and saving. To a very large extent that attitude is still prevalent in the United States and is, I am convinced, responsible for what is, on the whole, the most successful economy the world has ever seen.

I believe the basic question in the North–South dialogue should be, from the South: How can you, in the North, help us develop our structures so we can build successful economies? How can you help with investment and the transfer of technology that is built into investment? The developing countries have to realize that they must protect the investment they get because, if they do not, they will not get reasonable constructive investment. What they will get instead are investments that have a quick payout but are not long term and structurally sound.

One Case in Point: Patents

A case in point is patent protection. The developing countries say they cannot provide patent protection because they do not have the money to finance their own research and development, and they do not have the people to create appropriate R&D. This is simply not true. India, Latin America and Egypt, for example, do have highly competent people, people who are competent by world standards. But because the work of these people does not have protection, there is no motivation for creativity or discovery. The best of the people in those three countries go to the North, where their brains and their talent get the reward they deserve. If the developing countries persist in the attitude they now have on protection of intellectual property, the chances are very good that they will never get what they need.

Just as charity can never make you rich, if you enforce technology transfer, nothing really constructive will happen. Countries which made constructive use of technologies that were transferred to them provided the necessary protection. Japan is, of course, one of the prime examples of this. It bought a great deal of technology, protected it, gave inventors the incentive to create, and is now at a stage where it exports a great deal of technology. There is no reason whatsoever why countries like India, Brazil and Egypt cannot do the same if they provide rules and regulations that supply engineers and scientists and inventors with the incentives that are required.

It is true that a patent can afford the holder a certain monopoly position, but only for a limited time. This will certainly not lead to monopolistic structure in the economy. At the moment, in the pharmaceutical industry, we are talking of patent protection for eighteen or twenty years, which is not quite enough. At present it takes twelve years, and an investment of approximately $50 million, to come up with a new pharmaceutical product. So there are only eight years left for the innovator to make use of this protection. What the developing countries need is not only the quantitative growth that has been their fixation but also qualitative growth; and qualitative growth comes from technology and from invention. That, in turn, requires investment in brains and of brains, and these investments of intellectual property need protection exactly the way investments in physical property need protection.

Understanding Technology

Not only in developing countries but everywhere in the world we need better education for better technology. Not only investors but other members of society must at least understand the inventions and the technology that are being developed. We cannot live in two different worlds.

At present, in Europe, we suffer from people who make judgments of inventions by others without understanding, or even trying to understand, what is really involved. The paramount example of what is happening in this context is the whole issue of nuclear energy. The public debate on the desirability or otherwise of nuclear energy is conducted largely in slogans. The slogans claim that there is something naturally evil about nuclear energy; that it is incurably harmful to the environment; that the pollution it produces is infinitely worse than the pollution produced by other energy sources such as coal and oil. But this is simply not true. Coal and oil produce their own forms of pollution.

The truth is that the best solution from an environmental point of view is nuclear energy. For example, very few people in the current climate of sloganeering on nuclear energy know that less radioactivity is produced by a nuclear plant than is produced by a coal plant. Also, if we look at the real world, we see that if we add up the accidents, and the damage to the environment done by coal plants, and include accidents in mines, more people have died in one year from coal production than in all nuclear plants that exist. The truth, in fact, is that not a single person has actually died as a result of accidents at a nuclear plant. Nuclear plants are constructed so that they cannot explode. Human error can create problems, but there is no way, with the safeguards already in existence, for a nuclear plant to melt.

It is, of course, true that danger seems greatest when we deal in probabilities. Most people can't calculate the odds or understand them. At present, the odds are that a nuclear plant core can melt down once in a million years. There are risks in daily life where the odds are much greater than one in a million. It is, for example, considerably more likely that one can get run over by a car, or have a tile fall on one's head, or get murdered by a terrorist. The actual data for an individual getting hurt by the explosion of a nuclear plant is, in real life, infinitesimal compared to a whole range of dangers that all of us face every day.

One of the problems with atomic energy is that it is, of course, also mixed up in the demagogy, and therefore politically, with atomic war. But when you think that through, the existence in Germany of a number of nuclear plants is meaningless in terms of danger to individuals when compared with the Russian nuclear missiles that are already, in fact, aimed at German cities. One touch of the button in Moscow will obviously create infinitely more nuclear havoc than human error could possibly create in nuclear energy plants.

I believe that energy will play a major role in the future development of the world, including the developing countries. Many of the current development problems were created largely through two oil crises. But cheaper oil prices are not a solution. If prices go down too far, they will prevent exploration of synthetic energy projects. Energy is vital to the development of LDCs and to the nutrition of the increasing populations that all of them have. The only possible way to provide the cheap energy that is needed, with minimal environmental problems, is through nuclear energy, particularly through the breeder reactor when that becomes operational.

Education: A Cost-Benefit Approach

Our educational system, in the industrialized countries as well as in the developing countries, must become more technically and scientifically literate. It may well be that there has not been enough critical thinking and discussion in our educational systems. But we should beware of such critical engagement if it is not based on a solid knowledge of facts and a sense of reality. We must rid ourselves of the aggression and confrontation of groups whose basic attitude is that group interests—whatever the group may be—come before the common interest. What this kind of group-centered, confrontational and aggressive antagonism creates is, in fact, an anti-democracy. In Germany, for example, the Greens know that they represent a group interest and they can use emotional slogans to get a following for propositions that make no long-term sense at all.

What we need is an educational system that trains people in common sense for society as a whole. What we get instead, at present, is an educational system that stimulates and encourages the use of aggression and talks again of class warfare. The problem in the developing countries is not very different. The problem there is not so much one of illiteracy and the abolition of illiteracy as the use of newly acquired literacy for constructive, nonconfrontational purposes. What all of us are getting these days in the industrial countries and in the developing world—mainly from television—is indoctrination, not education.

In Germany, we had a system at the university where getting into college was a question of competition. The system provided equality of opportunity based on performance. Now students are paid to go to university, and what is asked of the students is not to prove through performance what they can do with their education; education has become instead a form of indulgence and entertainment. The present system also fosters the attitude that if it doesn't cost anything, it can't be worth much. Under the old system we had about forty thousand students in universities who, just as one measurement, won a considerable number of Nobel Prizes. Today we have 1 million students in our universities and not a single Nobel Prize. Expenditures for academic education and research have multiplied, but it is questionable whether this will result in an acceptable cost-benefit ratio.

The bottom line in education is that today we live in a technical world and we must learn to understand it. Not all drivers have to be car mechanics; but all drivers do have to at least understand how to use their brakes. What is true for car mechanics is also true for the more sophisticated areas of technology that are now an integral part of our world. One area where this clearly applies is nuclear energy. We must all understand the fundamentals. We must understand what the minimum risks are, and how they compare to other sources of energy. We must understand the cost-benefit relationship. Right now, as I pointed out before, the possibility of a core melting in a nuclear plant is about as remote as a meteor striking us. People do not go around speaking of the dangers of meteors.

When you get ignorance and ideology, as we have these days in the area of atomic energy, you have a truly lethal mixture.

Let me add here a small note on the risks involved with nuclear plants at present. Insurance companies, whose job it is to calculate risks, have made no change in their premium for the life or health insurance of persons who live near a nuclear energy plant as compared to those who do not. If there were a danger, a real and present danger, insurance companies would certainly by now have upped their premium for people who live near nuclear plants.

Freedom

A few words on concepts and perceptions: I start with freedom. I believe that freedom, dynamism and self-reliance are inextricably intertwined. But freedom is relative. We cannot live, indeed we would not want to live, in a society without respect and thought for others. If my freedom is a burden on others, it is not freedom. It is therefore important that we do not teach expectations that cannot be met without violence, or without depriving others of freedom.

Wealth . . .

There is another balance that must be carefully constructed. Wealth does not, in and of itself, create happiness. Wealth, like freedom, is relative. If, for example, demand grows more quickly than wealth creation, you get an imbalance that is socially precarious. As I look around the world today I see a list of demands, a large list of demands, all of which depend on others meeting them with no cost to the person who makes the demands. This is both impossible economically and dangerous socially and politically.

. . . and Values

It seems to me that the young nowadays, in both the industrial and the developing countries, are searching for values that give meaning to life. But religion as a value system is fading, and ideologies taking the place of religion are unable to command the attention and commitment of the young. This situation creates a good breeding ground for sects, which act as Pied Pipers to lost kids who have no roots anymore in their homes, their schools or their churches. None of these has apparently succeeded in giving these youngsters a picture of life that has meaning for them. There is more wealth in the world today than there has ever been before, but there are also social changes that have not been digested. There has been an undermining of the family and outright destruction of the extended family. And there are children who have the food, the clothing, the tools that they want and need and their parents cannot understand what more they want. But they do need more. They need a new sense of values, which will give them structure and meaning in their lives.

India

THE EVOLUTION OF A MIXED ECONOMY

G. P. Birla
Managing Director
Birla Brothers Private Ltd.

When you think realistically about private enterprise—which I do, being committed to it—you must start with the fact that, here in India, we have a mixed economy, composed essentially of three segments. We have a gigantic public sector, which includes operating companies. We have a second segment of our economy, which consists of joint ventures between the public sector and the private sector. Finally, we have a purely private sector. However, even that purely private sector has major intervention or, if you prefer, participation by the public sector because government financial institutions are big shareholders in private sector companies. As a practical matter, this means that the private sector cannot act alone and, in order to survive and even to function, must be attuned, sensitively and always, to working with government. This holds true whether the enterprise is small, medium or large.

The picture *is* changing somewhat. While some segments of the economy are still, in effect, government monopolies, other economic activities, which used to be exclusively in the public sector, have been opened up to joint ventures with the private sector, their shares widely held by the general public. The government has realized that it cannot do it all, and that most of the financial and managerial constraints it has imposed on the private sector are, in fact, counterproductive. Now government is allowing the private sector to function more freely, but is, at the same time, maintaining an active participatory interest in the private sector. Government insists on securing a piece of the action—not for purposes of bureaucratic constraint and control, but because it wants its own share of the wealth produced by successful private sector enterprises.

Another important change is that the basic industries, which used to be monopolies of the central government, are being devolved to state governments, and the states want joint ventures with the private sector in order to achieve faster development.

All this adds up to the fact that we are moving toward a better system—not better than private enterprise would be, but a great deal better than the public sector vise that gripped us before. An interesting example of what is happening is the relatively recent creation of a $1 billion Unit Trust—what in the United States you call a mutual fund—which is broadly held, and managed by the government, but the government invests all of the Trust's funds in the private sector.

Our most acute problem, in my opinion, is not this mixed and evolving system, which somehow we have all learned to make work, but a dearth of managers, especially at the hands-on level. Our best managers, indeed our best brains in many fields, leave India for the West, where they can make more money, pay less in taxes, and are more untrammeled in whatever career path they choose to pursue.

What we miss most are managers with decision-making ability. In the private sector, we still have family talent that can assume this function, but in the private sector good, competent decision makers get moved around, often for political rather than economic reasons, and become troubleshooters instead of managers. These factors taken together—decision makers in the private sector tempted by better opportunities abroad, and decision makers in the public sector, because of an absence of competent planning, tending to become troubleshooters instead of managers—add up to a serious impediment to a well-functioning economic system.

In this context, a vital issue that needs to be addressed is the spirit of entrepreneurship. I believe that there are basically two kinds of people: those who look for safety and those who look for challenge and risk. I am not making a value judgment here; it is a matter of talent and temperament. Nevertheless, in the real world, the former only want a job, preferably a lifetime job, and are content to progress gradually. They do not want to take risks, and they do not want to face the world in any way that creates problems, or even challenges.

Entrepreneurs, on the other hand, are people whose basic drive is to want to create, to show results. These kind of people do not mind hard work. They see as part of their task the creation of wealth and the creation of jobs for others. And they see no limit to the future: their own, their company's, their country's or the world's.

India has people who have the spirit of entrepreneurship, and so, for that matter, does China. I look at our farmers in the Punjab or at the thousands who have started small industries right here in Calcutta, for example, and I see that spirit of entrepreneurship alive and well.

As a matter of policy, India is opening up to new technologies and new methods, with a stress—and it is a warranted stress—on job creation. In recent months we have had delegations from Japan and Western Europe looking at investment opportunities in India. Unlike the situation in the past, the government now permits and to a certain extent encourages such investment, and industry welcomes it. We are aware of the fact that Indian plants have to modernize, especially in such areas as computers, telecommunications, petrochemicals. What people tend to forget about India is that we are already the tenth-largest industrial nation in the world, with an internal market of about 150 million people in the economically advanced sector. That is a very solid base on which to build.

At the global level, I see two basic problems. The first is

the superpower confrontation and all it implies, both in terms of danger to mankind and in terms of misallocation of resources.

The second problem is that the revolution of expectations around the world is too materialistic. It lacks spiritual content.

In India, we do have a spiritual dimension, and this leads to more patience and a longer view. But in most of the rest of the world unadulterated materialism leads to discontent, a discontent that affects the thinking of the older generation and poisons the minds of the younger generation.

The younger generation in the industrial countries, where there are very few pressing needs, seems to be heading for the escapism of drugs and addictions of one kind or another to fill the vacuum that has been created by an absence of spiritual values. These values used to be supplied by religion, but in many places around the world, religion has degenerated into a fundamentalism that is being used for political purposes. Coming as I do from a Hindu perspective, I believe what is needed is what, in Hinduism, is subsumed under the concept of *vedha,* a combination of devotion, knowledge, commonsense and duty. The principle on which devotion is based is the conviction that God is good, and good is God. And the most fundamental knowledge is the recognition that you achieve happiness by making others happy. This is true in all aspects of existence, with economics not necessarily paramount but emphatically included. It may sound simplistic—it is simple in concept, yet very complex indeed in application—but I consider it to be the prime task of leaders in the world today.

NEEDED: A LEAP IN SOCIAL TECHNOLOGY

Keshub Mahindra
Chairman
Mahindra and Mahindra Ltd.

I believe that we need, perhaps more than anything, a leap in social technology. In most countries, economic planning and development is designed to meet many goals and purposes, but at the center of it all it must be "man" who eventually benefits from this exercise. In order to achieve this, values need to be defined and education imparted so that man may move forward with confidence in his future. Man must be at the center of economic planning if the content is to have real meaning and not be merely an exercise in statistical spivery.

It is very important for the private sector to become more actively engaged in the process of development itself. For instance, in India we have a planning commission to which is entrusted the task of overall planning, but on this commission business is not represented. As agents of economic activity we in the private sector must involve ourselves more and more in the policies that determine the destinies of our societies. In the world of today, which is confronted with innumerable social complexities, we cannot just say that we must only allow market forces to operate and determine our economies, for wherever you look there is a greater tendency on the part of governments to intervene in our economic lives. The private sector has to face this reality and contribute its mite in the very process of planning and development so that it may offer its knowledge, expertise and services.

More Business in Government, Less Government in Business

One of the problems with socialism, or any other form of state-operated economy, is that the management of resources is totally divorced from market forces. In a mixed economy concept such as we have in our country, there are inherent problems in state-run enterprises. These are generally run by bureaucrats, and even if the bureaucrat is efficient, competent and dedicated, the system subjects him to the will and whims of the politician. The result is that, however energetic and competent, he cannot really operate because he is not left alone to do so. The system is not designed to leave him alone. There is a lack of a clearly defined accountability in state-run enterprises. We in the private sector have to recognize the existence of these problems and offer our help to governments. I do not believe enough of this is done.

If I sum up my conviction in a country such as India, and I do believe this goes for a number of other countries, what we need is more business in government and less government in business.

How to achieve free enterprise on a global basis is a challenging question and a magnificent goal, but I do not believe we are going to get there by the year 2000. A world economy could be genuinely global only if it were really totally free. That would require not only free movement of capital and goods, but also the free movement of people. And I do not see that happening within any future that I can conceive.

An ideal economic world, from where I sit, would be a world in which goods and services are produced where they can be produced at the cheapest price with the best quality for people. But I do not think we can get to that world while we have the different levels of development that exist. If we had levels of development that were somewhat more equal and if we could, conceptually at least, and indeed in reality, agree to free movement of labor as well as every other ingredient of economic productivity, we would have a splendid world from every point of view. I know that realities will not permit this in any foreseeable future, but it is sometimes nice to dream.

Interim Steps

But there are interim steps. What needs to happen, since we are obviously going to be stuck with nation-states for some time, is for nations to make a greater effort to understand each other's compulsions and needs. We have to appreciate and understand different cultures, different needs, different compulsions, and accept that there are different ways of achieving similar objectives. From the foundation of that appreciation and acceptance we can begin to build the kind of world we want to see.

This leads me to an observation on some interim aspects of development. It seems to me that development, per se, has both inherited and inherent constraints of its own. The inherited constraints derive from customs, values and systems that are traditional, but perhaps not optimal. The inherent constraints are problems that appear in the process of development. Let me cite a concrete example. In India, life expectancy in the 1950s was twenty-seven years; it is now fifty-two years. This has clearly been the result of developments in health, medicine, sanitation; but it has created effects—I hate to call them problems in that context—that did not exist before and that now need to be addressed. On such issues, obviously governments have a positive role to play.

More OPECs?

This raises two other complex and much-debated concerns that I personally regard as classic instances of interim steps. One of these is government-to-government aid; the other revolves around raw material cartels organized by developing countries.

On the subject of government-to-government aid, conventional—or, perhaps to be more accurate, fashionable—thinking maintains that this has been a failure. Astonishingly, though, the same people who argue that it has been a failure are also the people who demand vociferously that there should be more of it. As I see it, some government-to-government aid, such as, for example, aid rendered by the United States under the Marshall Plan, between the United States and Latin America in the Alliance for Progress, or between the United States and India in the seventies, has had a very constructive and large impact in the respective regions. In India in the seventies, people were still dying of hunger; now, in the eighties, we have had two bad monsoon periods and no one has died. That is to a large extent the result of government-to-government aid in the food sector in India, and of the Green Revolution and its transfer of technology which we have seen implemented here with highly successful results.

On the second issue, the formation of natural resource cartels by developing countries, the present oil arrangements may well become a pattern for other commodities. The reason for this is not ideological as much as it is a matter of capital requirements for the exploration and exploitation of basic minerals. These requirements are so massive that they will force, at least in most countries of the world, government participation in the enterprise. I believe this to be one of the most important, and often overlooked, effects of the recent years of inflation on our lives. By and large the private sector was denuded of capital, with the result that there is now not enough of it left to finance the kind of monies that are required for the tapping of resources in minerals and commodities.

Corruption

Such large-scale operations by governments inevitably raise the problem of corruption. Corruption is possible only if someone wants something from someone who has the power to grant it. Therefore, when you get an all-pervasive influence of government, you get all-pervasive corruption. So the answer to that one, I believe, is that as you get more economic freedom, you will get less corruption. Corruption comes from two sources: shortages and power. So the solution to corruption is wealth—in a relative sense, of course—plus freedom. But wealth plus freedom is not a complete prescription either. The first phase of the industrial revolution did have both of these aspects but fell down on its social concerns. The robber barons, wherever they operated, created enormous wealth; but they also created, or at least had no concern about, social misery. This is not possible anymore. Social factors, social responsibilities must now be factored into the creation of wealth.

The Time Element in Decision Making

One of the queries I have is whether we are on the right track with the election systems as currently practiced both in the United States and in India, for example. My question is whether that four- to five-year election cycle gives a chief of state enough time to do what needs to be done. It seems to me that when he is just about ready to implement his policies, he must begin thinking of the next election. My suggestion would be one term for seven years, not renewable. In that way a manager in the most important sense, that is, the manager of a nation, has time to put his policies into practical effect. He is also considerably less vulnerable, in such a context, to short-term pressures, which often distort long-term decisions in the public sector and, of course, in the private sector as well. What I see under the current political system is that too often long-term decisions are made in response to very understandable pressures of poverty and unemployment. But in a longer time context, the necessary decisions could be made with a longer and sounder perspective and could therefore devise more fundamental solutions.

Relations Between Government and Private Enterprise

I do see the threat to private enterprise of growing government intervention worldwide. But I think part of the blame is in the private sector. The truth is that when the private sector runs into problems, it has developed the habit of running to government for help. I could cite Chrysler in the United States, or British Leyland in the United Kingdom. But once you make this kind of conceptual compromise when problems arise, you cannot then go back later and complain about not having enough freedom to operate. As always, of course, the real problem is one of balance. Just where does the balance lie in creating the optimum relationship between government and private enterprise?

There is one sector where we really did it right here in India. That sector is agriculture. The government set a framework that was an incentive framework. It provided support prices, it provided credit, it provided research and development in the form of seeds and other inputs; and it provided irrigation. It then left the rest of it—that is, the actual production effort—to the farmers. And the farmers responded magnificently. India no longer imports food. To sum up, I think this represents what I would consider the proper relationship: for the government to provide the infrastructure and then leave the actual producers alone. In industry, the ideal would be for the government to provide such basic infrastructure as roads, railways, power and a school system. And after that let the private sector alone.

I believe that the system that controls everything, kills everything. But I also believe that some values and some disciplines are needed, and that governments have a role in instituting both. Governments should emphasize education, and in education it should stress ethical values. I have not been against dissidence, but object to those who think that the only way to be a dissident is to create mass movements that shout, that demand direct action and go to the streets for it. I believe in a system that allows people to voice disagreements and have a difference of opinion, for through such liberties are men "alive," and mature into responsible citizens. The "flower children" of yesterday have turned into men and women with some very constructive social ideas.

Disillusionment takes different forms in different societies. In the United States, what created some of the disillusionment is an excess of affluence. In India, on the other hand, it is that educated people cannot find jobs commensurate with their education. There are two ways to address that particular problem. We need more job focus in education, on the one hand; on the other, we need to create more jobs. And the only way to create jobs is through fast economic growth.

The Understanding of Business by the General Public

Part of the lack of understanding is really business's fault. Businesses generally give the impression that they are not engaged in the "public" business, and that they do not care to be engaged in it. Business gives the impression that its sole motivation is the buck. This is not true, but business must do a better job of explaining what it is really about and of framing that explanation in socially acceptable terms. Here, in India, we have a big debate over what is the socially acceptable profit. If we could explain that the wealth that business creates in itself meets important social needs, in terms of providing jobs as just one element, then this rather abstruse and sterile debate might dissipate.

It is also true that businessmen, at least here in India, do have problems in getting together for demonstrative displays of their concern with the public. For instance, I tried some time ago to get all the leading businesses to devote 1 percent of their profits to community goals. One of the first goals I had in mind was for the major business companies in Bombay to donate one hundred buses to the city. We've all seen the enormous queues that form at the beginning and end of the workday because there simply are not enough buses in the city. I wanted to create a business foundation to do that kind of thing. The problem I ran into was that the companies prepared to participate always wanted individual credit to their companies for whatever they were doing.

On the other hand, there is a legitimate question as to just where corporations should draw the line in terms of their social activity, their social involvement, and perhaps above all the allocation of profit resources to social ends. It probably depends on the society in which they operate.

I would argue that corporate responsibility needs to have some kind of relationship to its own activity. That relationship needs to be defined consciously, sensitively and imaginatively, and will undoubtedly vary from place to place, and even from time to time. In our own company here in India, we provide free education for the children of all our employees. Clearly this improves employee morale in a major way. But it also fits in with my conviction that the solution to the problems that face India today—population growth, poverty, hunger—can be met in only two ways: one is education and the other is fast economic growth. These are the two factors that I consider the major responsibilities of corporations like my own in India today.

Turning Full Cycle

Let me wind up by turning full cycle to where I began—the need for a leap in social technology. I see that need in three areas.

The first, and in many ways most pervasive, is religion. It seems to me that most religions are tolerant in principle, but not in practice. We must remember that all religions were, at one time or another, used to govern. Religion gives hope to people, and has great influence in old societies. Religion should be used to better man, not to govern him.

The second concerns social structure. In India, for example—and this is true for most developing countries, where the overwhelming majority of the world's population lives—we still have a feudal society. However, India, as well as some other developing countries, now does have a modern infrastructure and a modern democratic overlay. I am convinced that the modern facets will win out over the feudal because these modern values offer more to the average man than there is in the old feudal system.

The last area I want to address is the most important for the future of our life on the small planet we share. We need to design a social technology to intensify the process of interchange of ideas at all levels and between all segments of society. We also need more international education, by which I mean education from an international vantage point. But I think we are at a period where there is unprecedented opportunity for man getting to know man on an individual basis worldwide. And when that happens, I think we will all be surprised to discover how similar we are. Once that happens, all else follows.

The paramount social problem we have at the moment, on a global basis, is the wide disparity in development among nations, and all that it implies. The solution, I believe, is a closer understanding of what *is* implied in these differences and a true transfer of knowledge of all kinds—that is, scientific, technological, managerial. The problem is that nations do not talk about these things. Companies do, but governments don't. The tragedy is the fact that governments resist transferring that kind of knowledge, which is so clearly needed.

The fundamental long-term problem, it seems to me, is for people to learn to accept each other, to get it through their heads that no one, no group, no society, no nation, is superior to any other; that basically we are all humans, earthlings on a small planet. This does not mean that we are all the same. Equality, in the true sense, is the recognition of individual differences. To absorb these concepts will require education, discussion, mind-stretching, using the possibilities of the human brain to accept the fundamental notion that we are both different and equal.

DEMAND: THINKING THE UNTHINKABLE

Dr. Bharat Ram
Chairman
Delhi Cloth and General Mills Company Ltd.

Looking at the global economy, it seems to me that the core question in the short term, and certainly in the long term, revolves around demand. And the fundamental question is whether demand will be large enough. From where I sit, it is crystal clear that demand exists in the developing world. Unmet demand, that is. In many areas, demand in the industrial world has been satiated. Therefore, the basic challenge is to address demand where it exists, and to provide the purchasing power that can turn demand into a market.

In the past we have addressed this problem on an individual country level. The ingredients of the problem are known. They are science, technology, resources, with such allied problems as foreign exchange. Now I think we need to address this problem of demand on a more coordinated and comprehensive basis. I believe, for example, that IMF resources should be increased five times. Not, of course, immediately but over some reasonable period of time. These funds should contain some reasonable constraints, which need to be discussed. They have to be geared to individual countries, resources and absorptive capacity. But these constraints should also be imaginative. This kind of money and resource should not be applied only to projects. It must also be applied to what I think of as the raw material of projects, by which I mean, among many other components, people. This suggests that they must be applied to education in every sense of that word, but preferably and primarily to job-related education.

I know that the proposition of increasing IMF resources five times sounds almost impossible. And it appears at first glance as if this makes a substantial demand for sacrifice on the industrial countries. But I believe this is not an accurate perception. It seems to me to be the most evident self-interest. Not only will it create the markets that the industrial countries need, but there is the even more fundamental question: What is the alternative? Personally I cannot find any. I think we need to assume that there will be some waste in the developing countries, but that too is part of the learning process on both sides.

I see nothing wrong with at least asking economists to work out what would happen to the world economy if IMF resources were increased fivefold and largely invested in the developing world to increase purchasing power there. My response to people who say that this is out of line and that it will create all kinds of distortions is: "What really are the alternatives? And for how long?" I am convinced that demand where it exists, i.e., in the developing world, is the basic problem that must be addressed. I also believe that if we can address that problem successfully in the medium term, other solutions will fall into place or will be discovered. If we do not, I fear there are overwhelming problems that threaten to overtake us and make any solution impossible.

It is true that, in the past decade, we have all been too easy in choosing the soft options. We gave in to demand without insisting on responsibilities, and I mean responsibilities in terms of productivity. This was true both domestically and internationally. One reason for this is that after the war, technology was developing so fast it produced savings that exceeded demand. That is, the new productivity, the additional productivity that was made possible by technology, kept ahead of increasing demand. Now we still have the technology and what it can do, but we do not have the demand.

I believe we have to be careful in this context not to address all problems through the escape route of divine technology, which will make everything possible for all who are alive now and will be born in the future. It takes a proper combination of capital and demand, and to put together this kind of package requires both space and time. The key problem I see now is satiation of demand in some societies, and demand without sufficient purchasing power in others.

In technology, we have to reach for the optimum equation of technology and jobs. And the question to be answered is: Where is that optimum balance? From whom? But I do think that economic isolation is no longer possible for anyone, anywhere. I believe the most important reason for the transfer of funds—and I do mean massive funds—from industrial countries to the developing countries is for the transfer of technology and equipment. But there is also a demand creation aspect. For example, I consider education a fundamental demand creation mechanism. An educated man has, almost by definition, more demands than an uneducated man.

Entrepreneurship and Profit

With some imaginative leap, this leads me to the role, in developing countries, of entrepreneurship and, intimately allied, the role of profit. I believe that entrepreneurship is fundamentally a talent, but it also springs, and certainly the development of entrepreneurship springs, from need, or perceived need. Need becomes the driving force for entrepreneurship. Entrepreneurship can be encouraged, but it cannot be created. You cannot teach an ability to take risks. You can offer business training; you can offer management tools; you can offer an external environment in the area of taxes, laws, regulations and social acceptability that will encourage entrepreneurship. The most important ingredient in creating an environment that encourages entrepreneurship is the possibility for the entrepreneur to reap a reasonable reward for the risks he is taking. And there must be social approval. An entrepreneur must not be frowned upon. Entrepreneurship must be socially appreciated. Because entrepreneurs, to be optimally effective, strive not only for achievement in monetary terms; they also want social recognition.

As to profit, let me cite the example of India as illustrative. "Profit" was a dirty word in India for quite some time. It is not a dirty word anymore. Even in the public sector it has been recognized that any society, including a socialist society, must have profits in order to operate. In some societies the profit motive is coming back as an incentive. At this point, I believe that "profit" is a dirty word only for those people in society who do not want to work. In India, my guess would be that 80 percent of the workers understand the need for profit, and perhaps 60 percent of the academics.

The problem with profit is that in an uninformed society which is also poor, propaganda against profit is a good political tactic. What we in the private sector need to explain is "profit to whom?" Most people who are opposed to profit even on easy emotional grounds are not opposed to the kind of money that a typist makes in a corporation. Their problem is with the sums of money that they believe managers, and especially owners, appropriate. What they need to be made to understand is that the profit of a public operation goes to fifty thousand shareholders, that the successful create wealth and income on a very broad basis.

The Tricky Question of Management

The vital ingredient in the question of wealth is, of course, management. And that raises the question of what makes for optimum management. In India, as in many other developing countries, we used to believe that the best thing for us would be to copy the industrial world and get professional management instead of family management. I am not sure that is really the best road. I am convinced that family management must be professionalized, but it seems to me that unless management has a direct, long-term stake in the enterprise, it will not be as totally dedicated to the growth of the enterprise as would be people who do have a direct long-term stake, and therefore economic growth will not be as fast as it can be. So the question becomes: How do you give managers a really long-term stake in the enterprise? I am not yet persuaded that giving long-term managers an equity stake in the enterprise is any more effective than giving family members the appropriate managerial training. But I have an open mind. I would merely argue that the evidence is not yet in either way.

Government and Private Enterprise: The Odd Couple

Speaking of keeping an open mind on optimum relationships, I personally have the same approach to the relationship between government and private enterprise. We really cannot say that business and government should ignore each other and have nothing to do with each other. There must be interfacing and involvement between the two. But I think the best role for government is to set the ground rules and, after a point, become an umpire.

When the public sector is active in the economy, as for example it is in India, the most urgent task is to inject the philosophy of private enterprise into these government operations, and by that I mean the discipline of keeping an eye on the bottom line. These government entities cannot be allowed to generate surpluses by hiking prices. They must be persuaded to improve their bottom line by efficiency and productivity.

On the other hand, I would have to say that in developing countries there is perhaps a need for government to get involved in such fundamental economic enterprises as steel plants. I know, for example, that in India we could not have started the literally thousands of downstream enterprises and industries in the private sector without having the base, the foundation, laid by the big steel industry that was created by the government. I see no reason, however, indeed no excuse, for government to get involved in such industries as producing wigs, or small cars, both of which they do here in India.

What precisely the government role should be changes over time and it changes alike with the needs of a society, its sense of development and the capacity of its people. Therefore I see a real difference between the required economic role of government in developing countries and in countries that are already developed. For example, to start an enterprise with the purpose of job creation because joblessness will lead to unrest is perhaps an argument in a developing country over the short term. These enterprises are never economic in the long run, and therefore I find justification for them in developed countries much harder to sustain. But where there is really a social need, measured in terms of poverty, that can lead to chaos and explosion, the situation does seem to me to be different.

Now, the creation of wealth also requires captial, and there is considerable debate, much of it uninformed and impassioned, about where that capital will come from. I would like to address two of the more controversial aspects of the question, i.e., the function of foreign capital and the proper channeling of domestic savings.

I believe that foreign capital has an important role to play in development, including development in developing countries. In addition to supplementing the savings of the developing country and providing technology, it can also stimulate the entrepreneurial spirit by creating or giving the local entrepreneurs the incentive and ability, and indeed the demand, to create ancillary business. I have seen this happen here in India.

Domestic Savings

The problem in recent years in countries such as India has been that savings have been flowing into financial instruments with fixed returns rather than into the share market. This has resulted in less productive investment. The best vehicle for savings is a vigorous and expanding capital market, by which I mean a market for equities rather than a financially based structure of fixed returns.

Life on a Small Planet

Finally, let me offer a few thoughts on optimum relationships in the largest framework, that of individuals and nations on this planet we all share.

Much needs to be done in the area of living together on a small planet by both the developed and the developing countries, separately and jointly. First, there must be fresh thinking on development strategy in almost every sector. The links between action/response at all levels—from global and international to regional and national to grass roots and local needs—must be forged with a mix of competition and cooperation, each fortifying the other. It seems to me that we have come a long way since the 1930s. It seems to me also that we have been moving generally in the right direction. I hope that we continue to do so. We have been moving, and I trust will continue to move toward, if not an ideal, at least the best possible solution. But nothing will happen without awareness. Awareness is, I believe, a fundamental need.

Specifically, what I believe we need is a global dialogue that recognizes the danger of alternatives to interdependence. Just as an individual enterprise must see what is good for the country in which it operates, countries must see what is good for the world. But this is possible only if the individual is integrated in a true sense into the enterprise, and from there on into the role of the enterprise in the country, and then into the international community. This is the direction in which we must head.

Israel

IN THE YEAR 2000: A PLURALISTIC ECONOMY FOR MANKIND

Naftali Blumenthal, M.P.
Chairman
Koor Industries Ltd.

As we approach the year 2000, we must recognize and accept the continuing existence of a pluralistic economy for mankind, including public and private sectors.

Each one of these sectors, if it wishes to survive and keep up with the demands and needs of the future, will have to redetermine its goals and redesign its modes of action.

It has become increasingly clear that planned economies, that is, command economies and government-owned enterprises, have failed in this century. This failure is not theoretical. It is a fact, which has been illustrated, inter alia, in some major strikes that have shaken economies in both Western Europe and, significantly, Eastern Europe, where strikes have been unthinkable for many years.

New Directions for the Public Sector . . .

As a result, the men behind the planned economies and the government-owned sectors, wherever they are, are now looking for alternatives. Their efforts will be devoted to the achievement of essentially social goals: the prevention of unemployment; worker's welfare; self-determination of the labor force in one guise or another. Economic considerations will be bent, if necessary, to achieve these goals. But the public sector will have to adopt certain aspects and elements of the private sector, including the use of profit as a discipline. It will also have to pay more attention to management training, to the shaping of a future generation of managers capable of understanding and achieving a combination of goals, national, economic and social. Management efficiency and integrity will have to be improved by a stricter separation between the guiding and controlling level, that is, between policy makers and managers.

. . . and the Private Sector

The private sector will no longer be able to ignore social questions. It will have to recognize, for instance, the social and human aspects of employment and the prevention of unemployment. Even in profit-oriented market economies, it will have to include social goals and solutions in its target-setting and its strategic planning, so that in its basic thrust the private sector will be on the same wavelength as the public sector.

Another change called for in the private sector is its attitude to the worker. Private employers must learn to consider workers as partners, as having certain *ownership rights* in the enterprise which is the fruit of their labor. There are realistic reasons for this, created by the new technologies. For example: Only a decade ago, metal production consisted of twenty-five workers operating twenty-five lathes, each of which was worth $15,000; today, the same production is achieved by one worker, operating one machine worth $3 million. The motivation and competence of the worker operating that machine is vital. One man, operating a $3 million machine, being ill or badly motivated one day, can make an enormous difference to production. On the other hand, if properly motivated, he can make a considerable contribution to profit. Conventional theories of management do not address the increasing importance to the enterprise of individuals operating these powerful machines.

In a different context, take a biochemist who has the major thrust of the company's research effort in his head. That head can determine the future of the company. Management cannot deal with such creative and productive workers in the old way. I foresee a trend where more and more employees will be part of this vital, valuable category of individuals who are literally precious for the enterprise. An effective manager will have to manage, not hundreds of skilled laborers or technicians, but more likely a dozen creative geniuses. This, I believe, will bring about a change in ownership, since these creative people will want, and demand, a piece of the action. They will also want to play a different role in management. What I see, therefore, is more and more enterprises that are partly owned by employees, who will become one element in a new kind of participatory management. The difference between employees and owners will gradually diminish, bringing about a major change in private enterprise everywhere.

A Case in Point: Trifocal Vision

My own organization is a conglomerate of both industrial and commercial companies that operate worldwide. While we operate as private sector companies in terms of the bottom line, we are in fact owned by the trade union movement. At the same time, being a leader in our community (the largest industrial factor; the largest exporter; the largest investor and largest employer outside of government), we also assume national responsibilities. This gives our organization a trifocal approach: economic, social and national.

This trifocal orientation may be illustrated by our approach to the problem of unemployment. Our basic position is that at no time may any of our companies make a product that has no market, since, as a matter of policy, we will not close factories and create unemployment. What we do, therefore, is to invest heavily in new technologies, in anticipation of market demands. Indeed, we invest more than purely private sector companies operating in the same product areas.

We also carry out extensive long-term planning in order to avoid boom and bust cycles within our industries. This means that we cannot take advantage of a short-lived boom in a particular sector, hire additional employees, then fire them when the boom has receded or collapsed. The essence of our strategic planning, therefore, is not a blind drive to maximize output at all times regardless of the human and social aspects of employment. Our planning is based on long-term strategic considerations, which strive to anticipate market needs, new technologies, new markets and resources, in order to guarantee employment, modernization and profit at the same time. This is what I mean by trifocal vision.

Our planning horizon is the year 2000. This planning also devotes considerable effort to the constant training of our labor force, existing and new, at all levels, including management, to prepare our employees to keep up with the technological demands we know will be made on them between now and the year 2000.

Optimum Role of Profit

Another major change which will affect, in my view, all sectors of the economy, is a change in the meaning and role of profit. I believe that profit should be used in all organizations, whether they are in the private or the public sector, as a measure of success. The conventional thinking in much of the private sector is that profit is the target, and that the well-being and motivation of employees is a tool to achieve it. I consider this attitude wrong, the truth being the other way around. Profit and efficiency are tools to achieve the well-being of people in a productive enterprise. This approach creates a common target, a platform upon which everyone in the enterprise can stand. Indeed, profit is a tool we cannot do without. But the goal is the growth of the people within the enterprise, and all other desired ends follow directly from there.

People Are the Measure—and the Means—of Achievement

I am totally convinced that there is nothing superior in the world to the people living in it. People are the measure of all things—and the means to achieve every development, every improvement, great and small. Therefore, managers, whether they are managers of economic enterprises, political enterprises or technical undertakings, have fundamentally the same task. They must agree on a target, define it, devise methods to implement it, and then carry it out, together with their people.

One of humanity's problems is that many political systems are too weak to do this, both in the West and in the East.

Look at Japan

Even the Japanese success story is beginning to show its first cracks in the system. Take the problem of unemployment in Japan. At present, only 25 percent of Japan's workforce has unemployment insurance. And the system of lifetime employment, which the private sector was able to introduce for certain segments of the working population, is not sustainable in the direction in which the Japanese economy is heading now. The truth is that the success of the Japanese economic system has been based on the use—and I claim, the abuse—of subclasses in the economy. Women are one example. Small businesses are another. I am convinced that this is no longer possible and that the Japanese will have to change their system.

The Haves and the Have-Nots of the Planet

The relationship between the developed and the less developed countries is another area in which change is needed. Some real sacrifice will be required from the developed nations: not just a massive transfer of funds, but giving the developing countries the opportunity *to create wealth of their own.* This means, for instance, allowing goods manufactured in developing countries access to markets in developed countries; granting better trade terms for commodities produced by developing countries and perhaps, for a time, preferential tariffs; offering developing countries access to sources of energy and to modern technologies. In short, pulling together in an organized, concerted effort to give the developing countries the opportunity to make themselves productive, and to join in the race for economic and social growth in which developed countries already have such a substantial headstart.

Dignity and Democracy

From this trifocal vision two concepts emerge that seem to be both fundamental and common to all fields of human endeavor and to every community—be it a factory, an economy or a country. One of these concepts is dignity, the dignity of every single worker, of every working community, of every nation. Respect for that dignity is increasingly recognized as the key to economic, social and national success.

The other concept is democracy. I do not refer here to the concept of democracy in its political sense, but to an attempt to introduce democratic procedures into an industrial society which has been, so far, primarily a hierarchical structure.

The challenge of the year 2000 will call for a variety of approaches to ensure the well-being of mankind. Each one of the three economic sectors—governmental, public, and private—will have its position and its function in this global pluralistic marketplace, contributing in its specific performance to the creation of dignity and the preservation of democracy.

ADDRESSING REAL PROBLEMS IN REAL TIME

Dan Tolkowsky
Vice Chairman and Managing Director
Discount Investment Corporation Ltd.

What countries or individuals have to offer to the solution of world problems is fundamentally their thinking ability. It is the special approach, the special attitude they bring to a problem. An important ingredient in this contribution to solutions is that it must be free of time constraints that are ill-matched to the solution of the problem. The main difficulty with government thinking is that it is tied to terms of reference that are politically determined but have no particular relationship to the problems that need to be solved. The time frame needed to address some of the major problems mankind faces is longer than the time frame that is available to most political and governmental systems. Governments seek short- and medium-term solutions while most of the world's problems require long-term solutions. It is the lack of fit between these time frames that creates most of the imbalance, skewing and frustration in addressing global problems.

Private enterprise, too, is up against certain time constraints. There are, typically, the requirements of, say, quarterly financial reports (especially in the United States) or of the financial year end. Nevertheless, private enterprises are expected to address their own strategic problems, both medium and long term. The shareholders of a private enterprise are prepared to respond to the aims and conclusions of strategic planning when that planning is sound, whatever the time frame involved, if it can be justified in terms of the real issues being addressed. Governments rarely have that luxury. Or at least they believe they do not have that luxury. They think of voter response in a time frame that covers their own terms of office, while many of the problems they address do not fit into that time frame at all.

Also, the adversarial relationships that are built into the private sector, as against those that are built into the government sector, are different. The private sector must win the battle against its competitors, which definitely requires attention to both tactics (shorter term) and strategy (longer term). It addresses its fundamental problems in the time frame they warrant. Governments, on the other hand, are forced by their opposition parties into short-term solutions that in many cases are simply not responsive to the problems that need to be addressed. In sum, governments, and of course also the enterprises and societies they run, are essentially faced with a mismatch between their time horizon, the problems they face and the solutions that have to be sought.

In addition, especially in democracies, the political dynamic is heavily influenced by fringe groups, and the influence these have on the body politic makes it very difficult, if not impossible, for governments to address fundamental problems in good time. The illustration that I would cite is nuclear power. In Switzerland, for example, I have been told that they know they should be addressing the problem of nuclear power on a long-term basis, but they cannot do so effectively because of the opposition of certain marginal groups which nevertheless have a serious influence on the political process, an influence that is important enough to prevent the Swiss government from addressing the question of nuclear power production in the strategic sense, in true real time. Business is not up against this kind of constraint in designing its solutions; or at least to a considerably lesser extent. Indeed, this is part of the reason why business is solution-minded, while governments often cannot be because of internal and external constraints, to the ultimate frustration of the voter.

A Growing Gap

Another fundamental problem I see is that there are very few people above the age of forty who can really adapt. Usually at age forty people have a mind-set and a behavior-set that is difficult to change. But the problems the world will be facing will require great adaptability and flexibility. I therefore see as a major problem the difference between the rate of the need to adapt, and the ability to adapt in time. This is particularly true in the Western world where we have a rapidly growing elderly population. It may well lead to more unbalanced societies, in which a great mass of voters craves a deceleration of change, while an avant garde of scientists, technicians and businessmen wants to initiate and push for change, so creating an increasing gap between them and the mass of the population. This gap will express itself in culture, in the ability to communicate within society, in conditions of life. It will carry dangers that we have not begun to consider. I would urge all of us to recognize and address ourselves to this hurdle looming ahead.

The Nuclear "Threat"

The argument that mankind cannot survive and cannot function under nuclear threat is fallacious. Mankind has managed to survive all kinds of threats in the past. Here in Israel, for example, we have had a perception of threat to our lives for thirty-five years. Nevertheless, we have managed to raise normal children and grandchildren and to build a country that holds continual challenge with great promise for the future. Our specific experience in Israel convinces me that if we, meaning mankind, don't do something excessively stupid, we'll survive.

North–South

I am deeply troubled about the relationship of North and South. What I have suggested before in terms of the gap developing in the industrial countries, I see as even more hopeless in terms of North–South relationships. For example, look at the rate at which societies in Africa are moving forward. Their pace of movement is totally inadequate to keep abreast of what is happening in the rest of the world in terms of technological advance, and indeed the advance that is vital if they are to cope with their most critical problems. What bothers me even more is that the dialogue that is currently being conducted between North and South is irrelevant to the real problem. The real problem is organic rate of change, and, once again, the inability of national entities to address real problems in real time.

On the other hand, I do not believe that the nation-state can at this point be eliminated; nor indeed that it should be eliminated. It provides both cohesion and sanity to the ethnic or national group in question. It is important to accept the notion of a nation-state which can design specific solutions for specific cultures. The vital point is to develop wise and responsible leaders who would realize that they cannot look for an instant advance. They would recognize that their main task is to keep their society alive and secure until it can find its own way, in its own time, into the modern world.

In the developed countries, I see as the main problem the time constraints that I have outlined earlier and the fact that many of these countries are too hierarchical in their social structure, and therefore too rigid to face facts properly.

Certainly, no problem in the developing countries, or the developed countries, can be solved by preaching or rhetoric.

Social Limits to Growth

There may, in fact, be few limits to growth in a technological sense, or in terms of natural resources, but there clearly are social limits to growth. We cannot continue to provide more welfare with productive effort. The expectations that have been created cannot be met. There is a great deal of wasted effort around the world that serves no useful purpose but at the same time continues to generate expectations.

The Concept of New Frontiers

I believe in the advantages of an open, mobile, pluralistic society, of which the United States is still the paramount example. And I believe in an equally open, creative, pluralist economy, in which the creative entrepreneur has room for maneuver. What makes a society creative is mobility—mental, cultural and societal—the concept of new frontiers. The latter, in the United States, was a physical thing initially, but it has increasingly become a mind-cast. What makes a country creative is its psychological mobility. The United States illustrates this, and so does Israel.

I suspect that unemployment, high unemployment, is with us on a permanent basis and that increasingly people will move into the information and service sectors as well as into the gray economy, that is, the underground economy. Work will become a privilege, and the few dirty jobs that remain to be done by human beings will have to be paid for very highly indeed.

Finally, however, I believe mankind has a demonstrated instinct for survival that will see it through these problems which now seem so intractable.

Italy

THE CHALLENGE OF STRUCTURAL CHANGE

Dr. Ettore Massacesi
Chairman
Alfa-Romeo Auto SPA

The fundamental question we in Europe need to address today is structural change. The most volatile aspect of this, from a social and political vantage, is unemployment. It will take enormous courage and will to devise and implement solutions, and I have no doubt that new approaches—indeed, a new set of mind—will be required. Here in Italy, for example, when we talk about the reduction of working hours, which is a necessity in the Italian economy, industrialists oppose this idea. They point out that it is not possible, from a company's point of view, in terms of its bottom line. Nevertheless, economic need demands some such solution, and we must all seriously begin to think about it.

We had to think about a comparable problem after World

War II when there was also a need for major structural change. Then the need was for a different and differently structured job policy in industry. Now the new service industries require a new approach. This calls for value changes and cultural changes from both entrepreneurs and workers.

Take, for example, medical service. There have been many developments in medical service, and young people have gone into a great number of specializations within medical service. Now we find that if they cannot enter medicine in what they consider an optimum fashion, they will drop out and not participate productively in society at all.

The current culture also makes industry unfashionable. Educated young people refuse industrial work, do not accept service jobs, and what they really want is what they call "to be creative." In fact, all these young people, well educated, well trained, who go around wanting to be creative, in effect produce nothing and contribute nothing to their society.

The Role of Profit

In addressing structural change, the role of profit plays an important part. We need a new concrete definition of profit. Profit as a phenomenon has a lot of ideology surrounding it. In actual fact, today in Europe, especially in the industrial sector, there is little profit. Profit in the classic sense is now being made in finance, not in industrial production. The way the rules are written today, manufacturing is punished. People continue to think of manufacturing as a real source of profit, but that is simply an error. The real sources of profit today are finance and trade.

At Alfa-Romeo, for example, which is a public sector company, our industrial relations with the trade unions have created a situation in which the trade unions declare emphatically that they do not want to contribute to the company's profit. In fact, of course, we are losing money. Profit is the last item on the balance sheet, after labor, raw materials, *and* the cost of money, etc. The way things are at present, the only thing that is really floating is profit. All the others are pretty well fixed costs.

Profit is a reward and is needed for reinvestment. People don't realize that profit is needed for reinvestment in the continuing health of the company. Most of them think of profit simply as a reward, and very often an unearned and unwarranted reward. This is an illusion that badly needs correction.

There is a feeling that profit in private enterprise should not have personal value for the owner of the enterprise, but should have a collective social value. It is difficult to justify private profit when it does not serve both the individual and the community. But of course it can, and most often does, serve both.

It is important to improve the image of private enterprise and to make clear the valuable role that industry plays in making products and rendering services that contribute to everyone's life and well-being. The tendency in the private sector is to pride itself on making a profit per se. If profit is to be understood and accepted by the general community, it must be portrayed as a means to produce goods and services, and as a stimulus to development.

A Fabulous Period

The basic cause of stagflation is an arrest of development. The truth is that our generation has witnessed the most exciting, important development in the history of mankind. Returning to a normal pace of economic development is, for people of our generation, and especially for the young people of this generation, a shock and a strain.

Our period was a very dramatic one in terms of economic development. We see only the immediate consequences. History will have to give us a clearer perspective on what it all meant. Probably there are fundamental structural reasons. We had relatively inexpensive energy. We now have new sources of energy, and other material resources that never existed before. But we have been aware, since 1973, that we cannot count on an endless supply of both energy and natural resources and that, more and more, solutions will become expensive.

This brings us to an additional function of profit, which I think can also be explained to the general public. Profit is an instrument of measuring and getting efficiency. It is a stimulus and an incentive. The risk at present is that public opinion sees only results. It sees profit only as personal enrichment.

Profit in the Public Sector

We get a particular version of this whole debate in public sector companies. There are long and avid discussions on the role of profit and its moral and legal implications for an enterprise. Many people consider profit unnecessary and unwarranted. At the same time the public will not tolerate loss of money by state-owned enterprises for any period of time. There is indeed a big difference between the feeling of a private enterprise when it loses money and a public enterprise when it loses money. A public sector company can always draw on tax money to do what needs to be done. The drain is indirect and therefore not felt as deeply either within the enterprise or by the general public. The result is that public sector companies have lost some of the positive approach to profit and have slipped into making losses. In a perverse way, this is considered less dishonorable. This attitude is extremely dangerous.

Demand and Supply: A New Attitude

In Italy, a new mechanism and a new attitude are required. What is happening now is that people pretend we have all the resources needed for the quality of life that they desire. But people will not do, on the job, what is required to make that quality of life realistically possible. Everybody wants to have a washing machine, but there is almost no one who wants to make one. Everybody wants to have clean air and at the same time drive a car. Producing some of these things in the developing countries postpones the fundamental problem that is involved, but it does not solve it.

It must also be clear that state and government can provide only when resources exist from which they can give. Today in the political system of Italy there is simply a lack of balance, a discrepancy and disproportion, between the forces that demand and the forces that can supply.

CAPITAL ACCUMULATION

Professor Mario Monti
Economic Adviser
Banca Comerciale Italiane

The big problem in the world today is capital accumulation. Inadequate capital accumulation leads to financial crisis. It also leads to an even deeper structural dilemma, namely, the inadequacy of productive capital.

Worldwide, we have mismatched savings and investment. Too many savings are diverted not into real capital formation but into meeting current deficits. This has produced an excess of consumption over production.

Government Deficits: A Betrayal of Household Savings

In Italy, since 1971, our government sector has run financial deficits not only for capital formation but also for its current accounts. What this means is that the savings intentions of the household sector are betrayed, because private savings go into excessive consumption by public fiat over which the individual who pays for it has no say whatsoever. The same is true now internationally. At present, global savings do not go into capital accumulation but into meeting the balance of payments of individual countries, that is, into current expenditures. This is the real underlying cause of inflation we are experiencing worldwide. At present, borrowers pay 18 to 20 percent interest on borrowed capital that is not used productively and therefore cannot repay either the capital or the interest. Only inflation can reconcile this discrepancy. Under this system, whatever the specific cause, inflation becomes inevitable and brings real interest rates to zero. Because savings are not put to productive use, banks, money markets, financial institutions, the traditional accumulators of savings are now, in effect, engaged in a redistribution process, not in a capital accumulation process.

The Real Meaning of Recycling

The famous recycling that we have all heard so much about is really the international counterpart of consumer credit.

The solution lies in distinguishing between new flows of finance and the problems that have been created so far. We must deal with the problems that have been created in the past by consolidation of debts and rescheduling. But this must be either proceeded by, or at least accompanied by, a new method that will prevent a repetition of the same imbalance and the same profligate spending. The funds in the International Monetary Fund and in the World Bank have to be increased, but considerably more conditionality has to be attached to the disbursement of these funds.

Markets work on expectation, and therefore a debt is less dramatic if it does not need rescheduling each year. Commercial banks should have the same kind of conditionality as the IMF. This would give these disciplines a multiplier effect. What it should add up to cumulatively is that, as the IMF increases its funds, it should also increase its conditionality.

The State as Hidden Banker

What has been happening in the past in countries such as Italy is that the state has in fact been acting as a hidden banker, as a financial intermediary. What the state has done is to channel funds into public sector companies, and sometimes into subsidies for private sector companies, in the process substituting private sector banking, and crowding out of the capital market not only capital that should be available to the private sector but also the financial intermediation role of private sector institutions. A problem with all of this is that the state is not adept at the allocation of financial resources.

A second problem with the state assuming this role is that information on and transparency of its financial actions is limited. At least it is in Italy. It is somewhat different in West Germany, for examply. In Germany, the government must give Parliament each year explicit detail on the list of subsidies it has granted. It must do this by region, by industry, by sector and, I believe in major cases, even by company. When a government acts as a financial intermediary, there are also policy directions that undermine productive investment. In Italy, there is a portfolio policy which imposes considerable constraints. Among these constraints is that savings cannot be invested abroad and, perhaps more telling, there is a ceiling on growth rates of loans to corporations. In 1982, for example, that ceiling was 12 percent, when the inflation rate was 17 percent, meaning that there was a net cut of credit to companies engaged in productive enterprise in the private sector.

What really happens in such a system is that private savings are compulsorily channeled into government needs. This helps to bring down public sector interest and frees politicians from competitive market restraints. It makes public spending less politically expensive—and that is dangerous to the economy. The fact is that inflation is lowest where there are the least constraints on the individual savings choices of householders.

Companies have to be responsive to and responsible for their bottom line. Countries should be expected to do the same. What is happening now is that constraints are put on the private sector to drain money and savings away from the private sector for government use. And government use does not involve capital investment but largely meeting current expenditures. This is extremely dangerous.

Some Solutions

What is needed now in Italy, as an example, but really all over the world, is a decrease in labor costs; a decrease in the public deficit; and revised monetary policies. These monetary policies should also make all government intervention in the marketplace transparent, and require guidelines to make public sector investments as effective as those of the private sector. We need anti-trust laws that apply to the public sector as well as to the private sector, and we need, in Italy, a thorough regulation of the capital market to make all economic transactions more transparent.

A GLOBAL INDUSTRIAL POLICY: ONE MAN'S VISION

Dr. Amadeo Ancarani Restelli
Chairman
Soc. Ital. Catene Calibrate "Regina"

Let me begin by affirming that I believe deeply in free enterprise, above all because it is fundamental for democracy. If we fail to realize this, as we did in Italy for some time, we end up in a very dark night. It was free enterprise that kept our nation going in its darkest days.

Today there is a discontinuity between unions and managers, between workers and employers. It is a social conflict that is destructive and unnecessary. And I think constructive solutions can be designed. The essence of these solutions rests on the fact that within a society each segment, indeed each individual, has something specific to contribute. Internationally, in a truly competitive world economic order, the same is true for nations. Each country can play a special role, drawing on its natural advantages.

I believe nations should have an industrial policy. Society must be organized in a way that makes it possible for a nation to reach its industrial targets. What is true for a nation is also true internationally. For example, the world financial system is now faced with some very large problems. If that world financial system had more order, had cleaner and clearer guidelines regarding currency, exchange control and other purely financial instrumentalities, a better distribution between consumption and investment would result. There is such a thing as using world economic resources properly, not to produce junk but to produce good things that have quality and meet people's real needs.

What I would like to see is a group of international experts who would come together to focus on the world's most fundamental problems. They would have to have neither political nor economic prejudices, and they would have to be able to cut through the smoke and obfuscation of whatever theories are currently fashionable. Such a group could then set up a bank of realities, problems and possible solutions that would be at the disposal of all, in the public as well as in the private sector, who wanted to make use of this bank of expertise.

Three Ingredients

What we need in order to run the world more intelligently, at least from an economic point of view, is three or four basic guidelines on fundamental ingredients of the world economy. They seem to me to involve the dollar and its role in the world; food; and armaments.

I believe the world economy can be put back on track with a global version of the Marshall Plan. That is, there must be a few simple, concrete guidelines, plus the funds that make it possible to act on the guidelines. The guidelines must be such that we can all believe in them.

A New Democracy

We also need a new style of democracy. The old democracy, which consisted of the belief in freedom for the individual, the family and the company, is not enough. It is finished. Technology and information increase day by day, and laissez-faire liberalism, or socialism, can no longer cope. I believe that sociopolitical systems in the future will be a mixture of liberalism, democracy, socialism and special programs prepared by a computer. In this future we will use computers not just as intelligent adding machines but as good friends that can solve real problems. As we look to the future, we must also look at what is now happening in genetic labs. We may well be producing a new man, a new human being. That now seems dangerous, but then so did atomic power.

One reason why democracy is not popular in the world today is because democracy needs determination every day. Freedom requires dedication every day.

Multinational Corporations and State-Owned Enterprises

In structuring a global industrial policy, one of the main issues that has to be addressed is the relationship between private sector companies, big and small, and state-owned enterprises, which almost invariably tend to be, or to quickly become, gigantic. This relationship has both domestic and international aspects. Let me address the global facet first. I see no problem in big companies, private or public, competing in the international arena provided that state-owned enterprises are required, as are multinational corporations, to have balance sheets, audited balance sheets, that show assets and liabilities, profit, and a real solid bottom line.

In the Western industrial world, many state-operated enterprises claim that their basic function is to provide jobs. The truth is that if they provide jobs and are not profitable, they will soon stop providing jobs as well because, in the international competition, they will be squeezed out of the market. There really is no escape from economic realities. Time is an honest variable. It shows up the truth every time.

The international financial system should not subsidize state companies. It should finance them only if they present an audited balance sheet, the same kind of balance sheet that is required of private companies. If the government wants to borrow, let it do so, but not from commercial banks. Banks should force financial discipline on all their customers, whether they are private or public enterprises.

The Social Role of Private Enterprises

On the other hand, private enterprises must have a social point of view and there must be clear legislation to enforce this. For instance, there is a good argument for rules and regulations that govern urban planning or even for guidelines that, at certain times, prevent companies from exporting capital. This is analogous to the situation in a family. At home with my family I have a great deal of individual freedom in my room, at my desk. But at dinner there are eight of us and we have to make a concerted effort to be there at the same time, sit around the same table and communicate with each other. In a way, this is a restriction on individual freedom, but one that is completely necessary if family life is to be preserved.

To obtain freedom you have to see the value of what freedom means to others. Compromise is the ability to see another person's point of view and not interfere with another person's freedom. This requires imagination and generosity. We can all use more of that, in our family lives, in our corporate lives and in the world.

Industrial Policy and the Welfare State

In designing an industrial policy that is responsive to both needs and opportunities today, two other fundamental questions need to be answered. The first of these is a national question, the second an international question.

On the domestic side, we need to ask whether we can reconstruct the welfare state as it exists today to free up the capital, the people and the technology that are needed to create a productive state in which supply and demand are better balanced than they are at present, when the demand side weighs so much more heavily than the supply side.

The international question that needs to be addressed is the relationship of the developing countries with the industrial countries. In this context, it seems to me that the basic problem is to find a way to get on the same frequency of thought. We have young people in the industrial countries who are generous and who would be prepared to stay in developing countries for considerable periods, not so much to bring technology as to try to understand what the particular developing country wants, and how it wants to go about getting it. I think if that is understood, these young people could relay the message, and we could design ways and means of cooperating with these desires.

A New Philosophy

What we need, particularly in the industrial world, is a new inspiration to do our best. We need to discover a new element, a new relationship between our life and what we do with it. Put in somewhat different terms, we need to rediscover God in a new dimension of our relationship to the universe. What this will take is to design a new philosophy, a unified philosophic field theory, that will enable us to look at the core of problems, not at their periphery. In this new philosophy, in this unified field theory of the mind, money, work, family will all be important, but they will be part of a system, a system that has a human scale.

"I Am an Entrepreneur"

This leads me to my final point—the role of profit within this unified field theory, and the perception and image of the entrepreneur.

Today, it is difficult to say, "I am an entrepreneur," because that, in effect, is tantamount to confessing that you are a villain. The new philosophic reality, that unified field theory in which all the productive contributions to society will have a defined and understandable role, would change this perception.

The image of the entrepreneur and his activity are the result, in part, of personal ethics, professional ability and social setting. Of course, there exist political ideologies that can make a point of accusing, undermining and distorting entrepreneurship and its image. In Italy, for example, there are people who create difficulties for the private sector just for the sake of creating difficulties. With them it is an ideological matter, not a practical one.

In fact, decisions in the private sector are usually made for positive reasons, and reasons that serve the good of the community. The private sector does have its own bad apples, as does every other sector of society. I believe that the existence of a flexible and modern connecting tissue, composed of small- and medium-sized companies, is absolutely necessary for a civilized society willing and ready to improve the way of life of the entire community.

It is true that the tumultuous evolution of the industrial society in the last fifty years has created important new social and human problems, including such problems as pollution and urban congestion. My question is: What situation would the world find itself in if, with its enormous population increase in recent times, it had to cope without the important industrial developments that have occurred and that have created some of these problems to which solutions must be found? It is also important, however, that we keep a sense of proportion, on a global basis, of the cost-benefit relationship between technology and industry and the problems they create.

In finding these solutions, I believe two things are required. On the one hand, entrepreneurs must be given guidelines, if you like, a culture that will widen their vision to include the community in which they live. This must not be done through either violence or rigid direction from the top, but through clear, logical legislation that encourages productive entrepreneurship while at the same time it discourages, through punishment of one kind or another, activities that are narrow, or harmful to society. Within these kinds of parameters, freedom of entrepreneurship can be coupled with political pluralism, and the two together can devise a solution that is rewarding to all.

Japan

THE DELICATE BALANCE

Shuzo Muramoto
Director, Adviser and Former President
Dai Ichi Kangyo Bank

The major problem I see for the world at this stage is to make the world economy active again. Worldwide we have suffered from recession, the high price of energy. Countries, both in the advanced world and in the developing world, have been making themselves skinny. No one is in good shape. Everywhere consumption has been decreasing. I believe that if the price of energy is stabilized, this will go a long way toward making the free market around the world active again. It will make free trade reappear and reenergize the free market. Within this process, Japan is in a delicate position. We keep advocating the free market but we do not take our advocacy seriously at home. We must begin to do this and open our domestic market because otherwise we cannot ask the world not to indulge in protectionism in its countries. The problem for us is to strike the right and possible balance.

Energy and Action

I see the developing countries suffering now from many of the same problems, due to many of the same causes, that afflict the industrial countries. By this I mean primarily the price of energy and the lethargy that it has created in the economy of the world. If the world economy becomes active again, then the advanced countries have room to make new and serious contributions to the developing countries. I believe we should give them government-to-government aid for infrastructure, and we also need to open our market to their products. We have to import not only their raw materials and commodities but also at least their semi-manufactures.

A New Detente?

The third global area in which I see a compelling need for balance is a political one: the question of East–West relations. What the Soviet Union will do under its changing, aging leadership is still an open question. But it is quite clear that several years ago the USSR moved away from detente and created problems through its active intervention in the Middle East and in Africa, often with Cuban surrogates. Kissinger was right when he said: "We must draw the line." The USSR turned the corner and changed the global picture when it invaded Afghanistan. Since then, the USSR seems to have practiced some restraint, at least in terms of further invasions. There has been a relative period of calm. This may well have been due to the precarious state of health of the Kremlin leadership; but whether it is a real retraction of Soviet aggression or just a pause due to the limited capability of aging leaders still remains to be seen. We need to watch that very carefully. From what I can see, the economic situation of the Soviet Union is not good and there is not enough economic strength in the system to provide increasing power for outside invasions. Therefore I think there may be a chance for a new detente. At least, I'm crossing my fingers.

Technology: Problems and Solutions

For mankind as a whole, I believe technology is launching us on another wave of major change. Most of our recent inventions are good, but they do create problems in their wake as well. The classic example is pollution. It is clear that the problems created by technology will in turn bring along other problems. At the same time, the solutions that are devised to cope with these problems will also bring in their wake other solutions. Where all of this will end, I do not know. My telescope is not good enough to see as far as the year 2000. But if we face the fact that our advances will create problems, and address these problems with intelligent and sane solutions, then I think the chances are fairly good that we will finish another century in good shape.

Operational Tasks

Some of our more immediate problems are operational. The first that comes to mind is the world financial system, which is fragile. Its problems can be divided into two areas. There are the financial problems of the countries that are important to the United States, such as Mexico, Brazil, Argentina and other countries in Latin America. And there are the financial problems of countries around the USSR, that is, Poland, Romania, Yugoslavia. I believe the IMF, which is led by the United States, can devise solutions—and is indeed already beginning to devise solutions—for the countries that are important to the United States. Survival bridges are being constructed for countries like Mexico, Brazil and Argentina. For the countries that are in financial trouble in Eastern Europe, I believe we—and by this I mean Japan and Europe as well as the United States—have to be concerned but careful. We can watch the United States paving the way for the rescue of countries that are of concern to it, and we can see what aspects of this method we can emulate for the countries of concern to the USSR. I do believe we need to cooperate with these countries for survival, but the problem is that with these countries we never know just where they are going. For the moment what is needed is a very careful rescheduling of their obligations.

In Japan, it is of paramount importance for us to do something about the government deficit. The outstanding government deficit in Japan, in terms of government bonds, constitutes a greater percentage of GNP than in any other country in the world, including the United States. It is very important to put government activities in Japan under the same kind of discipline as the private sector and to give them the same kind of good management. Once this is done, and government is brought down to the kind of lean efficiency that we practice in the private sector, it may well be necessary to introduce new taxes, both in Japan and in the United States, to wipe out the existing deficit. As we reconstruct our government to make it as skinny as possible, this government skinniness will give new energy to the economy as a whole.

I also think we need to reexamine our tax system and possibly design a new, or at least a considerably amended one, to make the system more equitable. The way this needs to be done primarily is to eliminate loopholes. If that does not provide enough income to wipe out the deficit, we need to go to new taxes which, once again, have to be designed for equity. With government operations streamlined, and taxes designed equitably to wipe out the deficit, I am sure the economy will take off again. And what is true here in Japan is, I believe, true in all the advanced countries.

The Demographic Clock

It appears that the era of high growth for the industrialized nations is over. What we must aim for now and, I believe, can get, is slow and steady growth. We do need that because our working population is still growing.

It is also vital that we look at the demographic changes in our countries. In Japan, for example, when we originally planned our government pension scheme, the demographic facts were that there was one old person supported by ten working people. Now the ratio is one to seven. In twenty years it will be one to three, meaning that there will be one old person supported by three working people. This dictates structural change in the pension plan.

The private sector is setting a good example. Its responses are much more flexible. In our bank, for example, we are already looking ten to twenty years ahead to devise our own solutions. Our retirement age used to be fifty-five; now we are stretching it out to sixty to increase the number of people who want to keep working.

The New World of Leisure

The fundamental fact is that in the world, especially in the advanced countries, we will need increasingly fewer people to do the work that society requires. If the economic pie is big enough, we can accommodate the change. We will have room enough for people who will do the work that has to be done to provide goods and services, and we will have a leisure service industry that will respond to the growing requirements of people with more time to develop themselves. It is very important to educate people for this new society, to make sure that leisure becomes, not an incentive to make people lazy and wasteful, but an opportunity for people to develop themselves intellectually, artistically, and in every other area of human potential. Our universities need to address this problem as soon as possible. All of them should create faculties for citizens, not just faculties for students.

The Contributions of the Young . . .

Young people throughout history have been revolutionary, idealistic, dissatisfied with society as they found it. This was true in Rome, and Athens, and as a result of looking back at history, I believe one can be optimistic about the future. It is this idealism, impatience and innovation of youth that moves mankind along.

. . . and of Religion

I do think we should develop a more fundamental concern for the values that religion teaches us. In Japan, for example, Buddhism for most of us is just a matter of observing some ceremonies. But the true meaning of religion should be not just the ceremonies for special occasions or, as it is in many cases, teaching us how to die. The true meaning of religion should be to teach us how to live. I therefore believe it is important for religion, whatever it is, to become active again so that it lends meaning and perspective to our lives and to our culture.

Living in an Era of Change

We live in an era of very big change and an era in which everything makes very big waves. I learned something about how to live in such times when I learned about swimming. The most important instruction I got when I was learning how to swim was to keep my peace with the water. I was told not to fight the water, not to try to overcome it, but to try to live with the water. In an era of change, we have to learn to live with these changes, not to fight them, not to overcome them, but to live with them peacefully. We must not stand beside the stream of change, nor must we build barricades and bulwarks against it. We have to go into the stream and learn to live with the turbulent water.

MONEY, ARMS, FOOD AND FREEDOM

Shigeo Nagano
Former Director
Nippon Steel Corporation
Former President
Japan Chamber of Commerce and Industry

I see two major problems facing the world today. One is economic, the other is political-diplomatic.

The economic problem is recession and unemployment. The question is: How can we solve both of these problems and create a more stable atmosphere for all countries? I believe the major impediments are financial; that is, where and how do we get the money to finance an economy that will create more jobs?

The second aspect is: How can we create a world economy in which we can trade more freely?

It takes not only knowledge but wisdom to find the solution to these questions. I am certain that one of the ingredients of the solution is to decrease government and its activity in order to make room for expansion of industry and investment. Here in Japan we are now working hard for administrative reform that will make government smaller and less expensive.

Looking at the second problem, the political-diplomatic one, the real question is the whole complex of issues surrounding international armament. The sad fact is that, at present, arms production and other defense activities are necessary. But they are not productive. If we spent the money that we now spend on arms on productive uses, we would have a well-balanced economy worldwide.

The confrontation between the totalitarian and the free economy is with us and seems for the moment inescapable. Nevertheless the arms race does create pressure on the general welfare of people everywhere. Therefore I see the need for a real effort to lessen confrontation between the totalitarian and the free market economies. I know this is very difficult. It requires wisdom, and wisdom is hard to come by.

North and South

Another relationship that requires repair is the relationship between North and South. The developing countries that do not have oil have suffered grievously since the two oil shocks, and I believe the industrial countries must exert themselves to help them.

I see two ways of doing this. One of these is to meet the food needs of developing countries, not by exporting food to them but by helping them to produce their own. In India, for example, there is the Thar Desert which, if it were irrigated, could provide food for 100 million people. In the Sudan, there is the Nubian Desert which, if the headwaters of the Nile were properly diverted and used, could also feed tens of millions of people. Both these irrigations are technically possible. I intend to devote a great deal of my attention to making sure that the possible technology is translated into reality. There is no doubt in my mind that the shortage of food is the greatest source of instability everywhere. I am, of course, in favor of population control, but whatever control we develop and make available, and is used, especially in the developing countries, will not be enough to prevent mass hunger, nor the revolutionary and violent results that are an inevitable by-product of it.

Let me illustrate what I mean in the case of India. The Thar Desert could use waters from the Himalayas that now flow into the Indus through three tributaries. If these tributaries were properly diverted and used, the Thar Desert could be made a vast breadbasket.

The same is true of the headwaters of the Nile in the Sudan. The big earth-moving machinery that will be necessary for both of these projects could be developed for another major project that I am working on, which is a second canal through Panama. That canal would be deeper and wider than the present canal. It could be financed through the World Bank, the Inter-American Development Bank, and oil money. It would, of course, be very expensive, but it would be self-financing in fairly short order. Right now, shipping that cannot use the present canal—and there is a great deal of that—must make a forty-five-day journey from the eastern seaboard to get to the West Coast. With a new deep canal, that section could be transversed in seven hours. Cargo destined for Japan and Asia would save enormous amounts of time and money. The tolls and services of that canal would amortize fairly quickly the initial outlay.

We should help the LDCs with their infrastructure. The United Nations recommended, and the OECD agreed, that the advanced countries should set aside 0.7 percent of their GNP for government-to-government aid to the developing countries. At present, the ratio is 0.5 percent of GNP. If we increased our aid to the recommended level, or better still to 1 percent of GNP, we would have a huge amount available to undertake these fundamental projects I am talking about, like the new Panama Canal and the irrigation of vast deserts in India and the Sudan that could be converted into food resources.

Robots to the Rescue

In the industrialized world, our problems are different. They range from the role of the robot in our society to the relationship of the public sector and the private sector, and perhaps specifically of companies operating in each of the sectors.

Let me start with our friends the robots. In Japan, we have a tripartite labor/government/industry council. It consists of fifteen members only and it meets every month, so real discussion is possible and does indeed take place. At a recent meeting we were discussing industrial robots. Japan is probably the most advanced country in the design and application of industrial robots. The labor members raised the problem that the robots could become the enemy of labor. I pointed out that, on the contrary, the robot was the best friend that labor ever had. It would do all the nasty, mean jobs that men have never liked to do and indeed should not be doing. At the same time, robots will also increase the productivity, and the fruits of that increased productivity can be shared with the workers in the form of more leisure. There was a time when workers labored seven days a week. Then the working week came down to six days; now it is five. All of this was thanks to new productive technology. The robot is simply the impersonation, if that is the right word, for the next stage of this process.

The real question we need to address in the age of the robot is the question of sharing the work that is left for the benefit of the human spirit. This will require wisdom but it is a problem that can be solved.

We must design the work place of the future in such a way that everyone gets a crack at working, and that some do not hog work while others are left unemployed. Personally, I am certain we will find the answer to this problem. It is certainly a better thing for us to apply our minds to than thinking about how to kill each other. Finding the solution to this problem will in effect be the ultimate fruit of what science and knowledge in the nuclear age have provided in the way of opportunities. On the other hand, I do believe there is a limit to the number of people our planet can safely and sanely contain. So we need population control.

State-Operated Enterprises

I believe that there is a valid place for SOEs. That place depends on the country's economy and on the specific industry. In some areas of the economy, where both a better overall view is vital and a very long perspective is required, government can tackle this kind of project more easily than can the private sector. The price is always that government enterprises tend to be less productive than private sector enterprises.

Also in some areas, where advanced technology needs a long lead time, the government can act as a bridge between the initial stages in which private sector involvement may be economically unfeasible, to the stage where the private sector can take over and do it better. There is a problem connected with this. Once government gets hold of any enterprise, it is a struggle to pry it loose. But I have faith in the voters of democratic societies. They can see who does a creative and productive job and who does not. And politicians in democratic nations have to pay attention to this commonsense of the voters.

Values to Live By

On a number of occasions, addressing the problems that face us, I have stressed the need for wisdom. Wisdom is built on values. I believe that the most important value we all need to learn is that we are—all of us—human beings on a very small planet. We can share scientific development and create new development, but at the same time we need to recognize each other's individuality, including the values that are contained in every person's individuality. Real equality consists of recognizing differences.

Discussing values, one cannot avoid the subject of religion. Religion is good to the extent to which it acts as a brake on evil, on the evil that people want to do and that religious restraints prevent them from doing. Religion is also good to the extent to which it relieves suffering and the fear of death. Marx and Lenin said that religion was opium, but the fact remains that after sixty years of the Communist state, there is even in the Soviet Union a revival of religion.

There are disadvantages to religion as well. Khomeini in Iran or Qadaffi in Libya are obvious examples of the bad side of religion.

As in many other things in life, what is required in religion is a balance. If we look at the globe as a whole, religion overall comes out on the good side of the ledger. The truth is that we are humans, and we are foolish, and I believe that if religion were wiped out we would have more wars and more foolishness than we do now. We need religion as a restraint on our behavior. As the Chinese put it: "We should worship the gods as if they existed."

Nigeria

A THREE-TIER WORLD

Ahmed Joda
Chairman
SCOA Nigeria

The world is now divided into three categories. The first tier consists of the industrial countries of both East and West which, while they are ideologically opposed to each other, do provide decent living standards for most of their people.

The second tier comprises the newly industrial countries where, given good leadership and resources, there is at least a possibility that they will develop healthily and provide tolerable lives for the vast majority of their people.

Then there is the third tier—all the other countries of the world—and what is their future? They are not only not moving forward; they are slipping back. To get them on track requires understanding and a change of attitude by the United States and Europe, the countries that have political maturity and economic development. It requires from these advanced nations a change of policy vis-à-vis the third tier of countries. If that change of policy does not come quickly, the third-tier countries will continue to exacerbate their state of instability and violent change.

What is needed now is for the industrialized countries to develop a long-range policy toward the LDCs, and vice versa, to bring about stability with freedom, including freedom for enterprise.

But private enterprise is not enough. There has to be political understanding as well. The governments of the developed world need new approaches that will help to minimize the misapprehension that exists in the LDCs. The LDCs, for their part, need to emerge out of the distortions with which they tend to regard the developed world.

There are some problems that the very development of the industrialized countries creates for some of the LDCs. Take Nigeria, for example. Nigeria had access to the U.K. market that was free and easy, and very lucrative for all concerned. That was before the EEC was formed. Now that the United Kingdom is a member of the EEC, Nigerian access to the U.K. market is considerably more restricted. The LDCs have also been badly hurt by the fall in the price of raw materials and minerals that has accompanied a fall in demand.

The Private Sector in Africa

In Africa we badly need a forum where business and government can interact. The truth is that the private sector hardly exists in Africa in any modern sense. There is so much government control, interference, and unpredictable change of policy that it is difficult to imagine how free enterprise can take modern form. In Africa today, American and European companies feel better when they deal with government and government companies. The reason for this is that these government enterprises are the only ones that are big enough to make it worthwhile for private companies from the developed world to deal with them. The local private sector is too weak to justify involvement from mature companies.

On the International Front

There needs to be more understanding on fiscal, monetary and investment matters on a global basis. The problem is that while institutions that could do this already exist, national policies interfere with what these institutions could do. We should try to get sensible global rules in all these areas through the existing institutions. But I believe the private sector needs to be more actively involved in making sure that the guidelines and the harmonizations that are required really are evolved in these institutions.

Planning

In the three-tier world in which we live and work, economic planning has a different meaning and a different function in each of the tiers. In the United States and Europe, I don't think you need periodic development planning. Industry functions, and development occurs without government interference. In the developing countries, however, there is need for central planning, guidance, the allocation of resources to priority sectors. These aids, or crutches if you like, are necessary until a country reaches a certain level from which the private sector can operate on its own.

In Nigeria, for example, the textile industry has reached that certain level, and can be allowed to operate on its own. But while the textile industry can be turned over to private entrepreneurs, it still has to be protected in order to survive. If it is not protected it can easily be undercut by competition from the Far East, for example, or India. Beer and soft drinks are another industry that is perfectly capable of standing on its own feet from the viewpoint of being handled by private enterprise. But if we open the market to imports, these industries, too, would very quickly be in trouble. The same is true, in the agricultural area, for rice production. If we opened our market freely to imports, the United States would very quickly swamp our rice producers. They simply could not compete. In sum, developing countries have to reach a certain level of development before they can let the private sector operate freely and remove protection.

There are countries that seem to be doing this successfully. Brazil, for example, got there by its own efforts, taking advantage of a free inflow of capital. Korea, Taiwan, the Philippines had a similar development, and received considerable help because of their strategic political locations. India seems to be getting to a point where it can also solve most of its economic problems, and it is therefore beginning to free up its economy both in terms of what it lets its own private sector do and how it relates to the international markets and to foreign investors.

Corruption and Inefficiency

In the tier of the global economy that is described accurately as the tier of the developing world, there is considerable discussion of corruption and inefficiency, with the discussion focused on how both of these phenomena impair the public sector. I would be quick to concede that these are indeed serious problems, but they are as problematic in the private sector as they are in the public sector. If there is corruption, both are responsible. It takes two to create these problems. The cure, I believe, in developing countries, is for the companies to take the risk of saying no. If a number of companies did that in a country, the public sector that indulges in corruption would stop doing so.

Values in the Developing World

Corruption and inefficiency are, of course, inescapably connected with the values that infuse and define a society. In the developing world, the three segments of the value system that are of paramount importance today revolve around ideology and religion; tolerance; and how the young people of the future generation act in, and react to, the world.

Let me comment first on ideology and religion. I think they go together. Both are fundamental. Sometimes, however, they cannot be combined, in the case, for example, of communism and religion. The fact is that we now have very few religious wars in the world; the few we do have tend to have a political and economic basis, and the religion is just another dimension. The big wars that we need to worry about these days are wars between ideologies.

This leads me directly to the topic of tolerance. I am a Moslem, but I believe, for example, that we need more people like Pope John, who gave a sense of peace and understanding to everyone he met. What we need is a few good people around the world in positions of leadership who speak not only for the nation but for humanity, and who act for all.

Assessing the young people in the developing countries, the conventional wisdom is that they are disillusioned. I don't think that's true.

They are no more disillusioned than we were when we were their age. It is the nature of young people to want to change things and be critical, to look around and ask questions. As they mature, as they take a job, and raise a family, they tend to change and focus on the more realistic needs and requirements around them.

Speaking of the need to focus on realistic needs and requirements, this is even more incumbent on the people who are now in positions to make and implement policy. As I have said, I believe we live in three separate worlds. There are the developed countries of East and West, who can take care of themselves. Then there are newly industrialized countries, with the hope of solving their problems, but it is a hope that can be dashed quickly. What, then, about us, that majority of human beings who live in the Third World? The fact is that we now live in an era in which a few factories can supply the goods that the whole world needs. But what happens to people? We must resume talking to each other on the basis of these new realities. These discussions must take place now just among politicians; the heads of multinational corporations must participate, and so must thinkers from academia, wherever they are. And the ground rules must be that we negotiate, not as people representing groups of irreconcilable interests, but on the basis of the realization that we all need each other.

Philippines

DYNAMICS OF DEVELOPMENT

Jaime V. Ongpin
President
Benguet Corporation

I believe it is the prerogative of the private sector to be the principal vehicle for development. In some countries, and under some conditions, it may be necessary for government to set the framework and even to make direct allocations of resources to priority areas. Where that is necessary, a very delicate balance is called for. If the government exercises undue influence, you very quickly get distortion and disagreement, not development.

In the Philippines right now, I see an allocation of resources by the government that I believe to be seriously in error. Government is pursuing an industrial policy that is fifteen years too late. The Philippines is attempting at this stage to repeat the early experience of Taiwan and Korea. But, given today's costs for energy and long-term capital, I believe that launching large industrial enterprises at this stage will simply create white elephants that will be unable to compete with low-cost producers established before the energy crises of 1973 and 1979. This in turn will mean that we will not be able to repay the enormous foreign exchange borrowings required to create these white elephants. To me this is a classic example of where government allocation of resources can go wrong and cause serious, permanent damage to developing economies.

What we need now is investment in agricultural development, where investment costs are minimal and where we have inherent advantages and proven competence. If we develop agriculture the way we should, we would not only be able to feed ourselves, which I consider a vital priority; we would also be able to export agricultural surpluses and generate foreign exchange capital. Then we would be able to provide additional employment for our growing population. Our true unemployment statistic, despite what government claims, is between 20 and 25 percent, if you include severe underemployment, which I think we must.

The legitimate government role, I believe, is to set directions and provide the private sector with the incentives and support to pursue those directions. The government should nurture an environment in which the private sector can flourish. In a developing country, the government should work out a defined strategic plan, with priority areas identified, and then provide the incentives and the support for the private sector to exercise initiative and get the job done.

Even in a structured society, I mean a politically structured society as we have in the Philippines, the private sector is not helpless. It can speak up and speak out to assert influence, particularly in the economic realm. We have a society that operates with certain political constraints; but even within these constraints, we can exercise initiatives that are sensible and constructive if we are prepared to speak up, to be specific and to be unpopular. We can take a contrary position, if it is a constructive one. Right now I have the feeling, here in the Philippines, that the private sector has failed to speak up as it should, that it has not exercised enough initiative because it does not have enough intestinal fortitude to say what needs to be said.

The First Priority Is Growth

Profit is what makes the world go round. It is the incentive for investment and development. Whenever governments have taxed profits excessively, you get capital flight, and people flight. I am not speaking of developing countries only. I would cite as classic examples the United Kingdom and Sweden. I am persuaded that the role of profit *is* understood by the silent majority. This majority understands that profit constitutes both incentive and reward for individual investments of time, money and effort. It understands also that it is unrealistic to expect individuals, groups or societies to invest and make these kinds of efforts without reward. What we perhaps need to explain better is that there must be a healthy level of profit to sustain growth. By growth I mean, in the first instance, the growth of the enterprise which, however, is not possible without the concurrent growth of the individuals within the enterprise. I believe growth—of both the enterprise and the people in it—to be the first priority of business.

I would want to add, however, that the enterprise's own growth is difficult, if not impossible, without growth of the national economy as well. It seems clear to me that enterprises within the national economy are as interdependent as nations' economies are now interdependent in the international arena. Interdependence is a logical progression from enterprise to nation to the world.

State-Owned Enterprises and the Private Sector

In that context, an assessment of state-owned enterprises and the relationship of state-owned enterprises to the private sector is appropriate. There should be no state enterprises if they cannot be viably created and sustained. If a state enterprise cannot do that, it has no valid economic or even social role. To create a state enterprise with the purpose of providing jobs is shortsighted if the enterprise does not produce something that is inherently competitive, because, unless it is subsidized, there is no way for any enterprise to survive in the marketplace if it cannot compete.

I can see a role for the state as an investor in certain countries under certain conditions, but I cannot see the state as a manager. If state-operated enterprises are not economically competitive on a world scale, and, I would very quickly add, profitable, they are really just a burden on the taxpayer and a clear example of taxation without representation. What makes even very bright and competent politicians bad managers is that politicians respond to political pressures, as indeed they must, and the decision-making apparatus that is required for sound economic decision becomes distorted.

Finance: Lubricator or Diverter of Development?

Sound economic development is not only shaped—or distorted—by political influences. The financial system can also help or hinder. As I see it, the most fundamental flaw in the financial system, the international financial system as we have lived with it for the past few years especially, is that with the interest rates as high as they were, it was difficult to justify productive investment. And without investment, there is no development.

What is vitally needed now is a financial structure that is designed to help rather than hinder productive growth. One way of doing this is to arrange for patterns of co-financing by commercial banks and the World Bank and its regional affiliates, in which joint conditions are devised that reflect sound commercial practice and sound developmental policies. These conditions must be firmly policed, especially for loans made to developing countries. It is quite clear that here in the Philippines, for example, commercial lending in the past did not have the required disciplines, with the result that a great deal of money was wasted. Unless international lenders, especially commercial banks, clamp down on country lending with sound rules of conditionality and impose stricter discipline, this problem will not be solved.

It is important for the borrowers as well as for the lenders to have sound disciplines imposed on them. We in the developing countries have accumulated enormous debt burdens that were a result of the easy lending practices of the past few years. I personally used to worry about my children having to meet these debts. Now I've begun to worry about what my grandchildren will have to pay!

Let me, therefore, try to focus on solutions. I believe that the question of exchange rates needs to be addressed and the role of the IMF needs to be reassessed. The fundamental question is whether politicians should be allowed to determine how much money is printed by their governments or whether we need an underlying discipline that takes the decision-making apparatus out of political hands. Gold was such a discipline. While I do not necessarily advocate that we return to the gold standard, I do believe that an external discipline such as gold is needed for sustained progress. If we don't devise some such discipline, the system will continue to be out of whack. What I believe is needed is an updated version of the Bretton Woods agreement that addresses today's realities.

As to the International Monetary Fund itself, the evolution of economic realities around the world also requires a reassessment of the functions of the IMF. IMF functions need to be reviewed and updated, and a framework should be created, with carefully imposed disciplines, that makes possible co-financing arrangements between IMF and commercial banks. The rules under which the IMF was set up originally were fine for their time. Now we have about 2 billion more people than we had when the IMF was created. We also have more confusion, more unevenness in development, faster advances in technology, with applications that will not necessarily benefit everyone. Finally, we have a food gap that will not go away unless it is systemically addressed.

I am convinced that we can address these problems and design systems that will help to solve them. I believe that on the whole we are very competent as a race. By this, of course, I mean the human race. The problem is not so much our ability to design systems, but how to persuade people to abide by the rules we create. Therefore I believe we need to create external disciplines that act as rule enforcers.

Technology and Development

Another major ingredient in the dynamics of development is, of course, technology. It is important for developing countries to be selective about the type of technology they import. It is therefore important to get technology that makes practical sense in local terms. In the Philippines, for example, I believe there is no place for advanced technology except where we really cannot do without it. We do not need advanced technology just because it is the fashionable thing to have.

An example that comes to mind is energy. We have made a major geothermal energy investment, and I am not sure that that is really the best use of our resources because there are serious technical problems that remain unresolved. Or, for example, we are about to put $1 billion into an integrated steel mill, with advanced technology, when the world steel industry is suffering from serious overcapacity. I am not against advanced technology as such, but I believe the kind of technology we should import is the technology that fits into our specific situation. A good example would be genetic engineering, which could do wonders for our agricultural sector.

We should also import selected computer technology. We have a high aptitude for computer work, and there is no reason why we cannot create software or assemble computer components here in the Philippines where we do have a comparative advantage in the form of low-cost skilled labor.

Training That Works

In these areas where we do have a national aptitude, and therefore a comparative advantage, it is important to provide the training that will make sure our workers can keep pace with the technology we import. There are government attempts at this kind of training, designed to get better productivity per unit value, but even this sensible government approach does not work very well, primarily because it does not relate to a specific job. The best development of skills, the best retraining, is a worker taught a specific skill related to a specific job for which there is an existing demand in the domestic or international marketplace.

In my company we try to do precisely that, working with government training institutions. For example, in the construction industry, in which we are involved, we make use of existing government vocational schools, and we make use of the students who come to these government schools. We send our own instructors and our own equipment to these schools to teach the students skills that are related to the specific jobs to which we can assign them once their training is completed.

It's an ideal arrangement: The government provides the venue and the physical infrastructure as well as the social infrastructure training schools, and the corporation provides the specific skills, equipment and job opportunities.

To sum up, it seems to me that the real problem in developing countries is not that the technology is not available, but how countries can create absorptive capacity for the technology that exists. I am certain that the initiative for a transfer of technology that is effective must come from the recipient. The recipient corporation, the recipient individual or the recipient country. The recipient country must have, or develop, the willingness and the organization to absorb the technology that it can really put to use. It cannot, for example, come from the top down via a mechanism such as AID money. The emphasis has to be on absorptive capacity, and that means education, and education geared to productive uses of existing knowledge. Education has to be broad-based socially, has to make economic sense and has to be functionally oriented.

Living on a Small Planet

Having insisted on the importance of hands-on realism in our lives, I want to emphasize that to make development work in its most comprehensive sense, we need idealism as well. To make life on our small planet both possible and worthwhile, I am convinced that, as a value, materialism is not the answer. In Asia, the work ethic remains an ingrained value, but there has been a serious erosion in ethical values in government and in the private sector. In both, personal honesty has deteriorated, mainly, it seems to me, because there is no social sanction against dishonesty.This is now a phenomenon in many of the developing countries. There is, of course, a reason. Money means more in developing countries because so few people have it, and the implications of having money, or not having it, are so widely and deeply felt. Also, developed societies can afford to ostracize the people who are dishonest, while in poor countries most people cannot afford such social sanctions. Money in developing countries represents not only wealth but power, influence, achievement and opportunity, and it is in the hands of a very small minority. It becomes very difficult in such circumstances for the moneyless majority to bite the hand that feeds it.

Reverting to the inadequacy, indeed the danger, of materialism, I believe the revival of religion, especially in the fundamentalist sense, is essentially a reaction to materialism. We see it here in the Philippines. It seems that societies need religion, a belief in an afterlife and the system of rewards and punishments that all religions impose. On the other hand, I look at history and I wonder what has happened to religion as it is practiced today. I wonder whether the Christ we worship here in the Philippines is the same Christ who originally preached the Sermon on the Mount. I see the other extreme in countries like the United States, where the individual has become the be-all and end-all, where you get a self-centeredness, an egoism that also has a shallow side. The shallow side of this kind of individualism is that it does not look beyond itself. It is limited to self-gratification.

We could all use a lot more idealism, more altruism, more concern for the next person, ultimately on a planetary basis. But if the individual does not have this idealism, altruism and concern for the next person, then the family won't have it, the society won't have it, the nation won't have it, and finally the planet won't have it. It has to start with the individual, at home, and spread out from there. I do, however, believe that, as a race, we are capable of it.

Spain

FACING THE FUNDAMENTAL ISSUES

Manuel Marquez Balin
Chairman and Managing Director
Standard Electrica S.A.

In the world of today's economic relationships, there are some fundamental issues which I believe are of the utmost importance and which apply not only to the domestic economy of countries but also to the increasingly interdependent economic relations among countries.

I am a private businessman and therefore, by definition, in favor of private enterprise. I am convinced that private enterprise equals efficiency, and efficiency equals the creation of wealth. At present, this combination is being threatened or, if I want to be more positive about it, challenged. This is dangerous because it is the basic ingredient for development and growth for everyone, every individual and every nation.

In meeting this challenge, it is vital that public opinion be educated to the legitimacy of profit and to its importance as a necessary resource for the growth and welfare of society in general. In this area private enterprise has clearly not done its job. It seems to have failed to adequately explain its mission, its contribution to mankind, what that contribution was, is and will be. As a result, voices are often heard criticizing private enterprise for being profitable in times of crisis. I see as positive, however, the fact that there seems to be a recognition of this problem and that brains are being mobilized to meet it.

Bigger Is Not Better

It is important, of course, for government to understand the role of the private sector and not interfere unnecessarily. If you cannot do the job better, don't aggrandize yourself by taking it over. We learned this in the private sector. There was a time when our importance was defined by the number of people we employed. Now it is almost the other way around, and technology, competitiveness and efficiency—more than ever—are the keys to success. Government should come to the same recognition.

Learning to Say Yes

Government is responsible for legislation. The fundamental issue there is that legislation should be clear and permissive. Governments generally have learned very well when to say no to private enterprise. They should now learn when to say yes and how to say yes. It is also important that legislation not be discriminatory. This applies to individuals within a nation and it applies to corporate entities both nationally and internationally. We live in a single world. There is extensive management, technology and know-how, and the important thing is to spread these more widely everywhere around the world, including to governments.

In facing fundamental issues, it is important to be aware of obstacles that have to be removed or overcome. Let me list a few. The first of the obstacles is that in the absence of these positive ingredients, not only is a vacuum created but actual obstructions are moved into place. There is a real need for industrial restructuring. Industrial countries have been growing into patterns that have to be revised in depth.

Take Spain, for example. It grew in the sixties and seventies at a computed rate of 6.5 percent of GNP, and moved into the ranks of the top ten industrial countries. Now there are new technologies, and demand patterns have changed. It is true that this restructuring could be left to the market. But it is a question not only of price but of time, and there is a trade-off between these two. The market could do it over the long haul, but in Spain there is a question whether that time exists politically. Whether, if the restructuring is left entirely to the market, it would not result in social unrest and possibly even in revolution. That price I would consider too high. Therefore, there might be a need for a degree of government intervention. The question then becomes: What degree? What is the desirable hybrid?

I believe that the balance is both delicate and changing, and requires continual fine-tuning. It also differs with every society. The mixture depends on culture, basic societal values, which phase of industrialization the country finds itself in, and which phase of economic development the country finds itself in. An element of judgment is unavoidable. I believe that government intervention *today*, in a measured controlled way, may be necessary to avoid government intervention of major magnitude and a more dramatic kind *tomorrow*.

Unemployment . . .

Let me cite just one example. Unemployment is a worldwide problem today. Even in the United States, which is the economy with probably the least government intervention extant at this time, there was a movement to bail out Chrysler with government guarantees. A totally market-oriented ideology would claim that companies should have the right to be born, to live and to die without interference by government. But this ideology could be attenuated when a larger social good is involved as, in the case of Chrysler, unemployment.

On the other hand, we should ask ourselves if the market rules are not broken too often by another kind of major intervention. I refer to the power of the unions, which in many countries is playing a substantial role, frequently more dedicated to political issues in support of one or another political party than to the professional defense of the economic and social interest of their associates.

. . . and Technology

It is clear that you cannot stop technology just as you cannot unscramble the proverbial egg. In my own sector, electronics and communications, there have been discussions with unions who wanted us to introduce technology gradually. If Spain were an island living independently of the rest of the world, this might be possible, if not necessarily desirable. But Spain is part of the world and our industry must be competitive and be able to export. To do that, technology is a priority that must be applied. You cannot control unemployment by controlling technology.

This dichotomy of unemployment versus new technologies is particularly apparent when we address the much-discussed problem of transfer of technology. Modern corporations are accused of not providing developing countries with the *latest* technology. On the other hand, they are also accused of not providing them with *appropriate* technology, that is, the one that is more adequate for their stage of industrial development and their real economic and social needs. Finally, they are accused at the same time of creating unemployment with the *advanced* technology they do transfer. Since these accusations are mutually contradictory, the real problem becomes how the mechanism of technology can best be operated. I believe the market has to be the instrument. LDCs must learn to choose. They must learn to decide what they really need. And they must address the problem—as must all of us—of bridging the gap that technology creates in human resources through a continuous training effort.

Retraining and Recycling

I do not know how much looking back at history and the two previous industrial revolutions really teaches us. When we look back, it is indeed true that each industrial revolution has created more jobs than existed before it happened. Whether this will be true again, I do not know. Therefore I worry about it. But I do know that we now must make an effort in education, and in retraining and recycling people. This leads to the terrible question of what can be done with people who cannot be recycled. Early retirement is one possibility. But that carries heavy social costs. The way things look now, I am not certain how much of these extra social costs we can afford. I think of these people as the passive segment of society, and society must find a way of taking care of that segment. I do not believe that, as a basic concept, a state-organized effort mobilizing the young to do civic jobs is a good idea. To me, these are precisely the people who need to be retrained to fit into the new technological society. They are young; one can catch them. They have minds that are educable, they can be molded. But perhaps the older people in what I call the passive segment of society could be moved into some of these jobs, particularly in the service area for social needs.

International Cooperation

It is a matter of scale, of course, but conceptually the problem of international cooperation is not very different from the problems of national adjustment. We need to be more oriented toward real cooperation, and less inclined toward interventionism. At present, whenever the developing countries are confronted with a problem, the answer seems to be: Let us create an international body to address the problem. This is true in technology transfer, in management, in education, in any problem you can name. Indeed, technology transfer, management and education are an important part of the answer. The question is whether international organizations are designed to solve the problem. It seems to me that the international bodies that do exist suffer from a lack of imagination. They are perhaps necessary; but if so, a lot more innovation and imagination is required in them and from them.

The Role of the Private Sector

What should be, indeed what can be, the role of private enterprise in this process? I see that role as what I would call "stimulated generosity." When private enterprises go into a developing country, both should agree on the need for a contractual relationship which goes beyond the base sales agreement to include elements of training, possibilities of further industrialization to make the product that is initially being sold, or at least make elements of it. In other words, a close cooperation in terms of mutual understanding and benefits for both in the future.I am convinced that cooperation can be successful only if it is mutually profitable. Economic success and economic reward are not a zero sum game. A deal is a genuinely good deal only if it is good for both parties.

Ideally it would be desirable, in international bodies as well as in international interactions, if there was no intervention from public organizations or public agencies. The best model is freedom. Realistically, I do not see that as 100 percent possible, not within nations and not among nations. Therefore I believe that, at present, it is desirable to accept a degree of government intervention at the national level and the international level, if this intervention addresses the problem of how to attract and reward the private sector. Harmonization of legislation would help. Unless and until that exists, free trade will not function well or completely because there will always be a permanent excuse to shackle trade and introduce protectionism. But I know that we will get there only by stages. It will be a gradual process.

My suggestion is that meanwhile countries be grouped not by regions, but by wealth and by other economic parameters; in other words, that national groupings be organized, using as a yardstick elements of their economic strength. One indication of that would be the answer to the question: Whom do I meet in the marketplace?

Multinational Corporations and State-Owned Enterprises

One of the entities we encounter—certainly I encounter—in the marketplace are state-owned enterprises. In the relationship between multinational corporations and state-owned enterprises, the important thing is nondiscrimination. Codes of conduct are a good idea, possibly as a beginning for the eventual harmonization of legislation that I've described earlier. But these codes must be as identical as possible for MNCs and SOEs. The notion that there is a difference which you can tell by the flag on the roof is absurd. Let us judge companies on the basis of what they do, not by the flag they fly. As an example, I would cite the issue of the availability of internal credit. I would argue that credit should be available to whatever company can use it productively. There should be no other criteria and no discrimination.

As far as I am concerned, SOEs are fine if they follow market roles. This also means the government cannot tell SOEs to be social models in their employment practices, their social services, or other aspects. If they become social models in this way, they will not be able to follow the market and will become noncompetitive. There is a role for SOEs also in the parts of the economy where the private sector is not interested or does not have the resources. An example in Spain is coal mining, which requires huge investments of the kind that are not available to the private sector, especially given the long payout period in that industry. In the sector of new energy sources, perhaps there is a role for SOEs in a complementary way, to serve as a check on the private sector or to prevent market domination. In advanced technology sectors, we run time and time again into situations where governments say to the multinational companies, "Come in; we need you," and when companies are established, government agencies come in to compete in unnecessary ways. The argument made is that communications are a strategic sector and cannot be entrusted to private enterprise, especially if the private enterprise is a multinational company. This is a very weak and largely meaningless argument in today's world, where proper utilization of technology becomes much more relevant than its "place of birth."

To sum up, I think SOEs should have no discriminatory privileges and MNCs should have no discriminatory obligations. There should be a code that would provide SOEs and MNCs with the same obligations, the same privileges, and no demagoguery to justify discrimination.

"CAPI-COMMUNISM"—THE SYSTEM OF THE FUTURE

Dr. Juan Miro Chavarria
Chairman
Rio Rodano S.A.

The most pressing problem at the moment is that the value of money and interest in the United States is dangerous for Europe and for much of the rest of the world. The rise in the price of the U.S. dollar means a rise in all prices and all other trust actions and credits worldwide. This is also true of the credits that productive enterprises need. In such a situation, governments have to enter the market to help enterprises survive. But this interferes with the market economy; it makes it less free. It creates problems for the future. It clearly already undermines, and might even finish, the EEC.

My fundamental long-range conviction is that over the decades there will be an approximation of capitalist and Communist systems and countries, in which one assumes some of the more desirable characteristics of the other, and vice versa. I believe that within a century we will get what I call "capi-communism." That is, capitalism will include within its system more social justice, and communism will include within its system more efficiency and more freedom.

At present, we have a situation in Western Europe, and indeed in the United States as well, in which governments of the right were changed to governments of the left, and governments of the left were changed to governments of the right. What this means is that people don't know what they want. They only know that they want change. One reason for this, at least in Europe, is that businesses go bad and unemployment is growing and is, in my opinion, a bomb under the table.

It is also true that as we rush around with measures to reduce the consumption of energy, we have, in effect, compensated for the increasing cost of energy by a decrease in consumption that has meant a decline in living standards. This is true for Eastern as well as Western Europe.

Even within the OPEC countries, only a very few have benefited from the energy price explosion. Look at Mexico, Nigeria, Iran, Iraq today. All of them are in economic trouble. None of them has solved any of their structural or social problems. The only ones that seem to have benefited in an absolute sense are Saudi Arabia and the Emirates, and no one knows just how long that is going to endure. Therefore, even the countries which are thought to be rich as a result of the energy upheaval are not really rich at all. The reason is that all the money they have made has created almost nothing because almost nothing has been invested in profitable productive enterprises.

A New Beginning

What I see at present is a world in economic trouble, with future living standards lowered in one way or another. In addition, if the world economy continues on its present trend, the gap between the industrialized countries and the LDCs will become bigger, and that is dangerous. I see, therefore, a need to forget the past and start with a new beginning. Let me illustrate: If you play marbles with me and I win all your marbles, and if I want to continue the game, I must give you back some marbles. This is what the United States did with the Marshall Plan at the end of World War II, when the Western European countries were in shambles and only the United States had any marbles to play with. They then gave some of them back to Europe with the very effective result we all know.

Now I believe the time may well have come—and I know this sounds extreme and radical—to cancel all outstanding debts. In 1929, when we had a comparable problem, we solved it finally with war production. With atomic warfare, this solution is no longer possible. Therefore we need either to forgive all debts or, more plausibly, to extend them to twenty- to fifty-year maturities with very low interest rates, which is a de facto forgiveness. This can be done only through an arrangement, an agreement, between the OECD countries. I know this does not, in and of itself, solve the problems of the developing world.

What I see is another epoch in which the countries that have worked, which is largely equivalent to the countries of the North, must help the countries that have not, which is largely equivalent to the countries of the South, with de facto debt forgiveness ranging over two to three decades.

Perhaps with some productive discipline enforced in the interim, most of the LDCs can catch up, but it will take at least that amount of time. As I see it, the big banks, especially the big international banks, are now overextended; they have lent too much to the developing countries. I see no solution to this except a radical change in the monetary system.

Creating Jobs

On the question of unemployment, which is troubling us all, the fundamental reason is that today you can make more money on money than you can on investment. Even the best run companies cannot make a profit of more than 10 to 12 percent return on investment (ROI), while a minimal bank rate is 15 percent. One answer is for the banks to acquire equity in companies, but in my experience, when banks interfere in company management, the companies do not run right. Spain is a classic example of this. The problem is that once the value of money rises, investment in productive enterprise becomes unattractive. Savings go into money funds instead of into equity. I am convinced that the solution to unemployment is for interest rates to come down to around 5 percent, with ROIs remaining in the 10–12 percent vicinity. Then we will get major investment in productive enterprises, which will solve the problem of unemployment.

At present, there are fundamentally two kinds of countries just as there are two kinds of enterprises. There are enterprises with a strong equity base, such as 70 percent equity to 30 percent debt; and there are enterprises where the ratio is the other way around. The same is true with countries. Companies and countries that have a 70–30 percent equity base today can earn enough money on the equity portion of their assets. If the proportion is the other way around, interest charges eat up all profits; there is in effect no ROI. On a country basis, this applies to most LDCs, but it applies also to Europe as a whole vis-à-vis the United States, mainly because the United

States has 70 percent of its own oil and Europe has little or none. I believe that a timely restructuring of world debt is more desirable than a moratorium worldwide or a panic and inevitable depression.

Structurally, I have seen a solution at work in post–World War II Germany under Chancellor Erhardt. Erhardt created a very small money supply and free prices. Within two years, Germany was back on its feet under this policy.

On the fundamental question of how to get the South to work, I believe that when Eastern and Western Europe come together in the rapprochement that I call capi-communism, they can together persuade the South to adopt the kind of policies that lead to economic growth. What is happening at present is that the rivalry between Eastern and Western Europe, in which I include the United States and Canada, results in the developing countries holding their hand out to either the West or the East and not feeling the pressing need to put themselves on their own feet. Given the opportunity to hold their hand out either to the right or to the left, the developing countries do not feel the fundamental compulsion to work in order to live.

LESS IS MORE

Rafael Termes-Carrero
President
Spanish Association of Private Banks

Less is more: one of the world's most famous architects said that half a century ago. I submit that the same holds true today in the architecture of society, by which I mean the laws and regulations, approaches and practices that shape the social structures of our lives in the Western democracies. Our values depend on freedom, and free enterprise is an integral part of freedom. Unfortunately, our society—by which I mean Western societies, even the liberal ones—has been moving increasingly toward intervention. I think the reason for this is that when people or societies grow old, they look for more security. They look for protection, and they look for protection from the state. This propels the state toward intervention.

The function of the state is to provide public order, defense, justice and social services. In the economic sphere, the function of the state is to work to ensure the existence of a well-functioning market, not to interfere with the market and its operations. We are all better off with less government. I concur with the conviction of many American leaders that the government governs best that governs least. All our societies here in Europe need less government, not more.

In recent times, I saw a similar trend toward intervention even in the United States, and it worried me. Even in the United States the mentality and attitudes seemed to be changing. America was, and to a large extent still is, a country of pioneers, of dynamism, of belief in the future. But recently people even in the United States seemed to be afraid of the future. Fortunately, there are signals that things may be changing again for the better.

Perception

How can such change be achieved? First, we must change the social perception of the role of the entrepreneur. There is an attitude, now almost universal, that making money is bad. It used to be respectable to make money. Now people try to hide it when they do.

And the young want security: they want to be functionaries. The question is, again, Why? One reason is that, in the thinking of the young, their parents have become villains. As far as the young are concerned, we have given them a tired society without any initiative, without any challenge.

Education

Change has to start with education. Education has to teach that freedom is an individual concept; it has political, social and economic ingredients that are interdependent. Now youngsters are taught in school that being rich is bad, and there is a myth that profit is bad and entrepreneurs are villains. What we should be teaching instead is that men are not cheap. They are individuals. They need individual challenges, and only freedom provides these kinds of individual challenges.

Political Action

Having taught this fundamental orientation, entrepreneurship has to be backed by political action, political action in which private enterprise is encouraged for the good of society. Private enterprise is good for society because it is more efficient. The cause of this is clear. The goal of private enterprise is profit, while the goal of public enterprise is service. Profit provides a yardstick for measurement of competence and efficiency. Public service provides service without any cost consideration. Corruption creeps into the public sector when a functionary has the power to hand out licenses, for example, or issue permits for the action of private enterprise. This kind of power, with little or no accountability, prepares the ground for corruption. Where there is less public sector intervention, there is less chance for corruption.

State-Owned Enterprises

This trend of thought leads directly to an assessment of state-owned enterprises and their appropriate role. I think SOEs should exist only in areas where the private sector cannot or will not operate. Here is an example of where they should *not* exist: In Spain we have a public sector that produces aluminum. This is an economic absurdity. We do not have bauxite in Spain and we do not have cheap energy. There is no comparative advantage in producing aluminum in Spain, which is why the private sector has not done so. The reason given by the public sector for doing it was to provide jobs. The enterprise is, of course, an economic fiasco.

Multinational Corporations

As to multinational corporations, I think they are a fine institution. The role of the state vis-à-vis them should be to safeguard the free market. That is, if multinational corporations interfere with the free market, the state has to act. Otherwise they should be allowed to function with all the efficiencies and advantages they have, by which I mean their economies of scale and a global market in which they know how to operate. Specifically, if a multinational company does a job better than a national company, it should be allowed to operate freely in a competitive marketplace.

Competition

My answer to the critics of the capitalist system is that whatever is wrong with the system has been caused because the system has not been allowed to function, has not been allowed to fulfill its potential. And I believe that potential is best stimulated by competition.

The Social Responsibility of Corporations

Companies do have a social responsibility. It has two aspects. One is the company's responsibility to its international constituencies, the other is its responsibility to its external constituencies. Among the former I count stockholders, employees and management. A company has to give to each of these what they expect, to the maximum extent possible. That means dividends to stockholders, salaries to employees, and appropriate compensation to management. But the company can do this only if it creates wealth. That is its nature and main social responsibility. If it is saddled with too many other social activities and asked to provide too many other social benefits, it may not be able to meet its basic objectives. I repeat, its basic objective is to create wealth. The job of management is to balance the legitimate requirements of the company's internal constituencies.

A company also has external constituencies. These are its suppliers and its customers. In a bank, for example, the suppliers are depositors. A bank's job is not only to give these depositors their proper reward, but also to create an institution that is safe and sound, on which these depositors can depend for the long haul.

There are, of course, broader social requirements as well. Attention to ecology is one of them. I think of these not so much as responsibilities, but as constraints that must be honored.

The Question of Population

In the context of broader social concerns, I would like to offer some thoughts on the much-discussed question of population. The world has teetered toward a negative attitude on the subject of population. Fundamentally, I believe that reproduction is a matter of individual freedom and that countries can pursue policies that make for more growth, or policies that make for less growth, in which this individual freedom is exercised. In my view, the most advisable policies are those that favor growth in order to prevent the aging of population. In fact, Europe cannot replace its present generation, with the result that the population is aging. This process of aging is what has caused the old countries of Europe to become pessimistic. This, in turn, produces an ever greater burden for the young and more need for state intervention.

Personally, I believe that the young are an investment. What I see happening is that in societies where, from an economic point of view, the population battle is not necessary, it is being fought. In developing countries, the claim is that there are not enough resources. But the image that comes to my mind is if, say, you have a dance and sixteen boys have arrived but only ten girls, there are two solutions. You can either send away some of the boys or invite more girls. I am in favor of the second solution. I think there are enough resources in the world. The real problem is to find ways to use them. Overall, the reasonable solution is to move toward policies that produce a younger population rather than an older population worldwide, and then learn how to manage the planet's resources.

Managing Money: A Matter of Information

Learning to manage resources includes the management of money. I believe that the main problem of the international financial system is a matter of information. Take Mexico, for example, and its problems. We all thought that Mexico was a better risk, a better investment than Brazil. It had oil. It had a sound political system. But we had no information on its debt structure, particularly its short-term debt structure and the terms of those debts. By we, in this case, I mean the lenders.

As the international financial system operates today, the only organization that has this kind of information is the IMF. For political reasons, the IMF cannot make this information available to others, including commercial banks who make loans to these countries. Obviously, the IMF and the World Bank cannot make this kind of information available publicly. It has to be handled with great sensitivity. But I believe it would be a good idea if the IMF set up a kind of early warning system that would alert concerned parties. In Spain, we have in the central bank a Risk Information Center that knows what the credit exposure is of all companies in Spain, private or public. That Center cannot publish its information. But if someone in the banking system with a legitimate interest asks, the central bank does give out the information. I would like to see a comparable system, on a global basis, established by the IMF.

The conventional wisdom, at present, is that the major problem of the financial system is high interest rates. I don't believe this is correct. I believe that the basic problem is inflation, and high interest rates are the result of inflation, not the other way around. The answer, therefore, is that we have to fight inflation. The U.S. policy as it was pursued may have been painful, but it was necessary, and it has certainly produced the desired results.

A Free Marketplace of Ideas

Finally, I would like to note that it is true that our planet is now a small society and, like all small societies, it needs tolerance. We do want to have a plurality of ideas, but it is also logical, normal and good for people to defend their ideas, and even to defend them with passion. This is true of ideas in the religious realm, in the political realm, in the economic realm, even in the arts and in sports. The key is that this defense, however passionate, must be exercised with respect for the liberty of others. I believe it is vital for individuals to adhere to a principle; it is equally vital for them to respect the freedom of others not to adhere to the same principle.

We need not only a free market in the economic realm but also a free marketplace of ideas. There should be no pressure, no fear, no violence. Nothing constructive is ever achieved through violence. On a small planet, where human beings live with all their genius, with all their inspirations, with all their ideas and convictions, there should be freedom for the expression and development of all these. But however strongly and passionately a belief is held, in any aspect of life, the limits must be that others be free not to believe the same thing. Neither truth nor right is achieved by violence or compulsion.

Turkey

FREE ENTERPRISE: VALUES THAT WORK

Fuat Süren
Chairman
Transtürk Holding AS

Assessing free enterprise today, its validity and viability, I believe it is vital to look at the values that constitute its foundation and its framework. To do this, it is useful to approach the process with a historical perspective. In all societies, including the societies that now function as free enterprise systems, the first sociopolitical system was the reign of the priests, when rule was essentially based on metaphysical values. The next system was the government of kings, when rule was exercised by men who had armies and who could and did use these armies to pursue political and economic goals. The third system is the reign of the merchants, of which the free enterprise system is the apogee.

Each of the three systems has advantages and disadvantages, good points and bad. That includes the free enterprise system. Therefore, as with the two alternative systems, we have to ask the question: Will our free enterprise system last?

I believe that it will last only as long as the values that underlie and surround it make sense and are sustaining for society overall and for individuals within the society.

The problem with this is that free enterprise can only be based on moral values that cannot be explained by the free enterprise system itself but have their roots in a culture or a value system that is both broader and deeper. One reason why the young who live in free enterprise systems seems so disoriented today is that they see no values within the free enterprise system and have no outside moral structures to sustain them.

At the operational level, the free enterprise system, which needs and has fewer external controls than, for example, a centrally planned socialist system, inevitably evolves more internal controls. This is probably both necessary and desirable, but it does result in a build-up of internal bureaucracies and an accumulation of red tape that makes it difficult to reach decisions. I see this happening in multinational corporations today. They are losing, in many cases have lost, the spirit of enterprise. Multinational corporations today seem to concentrate on trying not to take risks, on establishing pervasive controls that often obfuscate and obstruct the decision-making process rather than facilitate it. They operate by using the funds at their disposal; but because of the bureaucracies they have built up, these funds are not used in a truly efficient way.

I see very little difference from that point of view between the way large private sector companies operate and the manner in which state-operated enterprises work, at least in the industrialized countries. I look, for example, at Renault, which is a state-operated enterprise, and at Ford, which is a private company, both in the automotive sector, and I cannot detect much difference between them. Both throw their weight around, primarily using their financial clout. Neither of them is truly innovative anymore, and both subdue and even subvert, rather than encourage, innovation. I make these observations not because I am against free enterprise, but because I am committed to it and believe that a critical appraisal of it is important and, I hope, useful.

It is true that if we look at the world from a purely physical viewpoint, we live on a small planet. But if we look at it in human terms, it is a very large planet, and people living on it are separated not just by national boundaries but, I believe even more fundamentally, by incomes. The lives of people who earn $200 a year and those who earn $20,000 differ not just in quantity but in quality. What is the value system that can deal with this reality?

Looking at the planet today, I see three major problems facing mankind: population, pollution, energy. My contention is that free enterprise can claim viability and validity only if it can devise successful, or at least workable, solutions to these three problems.

In solving problems within the free enterprise system, entrepreneurship is vital. One of the major bottlenecks I see in the developing countries—indeed, it is what makes them developing rather than developed countries—is that there are not enough entrepreneurs. On the other hand, multinational corporations which could fill that gap, at least on a temporary basis, have become too cautious. The result is political, social and economic tension that is further exacerbated by armament spending in both the industrialized and the developing world.

Having sketched the problems, let me assess some solutions.

On the microeconomic plane, I believe it is essential to find and allocate more funds to the developing countries, not on a charity basis, however formulated or disguised, but for innovative, productive undertakings. What the developing countries need, desperately and urgently, is venture capital in the true sense of that word, that is, capital willing and able to take risks—unlike the kind of enterprise MBA students at Harvard are taught to look for. Harvard and other famous business schools essentially teach their students how to avoid risk. This is not only wrongheaded but fundamentally counterproductive, since the very basis of a free enterprise system is risk-taking.

Despite the business schools, however, risk-taking seems to be alive and well in the United States; but Europe is hopeless, and the developing countries are more hopeless still. Concretely, therefore, we need to devise a system and a mechanism to promote risk-taking and raise venture capital, particularly for the developing world. Existing international institutions that address the economic and financial needs of the Third World, such as the World Bank and the IMF, are not good at this. This is not a criticism. These institutions fulfill a very important role; they give international depth to the global economic and financial system. But what we need are institutions specifically dedicated to the creation of wealth and income through risk-taking, institutions prepared to put up 100 percent of the capital needed by young entrepreneurs with good ideas or sound small projects.

The macro issue I see as most important is political and moral rather than economic. It is true that we have arrived at a crossroads where we have to pursue the hard options. The politicians we have in the world today have neither the stature nor the stamina to make these hard choices. If we do not find statesmen with character and vision to replace politicians who bend with the wind, we are heading for a very dangerous world.

Another fact that troubles me is that, as I look around me, I see a world in which people want to live life on credit. They want to consume before they contribute. And that is simply not possible.

We need a new moral system, or perhaps the creation of a new culture with values that explain man to man. We have an enormous amount of information at our disposal, but we do not have a working system to turn the information into knowledge. We must create a culture that systemically turns the plethora of information that surrounds us into knowledge that human beings can understand, deal with and live with.

This culture, and this knowledge, must be built on the fact that, for the first time in human history, we have to accept the reality that there is no afterlife, that here and now is all we have. We must come to terms with that.

In our bazaars here in Turkey, there are men who sell beads, or coffee, or a hundred other things; and there are men who tell stories. The men who tell stories have as many customers as the men who sell things. In one way or another, this has always been so. Mythology sustained our ancestors, and tales that fit the realities of our time are needed today. We need new storytellers, and the story they tell must be a strong one that speaks to all of humanity on the planet.

One ingredient in that story must be the moral imperative of human beings not taking advantage of each other. The story must illustrate how true cooperation can be achieved in a world of great variety, a world in which freedom is defined not only as freedom of expression but as freedom from being pushed around by others.

There is an economic aspect to this. To make possible a decentralized world, adjusted to human diversity, what is needed economically are efficient, small organizations. This is within our reach because new technology does make possible efficiency in smallness.

As a matter of organization within large undertakings, indeed within all economic enterprises, I believe it is important for the spirit of free enterprise to move up from the balance sheet to the human aspect. This means eliciting maximum participation from every member of the undertaking, bottom up as well as top down. It also means providing recognition, and reward for achievement, at all levels. In business, we must recognize that what makes any organization work is finally not causes, goals or systems, but people.

Therefore, the fundamental strategy and, I am convinced, the secret of success, is caring for people. No miracle or method can replace such human attributes as hard work, honesty and dedication. What the young need to learn is the joy of work, the fact that nothing is more fun than creation, and nothing provides more satisfaction than accomplishment. I know that I get more satisfaction from looking at what I have built in my life, and the people with whom I have built it, than I do from considering the dividends I have created. In the creation of wealth, it is, finally, the human dividend that matters most.

United Kingdom

SOLVING THE UNEMPLOYMENT CRISIS

Neville Cooper
Executive Director
Standard Telephones and Cables PLC
Chairman
The Top Management Partnership

To offer constructive solutions to the unemployment crisis, which seems to be haunting not only the United Kingdom but all of Europe, three questions need to be addressed:

Is the problem meant to be solved?

If so, how?

And what part should we, managers in the private sector, play?

To the first question, Is the problem meant to be solved?, I would reply decisively, Yes. Since work gives men dignity and satisfaction, since it is essential if human needs are to be met and society is to advance, and since it offers us the role of fellow workers in the process of creation, I cannot believe that it is part of the design of the universe that men should not have full employment for their hands, hearts and brains. I think this concept is important—otherwise we can rest too inactive, learn too easily to accept other people's lack of work, accept too readily clever definitions of employment in order to talk away the problem or persuade ourselves that work is not so great anyhow. The fact that we shall always fall short of the ideal of full-time employment for everyone need not deflect us. Good marksmen aim for the bull's-eye and expect to hit near it. I equate work and employment, and define them as producing value, giving the workman a reward, and imposing their own discipline, in that we sometimes have to do work when we don't feel like it. How it is organized and rewarded is an important but secondary question.

How will the solution to the current employment problem come about? The answer is complex, and we must first attempt to define the problem and its causes. What we mostly think about and quote statistics about is unemployment in the developed, industrialized countries. (Many Third World countries would dearly like to live with our unemployment figures.) Some contributing factors to the problem are: oil price rises; the recessionary cycle; production transferring to LDCs; new entrants to the workforce; the use of technology; and attitudes to work and change.

Causes of the Crisis

Obviously, the sudden oil price rises sucked in wealth to OPEC and other countries faster than it could be recycled to work-producing investment. Many governments borrowed to the hilt to maintain purchasing power, but this only postponed the effects. Clearly, we should aim for relationships which avoid sudden changes in future. OPEC is still too often the missing factor in discussions of North–South or of Japan–Europe–America problems. Nevertheless, even if we get these relationships right they clearly will not solve the whole problem.

The same is true of the recessionary cycle. No one expects unemployment figures to drop automatically to previous levels when we come out of the recession, and the long-term trend of increasing unemployment is independent of trade cycles.

As for the developing world making cars, textiles and so

on, what on earth did we expect them to do? We talked enough about helping those poor countries, but when they take obvious steps to help themselves we declare it to create an insufferable problem for us. If we are engaged in industries suffering because of the competition of less developed countries, we were lazy and stupid in not seeing the trends twenty years ago and maintaining our "margin of sophistication" by selling more advanced products or adding value in design or quality. This is elementary economics. At all events, since we cannot turn back the clock, this is a problem we must face rather than evade.

It is a fact that in many of our countries there are more jobs than ever before, and the increase in unemployed roughly equates to the number of married women who have entered the labor force. I am not going to spend time on this—nor do I draw a simplistic moral from it. The choice to do paid work or not is desirable, given that family responsibilities are being properly met. I would say, however, that among all the talk about the value of women's work, I wish we heard more about the value of love and care and family management, and I am conservative enough to think that talk about the desirability of men minding babies while women go out to work is trendy rubbish. At all events, we cannot deny people the right to enter the labor force although, with all the talk about work-sharing, we should recognize that earlier generations had their own methods of sharing it.

So, then, we come to new technology, which is too often blamed for the problem. My thesis is that the problem lies in our use of it, not in its development, which is as inevitable as the growth of an oak tree from an acorn. At the turn of the century, 30 percent of the labor force in this country was engaged in agriculture. New technology—notably the internal combustion engine—has reduced this to 3 percent, and they produce ten times as much. But did 27 percent of them become unemployed? No—largely because so many were employed in the new industries that developed because of the internal combustion engine.

Recent studies in Holland and Britain confirm that new technology can produce as many jobs as it destroys. Used as a manufacturing process, it reduces employment on new products. But used as a means to make entirely new products, it creates many jobs. The balance is fine—just as the unemployment totals in the United Kingdom are the difference between large numbers leaving and entering employment—of whom the majority are out of work for six months or less.

It has been said that we face greater change than previous generations. On the contrary, I believe we are more protected and prone to resist change than previous generations. People used to change jobs and move long distances to get work in new industries. For too long in recent times we have encouraged the belief that the government or someone else could meet a demand for us to stay put, change little, and have our old kind of work retained for us. Management and labor have both had their share of these reactionary attitudes.

Finding Solutions

Having identified some of the causes of the problem, we should address the question of how the solution may be found. It will clearly not come merely by organizing and by conscious action, although these are vitally necessary. Other factors are involved: people's values, their relationships, the spark of creativity which can be kindled or quenched in millions of hearts and which can lead to unexpected changes and initiatives.

Our Contribution

And so to our third question. What is our part? As always, I suggest it is to try to discern what is our Maker's design for development, and cooperate with it. We must take strenuous actions where it is appropriate and sensible. We must be concerned with the nonmaterial factors, which can be vital. Finally, we must recognize our relative ignorance and be ready to discern new trends and influences when they arise apparently spontaneously.

But what about the main issue? We know what we mean by work and employment. Can they be available to everyone? What is certain is that tomorrow's work will be concerned with tomorrow's products and services, and in that respect we are notoriously shortsighted. In the latter part of the nineteenth century there was a proposal that the British Patent Office should be shut down since it was clear that everything which could be invented had been invented. This was just before the development of electrical engineering and the internal combustion engine!

However, progress continued despite the Patent Office, and in due course an internal combustion engine was developed and harnessed to a carriage. There was therefore a law that a man with a red flag should walk in front of the vehicle so that its progress should not be dangerously fast. Maybe that was a good idea—but, unfortunately, if you had done that with the airplane, it would never have gotten off the ground. Some people might have it like that. It is said that in the early days of flying, an elderly lady opposed it on the grounds that "If the good Lord had meant us to fly in airplanes, why would he have given us railway trains?"

Before we laugh at her too much, we might reflect on the fact that there is a general tendency to think of our Creator as being mainly concerned with trees and lakes and nice "natural" things or, at best, low technology, whereas machines and skyscrapers and high technology are man's affairs. I believe, however, that we will only see the issues straight when we see Him as the Creator of the whole real and potential world—of nature, yes, but also of computers and electronics and an infinity of future developments which our minds cannot yet imagine and will never fully comprehend. Since progress is programmed into the universe, surely it is not sensible to try to hold it back, but rather to cooperate with it and to accept the challenge of developing the values and lifestyle that will enable us to live with it and channel it properly.

Resistance to change is like clinging to a sinking ship. It makes disaster certain. Reluctant acceptance is like sitting around in a raft hoping that something will happen. It is risky, and may only postpone disaster. Positive acceptance means striking out strongly for the shore and a new and unknown world, where there is work in plenty which needs to be done. In what is basically a benign universe, that shore has always been there, in the history of evolution and in the history of man.

What We Do at Standard Telephones and Cables

Since life is a whole, blended from belief and practice, let me now come right down to earth and explore some of the practical consequences of such a positive approach. In my own company, which employs some thirty thousand in the United Kingdom, we have a policy that we will continue to employ at least the same number of people during the next decade. We believe that this fulfills a social duty, and also makes sense, if we are to preserve the value of our management efforts as a proportion of the total economy. It will require a doubling of our sales in some four years, and a quadrupling in about eight years—and this will take a lot of planning and hard work.

Some people say, "But it's easy for you because yours are modern products in growing markets." This, however, misses the two main points. First, the effect of new technology is, for us, as for everyone else, to destroy jobs creating today's products. Indeed, a spokesman for one company somewhat similar to ours predicted that they will reduce employment from thirty thousand to ten thousand over the decade. This is the trend we intend to combat.

The second point is that we do not just soldier on making tomorrow what we made yesterday. Out of our annual sales of some £1 billion, two-thirds comes from products which have only been developed within the past five years. We constantly have to phase out products. This can be profitable when it is well planned, and should lead to a recovery of capital for reinvestment in relevant products.

I quote my own company not in the belief that we have all the answers. I am simply pointing out that, as a company facing typical problems of rapidly changing markets, competition and technology, we think it is entirely reasonable (1) that we should not accept a decline in profitable employment, and (2) that it will take all our efforts and energy to achieve this.

Life Moves On

Personally, I think that a back-to-nature, let's-slow-things-down philosophy is contrary to Christian faith. In the beginning, our tradition has it that man's task was to work in a garden. Later, tradition saw the task as taking part in the building of a city and of a kingdom. Life moves on, and the challenge is to change, to meet new global goals. Today, we might describe the task as the development of a new society. Communications will play a key part in this, for what men create together far surpasses what they do separately.

We can surely face the future with confidence and hope

provided we meet the preconditions. For I believe that the world is designed to work, even with imperfect people, provided they know their imperfections, realize their need of each other and genuinely seek truth and wisdom. In this process we will certainly make mistakes, but if we are quick to recognize them and change, we stand a good chance of making progress. For does not the whole mechanism of evolution and of human progress consist very largely of trial and error, feedback and learning, in achieving predetermined aims?

Information, Responsibility, Commitment

This has a significant bearing, I believe, on the solution of world problems, including the problems of employment. If truth emerges from trial and error, we must surely be prepared to share information and let other people make mistakes, rather than decreeing what is good for them and then trying to sell it, or impose it. I do not believe in a world in which a group of good and wise people decide what is good for everyone else—even if you could find such good and wise people. Nor do I believe that the developed nations know what is right and what products the less developed countries ought to need and want. Information, responsibility and commitment need to be shared.

Let me illustrate this principle with an example which also confirms to me that what is morally right and what is commercially wise can coincide—if we use all our intelligence and energy to achieve it. We have a plant in a small town in Northern Ireland where we realized that the product would be obsolete in about three years' time. We believe in being open and honest with employees, so the question arose: Should we tell them? It was tempting to keep the information to ourselves for a bit, in case of demonstrations or sit-ins or other negative reactions. However, we saw clearly that we must be honest, and that we must communicate the facts fully and intelligently.

To cut a long story short, our employees came up with the idea that, if we could not keep the plant open, they might offer it, and themselves, to other employers. They made approaches to companies throughout the world. Of course, during this period productivity was high and there were no unnecessary stoppages, because they wanted to demonstrate, as was true, what a fine investment they were for a new employer. I doubted they would succeed. You can imagine our delight, therefore, when it was announced that one other company had taken on about a third of the workforce, and another employer planned to offer further jobs which would take the total to more than we had employed. Incidentally, the additional work will be making garments, not electronic products—and I have no doubt that the employees will do it very well. For turning our hand to new things is essential if we want to go on being employed.

Thus, by sharing information and dealing with it positively together, a solution was found which we, as management, would not have found on our own. I am not advocating less management leadership but, rather, more leadership in tapping the creativity of people. We are not limited by resources. The Club of Rome was wrong—for the unlimited resource is the imagination and energy and creative spirit in man which, if given free rein, can find the way forward.

Clear Goals

I suppose we will only pursue the right answers with all our energy if we are clear on our goals. Some trends need to change. It is hard, for example, to have enthusiasm about a society devoted to the pursuit of selfish pleasure while the old and handicapped are pushed out of the family, and children left without the parental love and care they need. But can we not vigorously pursue the ideal of work for all, a good life for all, right relationships between people and the right development of society? This may help to determine some of the needs for work to sustain such a program.

Three Prerequisites

Summarizing, then, what are some of the ingredients of an answer? I suggest the following:

First, a clear picture of the sort of society we want.

Second, flexibility. The chairman of our company some years ago defined the highest skill as the ability to learn a new skill. We found that this faculty can be developed to a high degree, and no one is really short of it. It is our expectations of people that may need most to change. Any restrictions on people's ability to train and retrain at any age—and to have these skills recognized and accepted—are antisocial and reactionary.

Next, changes in attitudes to the economy. Those who believe passionately in competition will have to accept also the need for cooperation and planning. Those who hate private profit will have to reconsider, if the price of their prejudice is that millions are denied the jobs that might be created.

We must be ready to learn from experience and to apply the lessons fast and effectively. A recent study in the United States showed that, of several million jobs created over a period of two to three years, two-thirds were created by firms with less than fifty workers, and three-quarters by companies which had been in existence for less than five years. The measures so far taken by governments to encourage new and small enterprises are creditable but should, I believe, be greatly widened and extended. So also should measures to encourage investment by millions of people in their own and other companies. What better way of participating than having a stake? It seems to me that, too often, a mean-minded attitude comes with the legislation, which aims to ensure that such schemes shall not be too successful and that no one will get too rich.

Incidentally, why aren't we debating in the EEC a range of such wealth-creating, job-creating ideas rather than a tired series of rearguard actions against proposals to shift power or share misery, which are unlikely to butter any bread or create jobs? We must, at the same time, avoid the simplistic, false-alternative argument that new small businesses will be the solution or that they will not be the solution. Large industries also have a major part to play, both in subcontracting and in taking over small new enterprises when the time is ripe, in order to invest capital and management skills for the next stages of growth.

New Attitudes

We also need new attitudes to work and a new commonsense about pay. Many schemes for creating jobs are destroyed not by technology but by people's attitudes. When we offered, some two years ago, to cooperate with the British government's Youth Opportunity Scheme, we went through a good deal of discussion with the appropriate departments, only to be told at the end that there was not a single unemployed youngster in London who would be available or willing to take one of the places in our head office. I wondered whether this was because it was easier to dole out money than to fix people up with jobs. However, a group of career officers told us that one of the problems was that some parents told their children not to be fools—they would get very little more from being paid on the Youth Opportunity Scheme than they would by being unemployed. We did not accept these negative attitudes, but persisted and found some excellent youngsters. However, insofar as there was truth in the allegations, we need to change both the attitudes and money differentials in the direction of commonsense and realism.

The Moral Dimension

There is, of course, an important moral dimension to all this. I believe that a rightly concerned free enterprise system can meet the world's needs, whereas the control of a central bureaucracy can never do so. I also think that those who believe in such a system should be missionaries for it. But it is not just intellectual correctness that will win the day. The acceptance of ideas often depends on the quality of those who speak in their name. In this connection, there can be no condoning of city scandals or of dubious management practices. To condemn them utterly and to act to stamp them out is not an admission of the failings of free enterprise; it is a declaration that such practices are alien to such a system. The fact that governments, unions and others can be equally guilty is irrelevant. With clean hands we can work better. At the same time it must be made clear that we care deeply about people in our own and other countries. It is not just a question of PR. To be trusted, it is necessary to be trustworthy. To be seen to care, it is necessary to care.

Two Practical Propositions

I will end with two practical ideas—one at the micro and one at the macro level. It is often said that it will cost untold billions to create all the work places that are needed. But this sits uneasily with the assertion that there will be a diminishing proportion of traditional, manufacturing-type jobs, the assertion that so much wealth can be created by robots that we need to share out all the leisure, and the observable fact that there is a considerable shortage of people able and willing to clean windows, help old people, do simple maintenance work and a whole range of services that are not capital-intensive. Indeed, although we must applaud youth training schemes, it would be a pity if we found ourselves training youngsters for jobs that were not available. Training for higher skills is necessary, and it is a function of a healthy, vigorous economy. But training for simpler skills also has its place.

One of the encouraging experiences I heard of recently was a small private venture to give youngsters simple skills quickly—and then go out and negotiate jobs for them. In one town there were jobs which needed doing, including some nonspecialist repair work on the town clock, but the local council said it could not afford to pay for them. So the promoters of this scheme approached the citizens directly and managed to raise the money to get these additional jobs done by youngsters given the necessary minimum training. With concern and commitment on the part of such public-spirited entrepreneurs, who use unemployed or retired people to do simple training, we might bridge much of the gap between jobs crying out to be done and people who are unemployed. It would also be more self-respecting if people were required to do work in exchange for getting money, and this must surely commend itself to government and ordinary people alike.

A Marshall Plan in the LDCs

I suspect however that, despite all these necessary measures, we shall not, through them alone, achieve an adequate answer to this problem.

We need new, large and imaginative initiatives. I would like to give one example. At a conference of which I was a sponsor a few years ago, Professor Nakajima of the Mitsubishi Research Institute of Japan suggested the setting up of a global infrastructure program like an updated and enlarged Marshall Plan. He proposed that the developed industrial nations of Japan, Europe and the United States should undertake cooperative work in the developing world on projects that would have real value. They would include a second Panama Canal, the greening of deserts, hydroelectric schemes, and the like—all major projects which would cross national frontiers and which the nations concerned could not undertake for themselves. The benefits would include local jobs, work for the developed nations, the creation of wealth, and the fact that Europe, America and Japan would be working together to raise living standards and open up new markets rather than quarreling over limited existing markets in the developed world.

I confess that I originally thought the idea rather idealistic, and questioned how the capital could be raised. But when I see the billions our banks have been able to pour into bankrupt countries with no obvious benefit in cash-creating hardware, I think, on the contrary, that the professor was a realist. Surely we should be prepared to consider global action as masters, not victims, of the economy.

You realize that I am not talking about doing something for people in the less developed world, but something with them for our mutual benefit, which will demand change from all of us, developed and less developed alike. We need to consider, for example, the massive armaments bills, not just of the superpowers but of less developed countries. We must consider whether Western lenders have not exercised inadequate control of the purposes for which money is borrowed. We must deal with waste and inefficiency brought about by corruption, for which both bribers and extorters must share the blame. The prescription must include change for everyone.

The Challenge

We shall not make the necessary changes without conviction, determination, passion and sacrifice. The relevance of our faith is surely central. It should be a guide to desirable ends and to the means that will shape them. In addition, it should provide the impetus, the spur to action and the creative spirit which are needed. The existence of a global problem challenges us to find adequate answers. It is a challenge that can, and should, take all our skills, all our capacity for work. I suggest we accept it.

THE "SWISS ARMY" COMPANY

John Henry Harvey-Jones
Chairman
Imperial Chemical Industries

The most exciting perspective I see for the future is the opportunity for change in the way business is done that is provided by the new technology at our disposal. Specifically, I see the possibility, indeed the likelihood, of what I think of as a "Swiss Army" type of company. This applies to any size company, including large multinationals. They will have only a very small core of full-time professionals, while the rest of the work is done by people who are essentially self-employed and who make their contributions in their own time, in their own way, by using computers to communicate.

My main worry is not so much that human productivity cannot be improved, because I believe it can, but the disaster of capital productivity being limited by a shortage of capital. The amount of capital needed for each production unit is getting greater and there seems to be no way of stopping it. Plants are increasingly more complex. There are environmental requirements that cannot and should not be ignored, and all of that adds up to an increasing need for capital.

At Imperial Chemical Industries (ICI), we are concentrating on attacking this problem. We are doing it by working on plants that are small but cost-competitive, by which I mean, for example, plants that do not turn out 500,000 tons of a chemical, but 50,000 tons, and achieve their competitiveness by advanced technology and by being closer to the customers. This has social as well as commercial advantages, because closer local relationships are established. The product, the relationship to the market, the relationship to the community, indeed the size of the enterprise itself, all suddenly assume more human, more manageable and nevertheless cost-competitive dimensions.

There are additional advantages to this network of small plants. They are less vulnerable to disruptions through technical failure or through human intervention, which can range anywhere from strikes to terrorism. This makes the enterprise more flexible in every way and, since it is on a smaller scale, makes the investment risk comparatively smaller.

A New Management Philosophy

Another advantage is that we can make investments every year somewhere around the world, instead of having to do long-range strategic planning and making a mammoth investment only every ten years, which we then try to make as safe as possible. This approach is possible with available technology. What it does take is a new engineering and management philosophy.

I believe also that the new possibilities in automation—i.e., robotics and allied technologies—can, and indeed should, be used not to create larger assembly lines, which are mind-deadening, but to create greater flexibility. Since robotics can be constantly reprogrammed, it can be used to make a greater variety of products and require a greater variety of tasks from human beings.

The Humanization of Free Enterprise

As for free enterprise, I believe its most important task now is to make itself more human. Humanization of free enterprise would prevent its collapse and make it possible for free enterprise to seize and exploit and explore the opportunities that are presented to it by the world.

From a management perspective, this then poses the question of how one gets greater entrepreneurship by individuals. It is, I suspect, primarily a matter of education, but I believe people work best when they are self-motivated, when they are self-standing, in every sense of that word. This means that there is high risk and a high reward. From that point of view we are all entrepreneurs, knowing very well that finally no one can look after us except ourselves. Indeed, one of the problems that troubles me about large enterprises is that they reduce this spirit of self-entrepreneurship and tend to breed people to become dependent. In my concept of a Swiss Army corporation, this would not occur. The corporate core would provide a basically stimulating and rewarding center, but the real motivation would come from individuals who are self-motivated on an independent basis. On that level, too, it becomes very clear that if you are not socially motivated, you are dead. If you do not look after others, they will not look after you, and society becomes impossible.

As to the social responsibility of large enterprises, I am convinced that unless business meets human needs, the human needs within the business enterprise itself, it will fail. The argument is sometimes produced that, in the short term, taking care of human needs within the organization will not produce results for the ultimate profit line. I believe that even this is not so. Most human beings, most employees in large companies particularly, produce in fact between 30 to 40 percent of their potential. If their human needs were met more imaginatively, more completely, they would respond to this care with more self-motivation and more creativity. We would increase their productivity from the current 30–40 to 50 percent. If you had a superb leadership, you would probably get it up to 55 percent. Once an individual's basic material needs are met, and even when they are not met, there are fundamental human needs which are really very simple. Human beings want to be valued, want to be loved, and want to be held responsible, but they want responsibility asked for, not demanded. The fact is that we live in a world of increasingly intelligent, educated people who want to live full, responsible lives. I believe the best business strategy is to key into that motivation.

We are also faced with the fact that, at least in the industrial world, the young did not grow up with extremes of wealth and poverty, did not grow up with any material deprivation. They therefore see no need for these extremes and, I believe, will not tolerate them. For the young, our achievements so far are not enough. Understandably, they want to do more.

The young seem to be aware of the fact that there is now gross overcapacity for production and for material consumption in the industrial countries, while in the places to which they back-pack they see that a plastic ballpoint pen or an empty can of paint is wealth beyond the imagination of Croesus. Therefore, they come to life with a different perspective and different values. They are more concerned with their families; they are more concerned with the role of women; they are more concerned with human relationships everywhere and in all aspects of their lives. It seems to me that this different perspective is a great reason for hope.

Employees as Partners

I do not think that worker participation on company boards is a great help. But I do believe we need more evident accountability from managers for the stewardship they hold. This is true not only for the stockholders, who really do not have continual effective control of the enterprise, but also for the employees who are, in a final sense, partners in the enterprise.

I believe that top managers should be selected with the support of the workforce. The more obvious forms of accountability that I envisage can be handled by corporate boards that meet with the workforce on a regular basis. We, for instance, meet both with management and with our workforce at least twice a year and are open to questions from everyone. We try to provide our workforce and our management with explanations and elucidations about anything that troubles them. Instead of the supervisory boards that have been introduced in some of the countries of the European continent, I would rather see a trustee council made up of workers, owners and other public interests. At present, workers, in order to express their interest, can only strike, and the general public is in fact disenfranchised when it comes to management of corporations.

Nevertheless, I am convinced that only private enterprise can create the wealth that is needed. Planned economies seem to require at least three times the resources that private enterprise needs for the same production. I know, for example, that in the Soviet Union, the creation of certain pharmaceutical products has required many times the resources in time, work and raw materials to produce drugs comparable to those created by private enterprise in a free economy.

The Developing Countries

As for the developing countries, I believe it is not possible to move from peasant societies to a twenty-first-century society in a quick step. I cannot foresee this, for example, for either China or India. Therefore, what the developing countries need is not the most advanced technology but intermediate technology that makes it possible for them to move from where they are to where they want to be. This means, in the first instance, intermediate technology for agriculture, by which I mean such fundamental things as wells, irrigation, seeds, crop rotation techniques.

On the much-touted issue of the transfer of technology, I see no meaningful problem. The real question is the right kind of technology and the ability of the receiving society to absorb that technology and put it to use. To be specific, I believe 100,000 artesian wells would do more good for Somalia than its own airline.

The Global Challenge

Globally, we really must face the fact that fewer people will be needed to provide the goods that are required. At present in the industrial countries, agricultural production, for example, is limited to about 2 to 3 percent of the population who produce all the food the population requires. Manufacturing now uses 20 to 40 percent of the population to provide the goods needed, and I see that going down to 10 percent in the foreseeable future. In the past, people who were liberated from agricultural production were able to move into industry. There is no comparable form of output that would move people no longer required in industry, although services would absorb some of them.

The fundamental answer is to change our values from a position where a human being seems to be alive and have social status only if he or she is employed. Our political, religious, social and educational values in the past have all held that viewpoint. All of these must now face the fact that a different perspective and a different attitude are required, and that an individual's value can no longer be measured by his employment and by the work he does. We must create and sustain a system in which a human's self-worth is not dependent on being employed.

As to the socially desirable distribution of wealth, it seems to me that we must find a method—and that needs some very fine balancing—of distributing wealth in socially desirable ways without destroying the ability to create wealth.

United States

FREE ENTERPRISE: SETTING THE PARAMETERS

Dr. Lewis M. Branscomb
Vice President and Chief Scientist
IBM Corporation
Chairman
National Science Board

Free enterprise needs elucidation and redefinition. It also needs to be acculturated. For example, in the Philippines, the Minister of Transportation and Communications has pointed out that for fifty years the Philippines borrowed the U.S. system of free enterprise. The country did not transport the system and adapt it; it took the U.S. ideology wholesale and imposed it on the Philippine culture. It was an overlay, and it didn't work. In the Philippines, under present social conditions, the American version of free enterprise seems to be a doctrine of every man for himself. This, of course, is not a definition that we would accept in the United States, where we have a large array of internal and self-imposed constraints. But this is the way the Filipinos saw it and used it, with the result that while they did get some of its benefits, they also got with it a considerable amount of political and social chaos.

A substantial number of countries, especially in the developing world, do at this point need government action and active government intervention in their economic life. There is no point in treating this phenomenon with antagonism. Every country will finally have to design its own system of balancing free enterprise within its political, economic and social structures. Each country will have to set its own parameters in which free enterprise can operate.

There is a cultural context in which these parameters are set. Japan is an example of a good working environment for educated males; it is a terrible working environment for women. It is also not a very satisfactory environment for everyone employed in the second and third tier of Japanese industry; and it is not a very good environment for anyone over age fifty-five. Obviously, though, the Japanese system works extremely well for those who are within its productive top brackets.

Then there are countries that are small, have a particular geopolitical location, or are for the moment committed to the development of one of a number of resources. In all of these it is likely that government will play a more actively directive role. Therefore, the emphasis on the role of private enterprise within each country and each culture must be that it meets the realities of the country and its culture, and is appropriate as well to the most advantageous form of economic organization possible within that culture.

It must also be remembered that there is a price to free enterprise and the innovations and efficiencies it makes possible. The price is the possibility of failure, and some countries obviously can afford more failure than others. Everywhere it is important to manage failure. As a generality, government accounts for failure poorly, because it can disaggregate the blame.

A Division of Labor

The best division of labor between government and private enterprise is for private enterprise to assume responsibility for production, innovation and flexibility while government assumes responsibility for social welfare. This is not to say that private enterprise does not have social responsibilities of its own. I would argue, for instance, that the social welfare of its own employees is a company responsibility. Companies also have social responsibilities to the communities in which they operate locally, and perhaps even in a wider sense as well. The social responsibilities of a company should be where they overlap with an imaginative concept of the company's self-interest and they should stop there. Companies must be very careful not to lose the element of risk-taking, which is a basic necessity for any creative environment. Private enterprise is in a position where failure very quickly becomes evident and where accountability for that failure is clear, absolute and unavoidable. It is this risk of failure, and the clear responsibility for it, that prompts change and adaptation. This inevitably means that some companies, probably some industries, will sooner or later fail, and must be allowed to fail.

I believe government is essentially responsible for the efficient allocation of resources. It must, of course, obey the laws and play by the rules. If companies are efficient, and pay their taxes, government has the money to alleviate social stress. I disagree with the Reagan philosophy, which postulates that private philanthropy should alleviate social stress. I do believe that companies can and should internalize some social stress within their own enterprises if it does not interfere too drastically with economic efficiency. This constitutes, in fact, a form of hidden taxation and is dangerous if it goes too far. The reason it is dangerous is because there is no overt accountability. Just as the welfare state is dangerous when it gets out of hand, this kind of internalization of the assumption of social responsibility by private companies can be dangerous if it gets out of hand. Since there is, after all, no free lunch, the cost of a private enterprise assuming social obligations must reflect itself sooner or later in the cost of the product. And that leaves the question of who elected corporate officials to make social decisions.

In an appropriate government, by which I mean a democratic, reasonably effective government, people decide how they want to pay the price to compensate and take care of the basic needs of fellow citizens whom the private sector cannot absorb. This is a legitimate government function. Private enterprise cannot compensate for inadequacies and inequities of the social system. If it does not work the answer is not for private enterprise to pursue this responsibility, but for people in private enterprise to plan an active role in the political system and fix it so it will fulfill its role properly and efficiently.

Corruption and Inefficiency

When private enterprise complains about corruption and inefficiency, and rightly so, it should also look into the mirror. Government inefficiencies are difficult to measure. This leads to a problem in advanced economies where, at present, no usable measures exist for the service sector, which in the United States, for example, is already responsible for 70 percent of GNP. One reason why we cannot measure productivity in the service sector is that government is a large part of it, and there are no productivity measurements possible since government defines its input as its output.

On the subject of corruption, the United States is, at least in value commitment, and in some of the regulation and legislation that goes with it, probably pretty much on the right track. It encourages ethical behavior by the private sector. There are a whole slew of disclosure rules that encourage ethical behavior, and we have legislation such as the Foreign Corrupt Practices Act, which encourages it in overseas activities. The problem is that our performance is not necessarily up to our standards. We do have our DeLoreans, Equity Funds, Columbia Pictures, Lockheeds, and so forth. On the other hand, I spent twenty-one years with the U.S. government in the Department of Commerce's National Bureau of Standards, where the necessity for high ethical standards was evident and there was an almost total commitment to integrity by everyone in the Bureau.

Indeed, as I look around the world, I observe that there are other societies where the standards of ethics are at least as high in government as they are in the private sector. Let me just name two: Singapore and the United Kingdom.

State-Owned Enterprises

Any discussion of corruption and inefficiency leads almost inevitably to the subject of state-owned enterprises. One of the important problems in that area is that in many countries, especially in the developing nations, the view of capitalism has not evolved from what capitalism was in the days of Adam Smith. In some developing countries, private enterprise still functions pretty well as it did in the days of Adam Smith, while in mature industrial states there are a number of internalized constraints, which change the picture drastically.

Is Nationalism an Obsolete Idea?

I believe that the nation-state is a totally obsolete idea that runs counter to the natural trend of world evolution at this stage. But I observe that there is rampant in the world today what, for want of a better word, I call nationalism, which is the reaction of political and governmental groups to the recognition that they are indeed anachronistic. They therefore appeal to the sentiment, the fears, the passions, the insecurities of people, which are always easy to marshal. On the other hand, I do not see how states that still need to create viable governments can skip that stage. After all, you have to accumulate sovereignty before you can surrender it.

I also believe that the preservation of culture is very important. For example, at IBM we make a very strong point of employing nationals wherever we operate (and we operate in more than 150 countries) all the way up to the top. We do this, among other reasons, because we believe it is the most effective way to make us sensitive to the local culture.

A New Sense of Community

In a more fundamental way, I am convinced that our sense of community must change, and is indeed changing. Historically, a sense of community is based on shared interests. These can be economic interests, such as, for example, the ownership of oil, or the growing of coffee as a major crop. A sense of community can be based on age. Young people today in many cultures of the world share a sense of community, and some values, that are different from those of their parents. Scientists worldwide tend to share values, an approach to life, that gives them a sense of community. In a different way, so do artists.

Supporting these communities of interest, indeed both making them possible and intensifying them, are the new electronic media of communication. Our unprecedented technology makes it possible for people sharing the same interests to work together wherever they are, and worldwide.

The Global Network

This technology also makes it possible for large organizations to communicate not only from the top down, as is traditional, but also from the bottom up, and horizontally. At IBM, for example, where we have a network of over a thousand computers in some twenty-nine countries which largely manage themselves, a network interface on a horizontal level is now possible in a way that simply did not exist before. This in turn makes possible a fascinating combination of decentralization and integration, which has major organizational and psychological implications.

In the cultural arena, this kind of global network already exists, composed of movies, television and all the communications made possible through satellites. This raises a major challenge, especially for developing countries: the challenge of juggling the preservation of their own culture and traditions, where these should be preserved, with the requirements of development. One aspect of this is the much-debated transfer of technology. It is important not to force technology onto a culture or into a country either from a multinational corporation or from a government. The best way for technology to infuse the development of a country is to allow it to happen via the adaptability and flexibility of the free enterprise system. In that way, it will take root where it makes sense. That is likely to be very different in many countries and cultures. There is no getting away from recognizing the reality of diversity among countries and within countries or, for that matter, among and within multinational corporations.

The Political Problem

The political problem now seems to be, How we can average out the welfare of nations? This is the essence of the new international economic order. The way we are going about it is not realistic. It cannot be done by demagoguery and speeches at the United Nations. The developing countries, for example, should address the averaging out of welfare within their own countries, before they demand it at the international level.

A more realistic way of going about addressing the problem seems to me to be the creation, and above all the empowering, of more decentralized international organizations. Multinational corporations are a classic case in point. But there exists a whole range of nongovernmental institutions that play a role in the United Nations system. The tragedy is that the role played by nongovernmental organizations at the UN is peripheral and modest to a point of being meaningless in the UN approach to the world. These organizations, which really cut across national borders and across the limitation of sovereignty, could play a much more constructive role in international development that would lead to an averaging out of international welfare.

Technology and Decentralization

Technology makes large enterprises of any kind more viable, even on an international level, because it makes possible the decentralization of decision making. The future of multinational corporations, and indeed all other economically based or, for that matter, socially and scientifically based organizations on a worldwide level, is not the unmanageable hierarchical monster that has been depicted, nor is it the "small is beautiful" concept that has been touted. It is a body that has all the advantages of economies of scale, but is decentralized and localized in its decision-making ability. At IBM, for example, we have a few basic business principles that are corporate-wide; and we have a technology that is applicable, and in fact applied, wherever it fits. Not only applied, I might add, but created worldwide. Beyond these basic business principles, and our internationalized technology, we leave decision making to local management, and local management is indeed always local.

What Makes an Entrepreneur?

This leads to a very intriguing and very important question: What makes for entrepreneurship in a society? I would argue that it is a combination of culture, family, the educational system, and recreational patterns. I believe what children do in their extracurricular activities, at play, in the arts, in literature, when watching TV, is more important in creating entrepreneurial values than almost anything else. As Marshall McCluhan once put it: "Kids resent school because it interferes with their education." It is at play that children develop a sense of entrepreneurship, of risk-taking and its rewards.

One of the problems with encouraging entrepreneurship in our culture is, I believe, that we all look too much at economics. Economics is a science of resource allocation. It is quantitative and, in the final analysis, what it measures is money. This is not what makes for entrepreneurship. Governments have become the captives of economists, and I believe this is dangerous. Economists, for example, measure the GNP largely in terms of capital budgets, but they never measure a misuse of economic resources.

Companies, on the other hand, have different measures that are more realistic. Companies measure results essentially by production, and results are both planned and measured, not by economists but by a range of people whose concerns are more realistic in terms of producing goods and services that society wants and needs. The question is how one can get these kinds of people, rather than economists, into government.

Life on a Small Planet

Which leads me to the really big questions that concern government on our small but complex planet. Looking back into history for guidance, it is true that islands such as Japan and the United Kingdom—the historic analogies to our planet today—developed a degree of tolerance, but they did so only after long periods of their inhabitants killing each other off. The tolerance was developed among the tribe that was viable enough to survive. We cannot use that same process, that same tactic, on a planetary level. The fights on these islands were with bows and arrows or with muskets. On a planetary level we have different weapons, which we cannot use. So we cannot copy that system. We have to find other ways to develop tolerance and understanding for each other.

The most pressing problem in that connection seems to be,

How do we infuse ideology and religiosity with tolerance and reason? I believe I have the answer to that. We do it with science. Science has tolerance and reason as built-in components. It does not progress unless it has tolerance and reason. We have an example of that in what happened to Lysenko and his theories. What worries me now is the revival not of fundamental religion, but of anti-Darwinism.

On the other hand, I have seen how important and wholesome the influence of science can be on education, and even on politics. In the People's Republic of China, an important piece of the resistance that finally brought to an end the grim and destructive rule of the Gang of Four came from a scientist, a physicist in fact, who realized how dangerous to China and Chinese development were the principles espoused by the Gang of Four. He recognized that their policies simply killed off and totally stifled the innovations that were needed for Chinese development.

Connected with this thrust is the issue of knowledge. Our problem as human beings on this planet today is not a lack of knowledge, but how to use the knowledge that we have. I believe that this too has to be an international effort, governed by an international approach. One example I know of that could serve as a model is the Institute of Applied Systems Analysis which exists outside Vienna. It is now headed by a Canadian, but both the United States and the USSR participate in it. It examines systems analysis that can be applied to improve the welfare of mankind.

And connected with knowledge and its application is the process and pace of change that challenges us all. I believe the key concept in coping with change is resilience. This applies physically as well as to social arrangements. Let me offer as an example the electric utilities system of the northeastern United States. It was designed for stability. If there was a minor glitch, the system could pick it up and continue operations. It worked well for a long period, but it was not truly resilient. When a major problem occurred in the late sixties, the system failed catastrophically.

A comparable situation exists in relation to forests. Forests need occasional forest fires to clean them up. If they don't have these fires, then, if a fire occurs, growth is so dense that the fire becomes catastrophic.

Another example has to do with the Green Revolution. There used to be 100,000 varieties of wheat; in laboratories around the world, scientists have now concentrated on 10 varieties that are highly desirable from many points of view. That is, they are resistant to blight and to pesticides, and are highly productive. Say the world picks the three best out of the ten we have developed, and 75 percent of the world's wheat becomes one of these three varieties. We will certainly get both more productivity and stability worldwide. However, if microbes change, and they tend to do that, and a new form of wheat blight develops that affects one of these three varieties planted worldwide, then suddenly wheat production around the world is cut by one-third. That would be catastrophic. That is an example of an absence of resilience.

I see the same analogy in strategies for world peace. It is true that in recent decades we have had a stability of sorts. There have been only small wars. But we have also totally lost resiliency. If a real war breaks out now between the United States and the USSR, civilization will not survive anywhere. We need to build resiliency into our social and technological structures. On the technological level this means, among other strategies, that we need to have technology on the shelf.

We have to resist the siren's song of the economists. They do steady-state economics and want everyone to behave as a reasonable economic person. But the world is not made that way. There are economic fluctuations as well as social and political changes that the sweet dreams of the economnists cannot encompass. We must expect change, and prepare for change with resilient technologies. These technologies exist.

We have, for example, technology that both causes and fixes pollution. The two are intertwined. Technology is not an outside separate phenomenon; it is a product of life. We need it both to survive and to prosper.

AN ERA OF UNPARALLELED DEVELOPMENT

Maurice Raymond Greenberg
President and Chief Executive Officer
American International Group

Let me say first that I am not pessimistic about the future of the United States or of the world. Every generation thinks that its current problems are enormous, but future generations will look back at our time and see our problems as mounds, not mountains.

It is true that we have had more change in this generation than in all previous centuries. The next fifty years will see even more and faster change: in transportation, communications, information, medicine. We live, in fact, in a time of unparalleled and enormous development. And it is true that all changes also produce opposites.

The Real Problems: Capital and Government

Our real problem is that we do not have the capital to do everything that can be done. The great impediment, as I see it, is government. We have brilliant science and a private sector that can produce miracles, if only governments would not constrain it and restrain opportunity. Opportunities in our time are greater than they have ever been. Unfortunately, it is unlikely that governments will not interfere with the private sector. Our political systems are such that it is not possible. But I am hopeful that we, in the private sector, can make valuable contributions to political realities and steer them in a way that will prevent the misdirection of resources for political reasons.

The substantive problems we are struggling with at the moment are unemployment, inflation and social services to take care of those who cannot take care of themselves. Essentially, these are all economic problems. I do not believe that political solutions can be found. But it may be the price of a free society to allow for the inefficiency and experimentation of politics, where sound economic solutions exist.

I do know that we have to learn to balance our resources more efficiently. There must be a more pragmatic attitude by people in the democracies to realize that we cannot have more services than we can afford. If we provide services that are unfunded, we simply leave a burden to our children that I believe is unconscionable. For example, we simply must have a cutback in the Social Security System. In all social services we need more realism about what the government can and should do.

Basically, a government should intervene to the minimum extent possible. It should provide minimally for those who cannot provide for themselves, but government help should not be designed to encourage people not to provide for themselves.

If the private sector is allowed to use its dynamism, I see an unparalleled period of new frontiers offering opportunity on which entrepreneurs of all sizes can capitalize. The private sector created these opportunities and it will simply have to find a way—and I'm optimistic that it will—to exploit the opportunities of these new frontiers, even with government shackles. This is true worldwide. Recent and future developments in such sectors as communications, information and transportation make this a very exciting time everywhere, emphatically including the Third World

Entrepreneurs in the Third World

In fact, I have found in the Third World the most exciting, intelligent and innovative entrepreneurs anywhere. These people are doing what we in the United States were doing fifty years ago. They are nation-builders. They are tough, they are exciting, and they are very creative.

The New Frontier: Then . . .

Here, when we began, 150 years ago the new frontier was the industrial world. We made very good use of it for the manufacture of products. We created smokestack industries that, for a very long time, were unparalleled. Now the cost of labor, transportation, energy, capital and taxes may well have made many of our smokestack industries obsolete. It takes enormous capital to modernize these smokestack industries; it takes very little capital to modernize services. That is one reason I see the United States moving increasingly into services. Another reason is that in services most of our competitors are still in their infancy.

. . . and Now

When I say services, I refer to such sectors as technical and scientific innovation, banking, finance, insurance, hotels, transportation and the entire spectrum of leisure activities. In these areas, I foresee a whole series of new services that at this point we aren't even dreaming of.

In the service area, it seems to me that the United States is more enterprising and more innovative than other countries and has been for some time. We seem to have the instinct for services. In my own field, for example, the insurance industry, we have arrived at a position of leadership and innovation that was held by the big insurance companies of the United Kingdom a hundred years ago. We have a more global viewpoint, more long-range vision, more creativity and more imagination, especially in the marketing area.

Look, for example, at what we have done in holiday making. We have practically all of the Northeast moving to the South for vacations, and this with our leisure industries in California and Florida still in comparative infancy. The fact is that people in the affluent societies want quality of life, and providing the services for this quality of life is still in the earliest phase of development. I see, beginning already, for example, an explosion in the hotel industry, in all the print industries, in cable television, in telephone services. In our financial institutions I see an increasing array of multiple services which will be available not only to the domestic consumer but worldwide.

Opportunities for Many

In sum, I see in the service industry a brilliant future that will both replace and create jobs. It is true that people who must relocate and be retrained from the smokestack industries to services will often find this a very painful experience. This applies to many people in the short term; and for some who are too intractable, or will not move and will not respond to retraining opportunities, it may well be a long, painful road. But there are a great many who can be retrained and who can respond to opportunities where the jobs are created. For those who cannot respond to the necessary restructuring of our economy, we need the safety net that the government can provide. Indeed, must provide. I consider that, along with defense, its primary responsibility.

A Safety Net for Some

The people who will need the safety net are people who are now in their forties and early fifties. This also means that within twenty years we will come to the end of this particular problem. There will be no problem for the young ones. They will have grown up in the new era of computers, information, communications, and all the other services that characterize our particular period of history.

Much of our smokestack industry will be moving from North to South. The countries of the South will go through the same industrial process that we went through, only a great many things will be easier for them than they were for us in our time of industrialization. There is more and better communication, there is more awareness and more ability to develop solutions and to skip some of the hard lessons of experience that we encountered in our time. There are also more resources, physical and above all intellectual. The big problem concerning resources is the amount we spend on defense. I don't see the possibility of this expenditure disappearing until we have a meaningful arms agreement between us and the Soviet Union, and I have no way of knowing how long it will take to achieve this, and how plausible and possible it is.

A World to Build

Meanwhile we have lives to live, and a world to build. I would like to address some of the ethical aspects of that task. I proceed from the assumption that the disillusionment that characterized the young in the sixties, and perhaps even in the seventies, is not a permanent condition. The young have always been, and should be, idealistic, explorative and emotional. We have not lost a generation. The idealists of the teens have grown up to make a contribution to society in their twenties and thirties, when the most creative ideas they innovated have become distilled, and they have succeeded in pressuring the establishment to absorb these ideas. That is a good process that will and should continue. And it will, and should, take different forms in different societies.

Take, for example, the participation by labor in management. That is evolving everywhere, but taking different forms. In the United States, we are getting increasing manifestations of it in the form of stock options for employees, or profit-sharing plans. I do not believe that in the United States it is a good thing to have labor representation on the board. Most labor representatives don't think so either. In Germany, co-determination works because it is right for that particular society.

Corporate Culture

Just as there is right and wrong for the cultures of nations, there is right and wrong for the cultures of companies. Companies have to regulate their behavior vis-à-vis society so that they are more finely attuned to the mores and ethics of the society in which they operate. For example, the attitude of "buyer beware" is clearly a thing of the past. But the social obligation of business, the social responsiveness and responsibilities of business, have to be very carefully balanced. They must leave room for profit, because without profit everything comes to a halt. Generally speaking, U.S. business, at least, is conscious of this and behaves accordingly. This is not to say that there are not some baddies in business and these must be restrained.

In a sense, this is even more true when companies operate globally. They take more responsibility when they do that, responsibility to be good corporate citizens wherever they are. It is a simple case of survival. If a company is not a good citizen, it will not survive. Companies are very valuable to development everywhere, in the Third World as well as in the First. They create jobs, offer training, bring new goods, services and ideas. The reward for all of this is profit. If they cannot transmit the profit, the whole thing makes no sense. Profit is needed to create the reserve and the risk capital that makes it all possible. But we must do a better job of explaining just what it is that profit is and does, and why it is such an important and good thing for society.

Coexistence

My final point: Everything I have said assumes that somehow the diverse segments of the human race will find a way to coexist. In that endeavor, the first and most important imperative is that we continue to talk, however much we are fed up with the process. And we should continue to talk at many levels: through research centers, think tanks, international organizations, artistic organizations. All of these do create topics of mutual interest that can be discussed and they do solve some problems. In these discussions, in which I sometimes participate in my sector, as well as in some of my civic activities, it is true that my patience does occasionally give out. Nevertheless, we need these forums if we are going to learn to live together with the differences in attitudes and values that we still have.

When you think about it, it really boggles the mind that on this planet we still have religious wars when we've already landed a man on the moon. The fact is that we have made enormous scientific and technical progress but our emotional development has not kept pace. It appears that emotional maturity has to be relearned for each lifetime.

I believe multinational corporations make a very important contribution to this process of creating worldwide networks of shared values and experience, but whether there is a shortcut through this process of bringing our emotional maturity up to par with our scientific and technological abilities, I do not know. It may well be the most fundamental question of our time.

GLOBAL INVESTMENT: A TOUR D'HORIZON

Ambassador Robert Ingersoll
Former Chairman
Borg-Warner Corporation
Former U.S. Assistant Secretary of State
and U.S. Ambassador to Japan

Some developing countries have learned that the market system works; that the government that supports the market system provides better opportunities for economic growth, which in turn makes it possible to supply an increasing population with the necessities of life and sustain a desirable standard of living for the nation.

Jamaica is a very good example of a nation that tried the opposite tactic and found it led nowhere. On the other side, Singapore, Taiwan, Korea and Hong Kong, the Four Musketeers of Asia, are clear examples of what a market system can do for its people. Sri Lanka recently turned around, and Jamaica is now also in the process of turning around. It will be interesting to see how these two countries fare.

India, too, is finally moving away from a managed economy to a market economy, although in India I suspect the bureaucracy will prove resistant, and the change will be slow.

The evidence for the superiority of the market system, in terms of what it does for its people, is not limited to the countries cited. The USSR and China, each in its own way, have demonstrated the disadvantage of a planned and managed economy. In Eastern Europe the only economies that seem to be functioning with some reasonable success are those that have permitted a degree of operation for the market. Hungary is the best example of that.

What seems to have become clear worldwide is that Communist countries, or all countries that insist on centrally planning their economies and production, do not wind up creating the utopia they promise. And an increasing number of countries in the developing world see that this is true. It appears, however, that the developing countries have to go through a period of believing in this utopia and experimenting with a planned economy. It is only after they discover that this does not work that they move in a freer direction.

Economic Freedom and Political Freedom

The problem is that fundamentally, in order to have economic freedom in the full sense, you must have a basis of political freedom. It is true that political freedom is relative, as both Brazil and South Korea have demonstrated. But both of these countries, even with their relative political constraints, have made it possible for free enterprise to operate. And in both countries the dynamism and imagination of the people seem to find ways to surpass or work around and about whatever constraints the system poses. Nevertheless, for a truly and fully liberal economy in the long run, there must be a foundation of political freedom.

A Prescription for LDCs

The developing countries need primarily education and modern technology. To get modern technology, in a way that is effective and productive, countries have to make it worthwhile for investors to come who have this technology, and can transmit it in an effective way. Constraints on capital movement, on operations, and on the repatriation of profits, discourage investors. Classic examples of this, in markets that in and of themselves would be very attractive, are Indonesia, to some extent the Philippines, and India.

The truth is that a country really cannot have it both ways. If countries want to restrain investing, or nationalize it down the road, they have the sovereign right and power to do so. However, if this is their attitude, the only kind of investment they will get is one that will return to the investor a reasonable amount within a very short period. This tends to be short-term investment, and not investment of a kind designed to assist to the optimum in the development of the country.

What I see happening in the developing countries is that

the recognition of the need for technology, capital and managerial know-how is becoming more acute. Nations that in the past, for political reasons, obstructed investment—and the most effective transfer of technology, capital and know-how that investment represents—are beginning to recognize that they must open up their countries and economies to what is turning out to be the only effective transfer of the package of technology, know-how and capital that they need.

This is equally true in Eastern Europe and in what are now known as the NICs, the newly industrialized countries, like Brazil and Mexico, Korea and Taiwan. At present, the new global movement seems to be for capital to flow into the United States because it is perceived worldwide as having the greatest political stability and the most hospitable climate economically. An investor in the United States does not have to worry about nationalization. The problem with that is that the investment package is really needed most, and most urgently, in the developing countries.

Participation Is the Strongest Motivation

In the industrialized world, if I were to write a prescription, the main ingredient would be the concept of participation. In the sixties and seventies, young people in the Western world were in revolt. In the United States, they were in revolt against the war in Vietnam, Watergate, and the spoliation of the environment. All of these sentiments still exist. Now, however, they are not as wide and anarchic as they used to be; they are more directed, more focused, more practical.

Young people, in the United States particularly, see an opportunity of making a direct and concrete impact in community affairs. They are beginning to realize that they can get involved in local government and make things happen on that level. They are using the influence that they have. What the young are realizing increasingly is that instead of revolting against the system and trying to undermine it, they can take situations into their own hands and shape the system as they would like to see it. This is true in economics as well as politics. The young are realizing that they can start enterprises of their own, and that it is indeed these small new enterprises that they can shape, and that the nation needs to create jobs.

I think we have learned something from the Japanese challenge, something that does indeed move in the general direction that the young seem to be thinking about as well. What I'm referring to is employee relations, where we are beginning to recognize that the "hierarchy talks down" direction is not necessarily as productive as employee participation. I mean worker participation at every level: in design, planning and decision making.

It is, of course, true that in the most successful companies of the United States, decision making has been flowing from the bottom up as well as from the top down for a long time. Not only from the bottom up and top down, but also across, laterally. Some of the corporate leaders in the world such as Procter & Gamble, Caterpillar, Dow Chemical, Texas Instrument, Hewlett-Packard, IBM, Kodak, have known and practiced all along the need to motivate their workforce by involving employees at every level. Participation is the strongest motivation. Now, as a response to the Japanese challenge, more companies are looking at this and will be doing it. Things will, of course, take a while to change.

Participation has also altered the viewpoint of the rebellious young, who for some time were in favor of no growth. Now they realize all the basic things that are needed, such as road services, health, housing, science, art, all the things they care about, cannot be had without economic growth. Redistribution does not create. When there is a shrinking or even a static pie, the fight becomes over its division rather than energy flowing into creativity to enlarge the pie.

On the other hand, it does seem that it is the small enterprise that not only creates new products and services but also ideas and, most importantly, jobs. Increasingly, big companies are realizing that they must decentralize to the greatest extent possible and must, in effect, create small entrepreneurial units in their overall structure if they want to remain competitive.

Interestingly, even the Communists in China have made the same discovery. They are talking about the mistakes they made by centralizing too much in both planning and control. They say that they will now decentralize and introduce the market system. They seem to have recognized that without the market system, which provides feedback on products and services, they produce the wrong things. In a recent conversation with a leading policy maker in China, the policy maker told me that one problem with the Chinese economy is that too many decisions are still made politically and from the center. "I envy you," he said, "the way you can respond to market signals."

Evolution

Stepping back to assess the priority requirement of people everywhere on the planet, it is probably evolution toward universal harmony. In this, as in all interesting forms of harmony, individual strains—in this case, the strains of societies and cultures—must be retained and blended. Japan, where I have spent some time, is a model for this kind of society. It has been a small island for many centuries, and the result has been what I think of as a webbed society, in which everybody is beholden to everyone else. When a person breaks out of the web, he doesn't work either for the individual or for the society. For people living in this tightly knit society, a great deal of tension builds up. You see this when you live in Japan. I remember a strike on the subways in which the commuters finally got so irate they beat up the strikers. To me, this illustrates also what can happen in a world that is overpopulated. I believe human beings need elbow room.

Creating this universal harmony will undoubtedly be a long process. But there is the example of the United States, which shows that it is possible. Here we have a society of different cultures, languages, individuals from different ethnic backgrounds, who have managed to live together on the whole in reasonable harmony. I believe this needs a common language. In Indonesia, Sukarno, who did many unfortunate things as well, did realize that a common language is essential to a nation. Indonesia had seven hundred languages, and he insisted that everyone learn one common tongue.

To move toward this harmony, we need to make a greater effort to acquaint people all over the world with each other. Modern communications makes that possible. But it will take many generations, even with the communications facilities we now have, before we can make people everywhere think globally rather than nationally. Even in the West, with our special background, a lot of work still needs to be done in that direction.

Meanwhile, throughout the world there is no doubt that impoverishment and tragedies still exist. At least we have grown to deplore them. We still have not found the solution, but we are trying. Many of us are trying all over the world, and the fact is that there have been no major conflicts in the world for the last forty years.

We have tried, as well, to improve the human lot all over the world. We have not eliminated either famine or disease, but we have made gains in combating them everywhere. Poverty is still with us, but many people, indeed most people, are much better off today than was the great majority of humanity fifty years ago, and certainly a hundred years ago. Life expectancy has increased, and I would have to argue that this is a sign of major progress.

To Keep Moving

What we have to watch out for now is that we continue to meet challenges and responsibilities, and that societies that have moved up do not now begin to decline. I am, for instance, worried about Europe, where I see a lack of flexibility, a kind of cultural and economic arteriosclerosis that may produce a decline.

In the NICs I see progress. They are nipping at the heels of the industrial countries, and it has become expected in the NICs that the present generation will work and forego certain pleasures so that it can educate its children for a better life. That kind of dynamism can overcome many political and social legacies. It did precisely that in the United States when we began.

I worry here, as well as in Europe, about the lethargy that is created by welfare states. The most dangerous result of this system is that the young do not respond constructively and dynamically. We need dynamic response to the inevitable changes, the structural changes, that are now taking place. There is unmistakably, in the advanced industrial countries, a decline in smokestack industries and an increase in the information industries. We are inevitably moving to a post-industrial society. This post-industrial society brings along with it a trend toward regionalism, localism. There are more small enterprises, small new companies, and more local organizations backing and surrounding them.

On a national economic scale, this pushes decision making down both economically and politically. I believe that to be a very good thing, and I include in it the workman on the shop floor. After all, no one knows more about his job than he does. To get his ideas is vital not only for the enterprise but also for the motivation and satisfaction of the worker.

Knowledge

This leads me to my final point, which is knowledge and the best use of knowledge. We have an enormous amount of knowledge at our disposal now. The challenge, the effort, for this generation is to apply globally what we know. What we need to do is funnel the knowledge that we have, and have it circulate below, above, around, feed it into public consciousness at home, into the political process, into international institutions, into public consciousness everywhere. We have to make people realize throughout the world that we do have the knowledge that, if applied intelligently, properly, freely, can make for a better life for everyone.

As a practical matter, when that consciousness takes hold we will need a major conversion of the current global expenditures on arms for other economically more productive resources. The resources that would be freed when we no longer have to spend them on armaments should go, in my opinion, in the first instance into education, and secondly, into health.

I also believe that it is vital to spread knowledge, and particularly management techniques, in agriculture. This would solve basic problems not only in terms of feeding people adequately, but also in creating a saner balance between town and country, between rural and urban segments of a society.

A spread of the knowledge we already have can solve problems by economic means and, at the same time, will make possible a system under which sound political decisions can be made from the bottom up. This is a slow process, but I am convinced it can be done. I am also convinced that, given broad-based knowledge, the advantages of free societies will become crystal clear and will wind up becoming the global choice.

PAPER ENTREPRENEURISM

Charles W. Robinson
Chairman
Energy Transition Corporation
Former Deputy Secretary for Economic Affairs
U.S. Department of State

To assess world economic problems comprehensively one needs to look at them in two contexts: domestic and global.

In the domestic context, the United States faces problems that are quite different from those of all other countries—including such roughly comparable economies as those of the industrialized democracies of Western Europe and Japan. These special problems arise from the leadership the United States held for three decades in industrial organization; in such areas as the development of mass production techniques, the systemic organization of industry, scientific management and other important innovations. The ideas and techniques that initially led to United States leadership in industrial innovation, however, also built rigidities into the economy that are now difficult to overcome. The United States steel and automotive industries are glaring illustrations of this.

The problem with these rigidities is not only that they have impeded structural adjustments that are both unavoidable and urgent, but that they also have exacted and continue to exact a high price from the American consumer. It is estimated, for example, that the voluntary car quota system, made necessary by these rigidities, has already added $400 to the price of every U.S. car and $1,000 to the price of Japanese imports. More important still, there are estimates that the car quota system, the main thrust of which is presumably to save or create U.S. jobs, in fact costs U.S. consumers $100,000 for every job that is saved.

Interestingly, Japan, less hampered by these rigidities, is reacting quite differently. It has, for example, moved most of its textile industry out of the country and it is handling its steel situation, where it too is affected by the new low-cost steel producers of the newly industrialized countries in the Third World, by selling technology and machinery to the appropriate LDCs and making a great deal of money in the process. Concurrently, its own strategy is to move to high price, high-technology specialty items.

The Global Perspective

The global context of world economic problems for the United States has two major elements. One is a by-product of the death of colonialism; the other is government intervention in economic decision making. In most LDCs these decisions are made largely for noneconomic reasons that frequently run counter to market realities.

Take the case of copper. In the copper-producing LDCs, government decisions have called for an ever-increasing production of copper as food production plummets and the need to earn foreign exchange for food and other imports continues to rise. As copper prices fall, owing to a weak market for the metal, LDC governments react by producing more copper, which inevitably results in a further glut and a further fall in prices, followed by greater production to keep up income. In effect, LDC governments, by following a policy counter-indicated by the market, first created and then accelerated a downward spiral in prices deeply inimical to the income goals they purportedly tried to pursue.

The Role of the World Bank

The World Bank has contributed to this problem. Political instability has made major private investment in natural resources almost impossible in LDCs. Governments stepped in to fill the gap, investing very large amounts, strongly supported by the World Bank. As the private sector of colonial times opted out of these countries, more government money—and government decision making—poured into the system, backed by the World Bank and completely oblivious to market forces.

Personally, I believe this is a misuse of World Bank resources, both financial and political. I am convinced that the World Bank's equity branch—the International Finance Corporation—could and should play the major role in economic development of LDCs instead of the rather marginal role it plays at present. The World Bank should use its political muscle to encourage private investment through the IFC in the developing world. The best method, in my judgment, is trilateral investments with participation from the IFC, local governments, and private investors. In such a constellation, I see the IFC eventually selling out its ownership to the private sector, both foreign and domestic, but retaining the political risk. This would induce LDC governments not to violate their contracts and thereby eliminate, or at least substantially reduce, political risk for the private sector.

There may also be a place for government-to-government concessionary aid, but the danger is that such aid can be, and often is, addictive. A case in point is what international food aid has done to food production in many LDCs, that is, it has created a dependency on external supplies of food instead of encouraging domestic food production.

Perhaps the best type of foreign aid is aid that develops human resources by training people at all levels and in all productive areas, including science, technology and management.

A Major Menace

On the U.S. side, the major problem, aside from the rigidities discussed earlier, is what I think of as "paper entrepreneurism." U.S. industry has teetered into a dangerous habit of straining for short-term profits rather than long-term returns, and of achieving these profits by putting together financial deals and mergers rather than creating new facilities, products and services.

The institutions most responsible for this dangerous trend are business schools, on the one hand, and the financial markets, on the other. The schools turning out MBAs—and this includes our very best schools—spend far too much time teaching their students how to manipulate paper instead of how to mind production.

The second institution pushing industry in the wrong direction is the financial community, specifically the security markets and their obsessive concern with short-term results. This obsession is fueled by institutional investors who generally have numeric goals that have nothing to do with the health of the business. The result of all this is that the CEOs of companies are maneuvered into a situation where they must worry about short-term bottom-line results in order to keep their jobs; they cannot give enough time or thought to a ten-year strategy because they may not be around to implement it. The tenure of CEOs today is half what it used to be. For all these reasons, investments that would lead to long-term strength, sound growth and employment creation simply do not happen in large companies. The only people who can avoid this trap are owner-entrepreneurs, who can afford to ignore the stock market and make investments that have a long-term payout.

SEC to the Rescue?

Public bodies presumably designed to create a healthy investment climate and protect and encourage the investor, such as the Securities Exchange Control and the Financial Accounting Standards Board (FASB), are no help, at least in the way they operate at present. The methods of reporting and accounting that these two agencies require encourage short-term orientation and lead to short-term decisions.

The rules should be revised to require reporting and accounting that reveals and that reflects the results of investments that have a long-term payout.

Another system that urgently requires revision is the compensation method now in force to reward managers. At present, that system is also geared to providing bonuses based on short-term profits instead of compensation geared to long-term strategies. It should at least be a mix of both.

Finally, with SEC cooperation, stock prices should reflect long-term corporate prospects, not just quarterly returns.

Free Trade or Fair Trade

Free trade is an optimal goal, but it is politically unrealistic at this time. The rate of technological change is so rapid that society must step in and provide some kind of protection, if necessary by slowing down changes in production patterns.

Since we live in an interdependent economy, I suggest, for example, that we limit changes in the volume of imports to 25 percent a year in any given industry so that the industry and the people in it get a chance to readjust. I would suggest that exporters to the United States who exceed the 25 percent limit be fined by the imposition of higher duties and that the money collected in this way be used to provide adjustment to the affected domestic industries.

Historic Discontinuity

I see all this in the context of the period of historic discontinuity in which we find ourselves, a discontinuity caused by the technical revolution, the death of colonialism, and economic imbalance. We need to look at the world with new eyes, and determine what are the new questions that need to be asked. This is the paramount priority facing us.

THE SHAPE OF THE FUTURE: BRAIN VALUE ADDED

Herta Lande Seidman
Managing Director
International Trade Services
Phibro-Salomon Inc.
Former Assistant Secretary of Commerce

The far future is inevitably shaped by the near future, and in the near future I see the quality of life being changed in major ways. Three factors will shape that change: technology, genetic engineering, and the service economy. These three will fundamentally affect, if not dominate, both wealth accumulation and wealth distribution. They will also provide the framework for society in general as well as for the work place specifically. Therefore, the most important requirement for any society, and the individuals in it, is a psychological readiness for change.

In the technological area, laser power generation through

nonfossil fuels, and the possibility of engineering changes of matter, including human matter, will create major changes and challenges.

In services, transportation, communication, information will create a very different working environment. What will increasingly matter, and what will make the fundamental difference between countries and between individuals, is the factor of brain value added. Among many other things, this makes the old division between North and South increasingly irrelevant. Countries can make the leap into this new area whether they have been traditionally developed and industrialized or not, because what will matter is not the brawn power that was needed in the early days for the successful development of agriculture, not the machines that were required for the development of industrial societies, but brain power.

Individual Excellence

This leap will depend to an unprecedented extent on individuals, anywhere in the world. That, in turn, will create unprecedented stress because both individuals and societies can no longer blame their lack of development on givens, such as land and territory, or achievements that have capital-intensive requirements such as machinery, or even on such old sociopolitical arguments as colonial exploitation or unfair terms of trade. What will be required to function in this new society is simply individual excellence, the optimum use of individual brain power. We will have, indeed we already have to a large extent, the knowledge; needed now is the courage, the commitment, the discipline. In a very real sense it will no longer be possible for any society, or for that matter for any individual, to say, "They didn't let me; they impeded me; they exploited me. They wouldn't let me do it." In this new society every individual has the opportunity to use his or her individual talent, and to demonstrate achievement. Individuals and nations will be measured by the reality of their achievement.

Successful Societies

There is of course a reverse side to this coin. Failure will be punished more drastically, for both individuals and countries. For countries, the most important factor will be whether society can be organized to make it possible for individuals to succeed. Successful societies will be those that are the most flexible, the most open to change, the ones best designed to let individuals identify opportunity and pursue the opportunities they see. Looked at from this perspective, some countries that now seem very strong, such as Japan, may well turn out not to be strong because they are socially too rigid. While other countries, for example Brazil, that are now still relatively weak, will be able to make the required leap because they are basically open societies geared to flexibility, change and risk-taking.

The existence of natural resources in countries will be increasingly less important. Take, for example, countries that are rich in copper. Fiber optics will replace copper in telephone cables and other traditional uses. Therefore, countries that rely on the exploitation of natural resources that have traditionally been a source of wealth may well run themselves into a dead end if they do not apply the added brain power that will provide new directions and, of course, will also provide new opportunities.

Another example of this change is steel. Steel has been replaced in some applications by synthetic rubber, by plastics, even by cement. The net result has been that in many ways steel has become a dinosaur, and feeding the dinosaur is becoming increasingly expensive. What will matter in the economy in the future is not the existence of raw materials, not the existence of machines, but the human applications of available resources, including new resources that can be engineered through the new technologies.

Robots—and Other Workers

Paramount among these new technologies on the production front are robots. There is no doubt that robots will take the place of humans on boring, dead-end jobs on assembly lines. One would have to concede that is fundamentally a very good thing. Good or bad, however, it will certainly happen. The question then becomes, What can be done to retrain the people who did the jobs that the robots do better? If they are adaptable and young enough to be retrained, that has to be done. We also have to face the fact that there will be segments of the population that cannot be retrained for the jobs that are available. For them we have to create safety nets. Some of these safety nets can consist of interim jobs that are not in themselves highly skilled. For example, I can see no reason why steelworkers who are no longer needed in the steel dinosaur cannot be trained to build bridges, railroads and other infrastructure ingredients that clearly are needed. But in a fundamental way a major period of transition is unavoidable. It is like the forty years that the people of Israel spent in the desert after they left Egypt. During those forty years, the ones who grew up as slaves died and a new, differently minded generation arose. It was only when that new generation had grown to maturity that the people of Israel found and entered the Promised Land.

High Tech or Subsistence?

All of this is not to say that either agriculture or industry will wither away. They should, and indeed will, continue to exist. The real question is whether there will be an agriculture and an industry of high technology, or of subsistence. To put it differently, whether once again we will be applying brawn to these sectors, in which case it be a sluggish, slow process, or brain, in which case it will lead to success.

Applying the same reasoning to the relationship between multinational corporations and state-owned enterprises, it seems clear that sooner or later SOEs will have to get out of business. We will be entering a world where efficiency and competence will decide survival. This is true for individuals, societies, and components of societies, such as companies. In such a World I do not see state-owned enterprises, with their built-in incompetence, clumsiness and rigidity, surviving very long. I also believe that small business will have an advantage in this kind of world, because small businesses seem to be more capable of drawing on brain values. In the United States we have already seen during the past decade the vital importance and survivability of small companies based on human resources, on brain value added.

Measuring Productivity in Services

One of the problems in this emerging world is that we have not developed measures to judge human productivity in the service area. Traditionally, productivity is measured by return on capital investment and output per man-hour. In the service industry, particularly in the new high technology, information and brain power–based service industries, capital investment is minor. Output per man-hour as a measure does not apply because we do not have the tools or mechanisms to judge this kind of output in the traditional manner. Just as I believe that inflation rates in a country need to be measured in relative terms according to a basket of criteria, so the judgment of output must be very different for nations whose output can be measured in terms of agricultural output and industrial output as against a country like the United States where today more than 70 percent of the workforce is employed in services.

For example, to measure a company like IBM by the old standards of an industrial company makes very little sense. Most of what really makes IBM the kind of company it is is not its production of hardware, but the kind of brains that go into software, design and service. How are these outputs measured? The same is true for a Japanese company like NEC, or Bull-Honeywell in France. At present, the truth is that we have not evolved measurements which make any sense in terms of reality that can give us an accurate assessment of productivity in the service sector.

A Demanding New World

As I look at our world today, I can see within the next fifteen years not only the possibility of extraterritorial production, which has already been signaled by the space shuttle and its experiments, but also the possibility of the colonization of other planets. This will make sense as high technology succeeds in changing both material and human capability. We have already succeeded in changing, through high technology, such crops as rice and wheat. There is no reason why comparable changes should not be possible with a wide range of other products. This includes the possibility of human life moving from earth to other locations in space.

I do see the period ahead as a time when there will be more opportunities, wider horizons, greater chances than ever before in human history for those individuals and societies that can deal with them and take advantage of them. This is technically true and economically plausible.

A Political System That Can Cope

The question then remains, What kind of political system deals best with the opportunity? There is no doubt in my mind that that system is not just democracy, but democracy after the U.S. model. I look at the values of liberty, equality and fraternity that underlie the French Revolution. Aside from liberty, which is fundamental, the other two are values that are designed for community rather than for the development of individuals. Therefore, the values that underlie the French Revolution inevitably lead to socialism, and from then on to communism, while the American values are designed for individual fulfillment coupled with a respect for liberty, which is, in a second dimension, tantamount to respect for the freedom and opportunity of others. The system that provides the greatest leeway for individuals and their creative potential is also best designed for flexibility and adjustment to change.

As a bottom line, I see a yawning gulf developing between those who will make it and those who will not, on both an individual and a national basis. This division will transcend the current North–South split. Those who will succeed are those who will accept responsibility for success *and* failure, and will be not only trained but ready to deal with changes. At present, the real problem of developing countries is still that, with rare exception, they will not accept responsibility for their failure and therefore cannot get themselves ready to deal with it. There is nothing inherent and intrinsic in any developing country that could not be overcome if the country adapted its values to cope with change, and used the brain power that every country in the world has to help it design and meet that challenge.

I would have to concede that surrendering to government care and welfare is comfortable, and that leaving this safety blanket requires a readiness to deal with contradictions and complexities that is difficult both for individuals and for nations. But it is the willingness and ability to take this risk that will make the difference between successful people and unsuccessful individuals and societies.

I take a long look back into history and I see that in some ways we have really gone through this process before. When society moved from farm to factory, enormous changes of values and attitudes were involved. There were changes in family structure; there were changes in art; there were major psychological adaptations that had to be made, and indeed were made. We are now in the middle of a second industrial revolution, with all that this concept implies. The basic reality is that in this industrial revolution, what really matters is brain power added. In the last one it was machine power added. Then, as now, this implies a change of structures and of players.

World Bank

FUTURE CHALLENGE AND POLITICAL WILL

A. W. Clausen
President
The World Bank

The future offers us an awesome challenge. However, in this age of the space shuttle, electronics for the masses and instant global communications, there can be no doubt that the means exist to meet it. The obstacles to a decent dignified standard of living for hundreds of millions of people in the Third World lie not so much in the halls of modern technology as in the hesitations of those with the political power to make that standard possible. What is lacking is a firm commitment on the part of the international community to act while the window of opportunity is open to us.

It makes sound economic sense—and prudent political sense—not to let programs of development assistance to low-ncome countries weaken and decline. In this period of global economic uncertainty, it is not only the low-income countries themselves who need fear the awful consequences of their own economic retrogression. The whole world should fear them, and not least the donor countries. For them, the economic, political and strategic consequences of chronic decline in the poorest countries will certainly be grave.

Self-Interest, Not Charity

For this is not an issue of charity. It is one of national self-interest in an interdependent world economy. I refuse to believe that it is so complex that rich and powerful nations cannot see where their self-interest lies, and cannot recognize the political, commercial and security arguments for doing more.

We at the World Bank are the first to acknowledge that it is a formidable task. We are not blind to the fact that the global economic environment today is far less hospitable than the environment in which many developing countries made progress in the preceding decades. Unfortunately, the capacity of the international community to solve these problems is being underestimated, and adequate support for the effort has not been forthcoming.

A Time Bomb Ticking Away

It is still not too late to utilize the tremendous resources which are as yet untapped in a major effort to accelerate the growth of the low-income countries and to reduce their poverty. However, the procrastination must end, and it must end now. The economic distress of the poorest nations is a time bomb ticking away. We delay defusing it at our peril!

The World Bank is doing what it can to speed the development process. In addition to its direct lending to the developing world, the Bank is trying to maximize its effectiveness by pressing for policy reform in the developing countries, by cooperating more closely with other agencies, and by expanding our collaboration with private investors.

Policy Dialogue

Perhaps the most important resource The World Bank can offer is not money, but professional advice and assistance. We conduct what we call a "policy dialogue" with our borrowers. It includes suggestions on a whole range of policies, from the macroeconomic to specific sectors such as industry or agriculture. The advice is independent and candid. The Bank is also doing more structural adjustment loans to support programs of policy reform. Our objective here is to help countries put into place appropriate economic policies so that development projects can have higher economic rates of return to the country.

Raising the Productivity of the Poor

This stress on policies that encourage efficiency doesn't mean that The World Bank is backing off from its concern about poverty. We intend to maintain the share of our investment focused on raising the productivity of the poor. But, as the experience of Africa demonstrates, you can't improve the lot of poor people in a country if the whole economy is sliding backward.

Second, the Bank is working more closely not only with the IMF, but with its fellow development agencies, particularly in the process of policy dialogue. In many instances, donor nations have asked The World Bank to give recipient nations more help in coordinating bilateral and multilateral development programs. We have already set up consultative groups from some twenty countries, and we intend to organize more consultative groups when they are needed and when they are requested.

Direct Foreign Investment

Third, and most important, we have significantly expanded our collaboration with the private sector. We believe that international private capital is essential to the development process, in the form of both direct investment and commercial lending. Constrained commercial bank lending, together with high real interest rates, makes direct foreign investment more attractive and important to developing countries. Such investment should be encouraged to complement and supplement local entrepreneurial resources.

Co-Financing

One area where much progress has been achieved is our co-financing program. Co-financing has enormous potential for channeling additional funding for projects from bilateral aid agencies, export credit institutions and commercial banks. For instance, over the last ten years the Bank has obtained co-financing worth $16 billion from official sources, almost $12 billion from export credit agencies, and $8 billion from private lenders. These have combined to provide co-financing for over eight hundred projects representing a total project investment of $141 billion.

We have also introduced new co-financing approaches that will make going into partnership with us more attractive to commercial banks. Over time, these co-financing initiatives should draw significant additional resources to the developing countries.

One other fact is worthy of mention. Cooperation with The World Bank group has resulted in substantial real benefit to the private sector. Over the years, the Bank and IDA have disbursed more than $50 billion to companies in the industrialized countries that have won contracts to supply equipment to projects we have financed.

The Private Sector: A Powerful Engine for Development

I have spent most of my professional life working in the private sector, and I am proud of my private sector bias. The private sector has made an immense contribution to human progress and remains a powerful engine for development. In most developing countries, the private sector accounts for 70 to 80 percent of economic activity. Thus, economic growth depends mainly on whether the private sector is given the incentives and support it needs to expand production. However, the private sector cannot do it all. The case for increasing official capital flows, both concessional and nonconcessional, is compelling.

A Peaceful Global Order

Official Development Assistance (ODA) is desperately needed by low-income countries which do not have access to, and cannot afford the terms of, significant commercial borrowing. Yet for more than a decade only 30 percent of total bilateral ODA has been allocated to the low-income countries. It is shocking that those who need it most receive so little in both absolute and relative terms. These nations have special and pressing problems, as all of us well know. Yet the irrefutable economic arguments for channeling a large share of bilateral assistance to these countries continues to fall on mostly deaf ears.

Those of us who are working to encourage Third World development have powerful historical forces in our favor. The last half millennium has been dominated by the spreading dynamic of economic development. Nothing has so profoundly marked our century as the political and economic progress of Asia, Africa and Latin America.

Over the long term, whether or not the Third World will develop is probably not at issue. The issue, rather, is whether Third World development will be tortuous and profoundly divisive, or whether it will be continuous and interwoven with the construction of a more peaceful global order.